Library of
Davidson College

TRIBESMEN AND PATRIOTS

Political Culture in a Poly-Ethnic African State

Ndiva Kofele-Kale

UNIVERSITY
PRESS OF
AMERICA

Copyright © 1981 by
University Press of America, Inc.™
P.O. Box 19101, Washington, D.C. 20036

All rights reserved

Printed in the United States of America

Library of Congress Cataloging in Publication Data

Kofele-Kale, Ndiva.
  Tribesmen and patriots.

  Bibliography: p.
  Includes indexes.
  1. Cameroon--Ethnic relations. 2. Cameroon--
Politics and government. I. Title.
DT570.K62   306'.2'096711   80-5734
ISBN 0-8191-1395-6
ISBN 0-8191-1396-4 (pbk.)

I dedicate this work to the memory of
EMMANUEL NJOYA MARTIN whose senseless
and premature death from a car accident
in 1970 robbed me of a close childhood
friend and Cameroon of a promising
leader.

Contents

		Page
List of Tables and Figures		ix
Preface		xiii
Acknowledgements		xv
Introduction:	A Brief Political History of Anglophone Cameroon	1
Chapter One:	Political Culture, Ethnicity, and Environment: An Overview	7
	The Concept of Political Culture	7
	Why Study Political Culture	12
	The Historical Discontinuity Argument	14
	Ethnicity/Tribalism Argument	19
	Inconsistencies in Patterns of Socialization Argument	46
	Theoretical Framework	50
	Hypothesis to be Tested	58
	Footnotes	61
Chapter Two:	The Socio-Ethnographic Context for this Study	77
	Selection of Environmental Locations	79
	Urban Centers/Towns	79
	Rural Villages	84
	Plantation camps/Labor villages	87
	The Period 1884-1914	89
	The Period 1916-1938	90
	The Period 1939-1959	91
	Post-Independence (1960-)	93
	Criteria for Selection of Ethnic Groups	94

	The assumption of heterogeneity	97
	The assumption of homogeneity	99
	Description of the Ethnic Groups	100
	The Grassfields	100
	Bafut: A Tikar Chiefdom	103
	The Kpe	108
	The Banyang	115
	Summary	126
	The Sample	134
	Footnotes	136
Chapter Three:	Contrasts and Similarities Among Three Ethnic Groups	145
	Background and Demographic Variables	145
	Age and Education	145
	Occupation	146
	Religious Affiliation	148
	Family Status	156
	Residential Patterns	157
	Ethnic Group Values	157
	Patterns of Authority and Decision-Making	160
	Patterns of Intragroup Contact	170
	Orientation to Change	180
	The Socialization Process	185
	Socializing into Specifically Ethnic Traditions and Values	187
	Transmission of Political Values	190
	Summary	201
	Footnotes	206
Chapter Four:	Environment and Ethnicity: Contrasts in Rural-Urban Attachment to Ethnic Group Values	209

	Patterns of Authority and Decision-Making	214
	Childhood Images of Parental Authority	214
	Allocation of Domestic Authority	215
	Structure of Intra-Group Decision-Making	216
	Patterns of Intra-Group Contact and Solidarity	222
	Language Fluency	222
	Structure of the Extended Family	228
	Orientation to Change	231
	Summary	235
	Footnotes	239
Chapter Five:	Environment and National Identity: Contrasts in Rural-Urban Orientations Toward the Nation	243
	Sense of National Identity	244
	Political Awareness	244
	Political Knowledge	252
	System Affect	260
	Attitudes Toward National Independence	260
	National Attributes Evoking Pride	261
	Socio-Economic Development	266
	Strength of Attachment to Fatherland	266
	Sense of Community Identity	267
	Degree of Neighborliness	267
	Degree of Friendliness	268
	Propensity for Cross-Ethnic Marriage	271
	The Symbol System	274
	Summary	276
	Footnotes	280

Chapter Six:	Environment and the Belief	
	and Rule Systems	285
	The Rule System	285
	Decision-Making Pre-	
	ferences	286
	Conflict Resolution	289
	The Belief System	291
	Social Welfare	292
	National Unity	294
	Moral Society	296
	Summary	300
	Footnotes	302
Chapter Seven:	Conclusion: Political Culture in Anglophone Cameroon	305
Bibliography		325
Name Index		347
Subject Index		353

Tables and Figures

Tables

3.1	Distribution of Christians in the Division of the South-West Province of English-Speaking Sector of the Cameroon Republic, According to Denominations	150
3.2	Distribution of Christians in the Divisions of the North-West Province of English-Speaking Cameroon	151
3.3	Distribution of Christians in Areas Occupied by the Ethnic Clusters Surveyed in this Study	152
3.4	Pre-World War I Missionary Activity in German Colony of Kamerun	155
3.5	Marital Status and Family Size of Respondents by Ethnic Groups	158
3.6	Number of Years Respondents Spent in Locality by Ethnic Group	159
3.7	Childhood Confidants	164
3.8	Whose Voice Had the Most Weight in Family Decision-Making	166
3.9	How Decisions Were Made in Respondents' Family	166
3.10	Responsibility for Day-to-Day Decisions Taken in Respondents' Family	166
3.11	Children in Family Decision-Making Process	167
3.12	Respondents' Choice of the Ideal Method of Arriving at Group Decisions	169
3.13	Respondents' Projections of What Fellow Ethnic Group Members Would Consider Ideal Method of Arriving at Group Decisions	170
3.14	Respondents' (as a parent) Feelings Should an Offspring Choose to Marry Outside the Ethnic Group	174
3.15	Respondents' Preference for Ethnic Group of Children's Spouses	175
3.16	Relationship Between Sex and Non-Ethnic Marriage Partner	175

3.17	Orientations to Change	185
3.18	Projections of Fellow Ethnic Group Members' Orientations to Change	185
3.19	Ideas to What Cameroon Should be Like in the Year 2023 A.D.	186
3.20	Amount of Time Spent With Co-Ethnics During Adolescence	189
3.21	Amount of Time Spent by Respondent Learning About Ethnic Group Values and Traditions	189
3.22	Persons with Whom Respondent Associated During Adolescence	190
3.23	Persons from Whom Respondent Learnt the Most About the Values and Traditions of Ethnic Group	191
3.24	Events that Started Respondents Thinking Seriously about Government and Politics	196
3.25	Parents' Discussion of Politics	200
3.26	Elders' Discussion of Politics	200
4.1	Participation in Family Decision-Making	218
4.2	Allocation of Domestic Authority	218
4.3	Group Preference for Decision-Making Models	219
4.4	Ability to Speak Ethnic Language by Traditional System	227
4.5	Languages used in Communicating with Fellow Ethnics Among Segmentary Peoples	227
4.6	Languages used in Communicating with Fellow Ethnics Among Centralized Peoples	228
4.7	Family Size Among Segmentary and Centralized Group Members	230
4.8	Family Composition Among Segmentary and Centralized Group Members	230
4.9	Respondents' Own View of Change by Location: Segmentary	232
4.10	Predictions of How Ethnic Group Members see Change by Location: Centralized	233
4.11	Predictions of Group Members' Predispositions Toward Change	237

5.1	Relation Between Community and Political Awareness: Input Cognition Aspect	245
5.2	Reasons Given by Respondents Who Found Government Impact Unfavorable	253
5.3	Reasons Given by Respondents Who Considered the Impact of Government to be Favorable	253
5.4	Ability to Identify Cabinet Ministers	254
5.5	Ability to Identify National Party Leaders	255
5.6	Ability to Identify Party Leaders	255
5.7	Pride in Country: As a Cameroonian, What Things About this Country are You Most Proud of?	261
5.8	System Affect as Evidenced by Willingness to Change Nationality	266
5.9	R Factor Analysis: Rotated Factor[a] Matrix Showing Factor Leadings on Dimensions of Inter-Group Contact	269
5.10	Symbol Subsystem: Meaning Attached to National Flag and Anthem, by Location	275
6.1	Choice of Decision-Making Models by Location	291
6.2	Choice of Conflict Resolution Models by Location	292
6.3	Opinion of the Social Welfare Goal by Location	300
6.4	Opinion of the National Unity Goal by Location	301
6.5	Opinion of the Moral Society Goal by Location	301

Figures

2.1	Map 2: Major Plantations and Administrative Areas, C.D.C., 1969[a]	95

Preface

Since independence, the leaders of Cameroon have struggled with the task of instilling a sense of national identity among the 7 1/2 million people who live within the country's borders. Yet after two decades only modest progress has been registered. What accounts for this slow progress? Conventional opinion has put blame on the persistence of ethnic/tribal loyalties. Indeed, given the approximately 200 ethnic/tribal groups to which Cameroonians belong, it can be said that every Cameroonian is in a very literal sense a tribesman or tribeswoman. Attachments to these subnational groups often overshadow loyalties toward the Cameroon state. Thus, there is some truth in the observation that primordial attachments flowing from the bonds of blood, speech, and custom have proved more powerful than any ties to the relatively abstract concept of a Cameroon nation. But this position is at best a partial explanation of the absence of a pervasive sense of common nationhood among the diverse people of Cameroon. The explanation is incomplete precisely because (1) it puts too much stress on the issue of tribalism while neglecting more fundamental contradictions in Cameroonian society; (2) it is overly concerned with cultural differences that divide rather than with the many cultural similarities that unite the Cameroonian peoples; and (3) it presumes that all members of polyethnic societies are uni-dimensional people who see themselves either as tribesmen or national citizens but never both. Without in any way minimizing the explosive and threatening character of subnational loyalties, there is reason to believe that other divisions within Cameroonian society to an equal degree undermine efforts at creating a transcendental sense of "togetherness."

An examination of the disparate peoples who make up Cameroon reveals that they are segmented not only along ethnic/tribal lines but also along occupational, educational, religious, and environmental lines. Among these tribesmen are some of the wealthiest as well as some of the most impoverished people on earth; in their midst is a small elite of highly educated, urbane, and cosmopolitan individuals, while the mass of their compatriots are in the main illiterate and parochial. There are Moslems, Presbyterians, Catholics, Jehovah Witnesses, Animists, and so on. There are peasant farmers tied to the soil by necessities of their work, and unemployed youths deeply rooted in the urban centers. In short, Cameroonians in addition to their ethnic/tribal affiliations belong to a congeries of membership groups each of which elicits loyalties at cross purposes with the ideal of an over-arching national community. To suggest, therefore, that only ethnic/tribal cleavages prevent the emergence of a collective sense of Cameroonian identity is to misconstrue the problem. This then is the message contained in this book. I am suggesting that environmental cleavages, i.e., rural-urban distinctions and differential access to the fruits of socio-economic development, account more for peoples' orientation <u>vis-à-vis</u> the national political system than does tribalism. In taking this position, I also try to show that in polyethnic states like Cameroon, tribesmen can also be patriots: that ethnic/tribal loyalties and national identification are not mutually exclusive.

Acknowledgements

Field research for this book was undertaken between 1972 and 1973 with the support of a generous grant from Northwestern University's Program of African Studies and a fellowship from the Woodrow Wilson National Foundation in Princeton, New Jersey. I am deeply appreciative not only for the opportunities provided but for the expressions of confidence which these awards implied. A summer at the University of Michigan, Ann Arbor as a Visiting Scholar and participant in a College Faculty Workshop on Computer Related Instruction (CRI) in Political Science offered me an opportunity to review my Cameroon data (part of which was incorporated in a jointly-authored monograph: Comparative Political Culture and Socialization: A SETUPS published in 1976 by the American Political Science Association as one of its CRI packages on Cross-National and World Politics). I am grateful to the National Science Foundation whose funding made possible the 1975 summer faculty workshop and the APSA for making it financially possible for me to attend.

My interest in micro-political behavior in general and political culture in particular was stimulated by Professor John N. Paden whose magisterial study on Religion and Political Culture in Kano continues to serve as a model. I am grateful to him for his support and encouragement throughout my stay at Northwestern University. I also wish to acknowledge the immense contribution of Professors Remi Clignet of the University of Maryland and Ronald Cohen of Northwestern University to my intellectual development. Particular gratitude to Mr. Joseph Meredith and Dr. Donald Miller both of Governors State University; Ms. Margaret Trapp, my copy editor and several anonymous readers for their incisive critiques of portions or all of this manuscript. Special thanks to the several hundred Cameroonians who patiently responded to the lengthy questionnaires which served as the basis for this study. Although it is not possible to recognize individually all those who rendered valuable assistance while data were being collected for this study, I would like to acknowledge the contributions of my research assistants: Miss Maureen Ashu, Messrs. Nani Hamza, Ndiva Njoh Ifase, Mbella Fal'a Kale, Molua, Ndumbe, and Sati. My profound gratitude to Dr. S. J. Epale (former Secretary-General), Messrs. Elundu (Plantation Manager, Tole Tea Estate), Epie (Divisional Manager, Missellele), Ilongo (Manager, Tiko Rubber), Mesembe (Plantation Manager, Tiko), and Wem Mwambo (Public Relations, Bota), all of whom were associated with the Cameroon Development Corporation at the time this research was conducted. That these people are absolved of all errors of fact and judgment found in this book needs no emphasis.

The mammoth task of indexing was undertaken by Mr. Semei Tamukedde Zake. I am most grateful to him and to Dr. Robert Milam, Dean of the College of Business and Public Administration--my academic home these many years--for providing funds for meeting the costs entailed in preparing the index. My deep gratitude to Dean Milam also for his efforts in creating a climate conducive to reflection and writing within the College of Business and Public Administration. For the typing and proofreading, I find myself once again in the debt of Ms. Marsha Doyle who performed this labor with the speed, care, patience, and excellence which has long been her distinctive trademark.

Sections of chapters 4 through 7 are reproduced after revision and updating from two chapters I contributed in <u>Values, Identities, and National Integration: Empirical Research in Africa</u>, ed. John N. Paden (Evanston, Illinois: Northwestern University Press, 1980), pp. 121-172. I am grateful to Northwestern University Press for permission to adapt or reproduce this material.

Ndiva Kofele-Kale
Park Forest, Illinois

Introduction: A Brief Political History of Anglophone Cameroon

On October 1, 1961, the former Cameroun under French trusteeship (which had become independent on January 1, 1960, and assumed the new name of the Cameroun Republic) and the former Southern Cameroons under British trusteeship joined together to form the Cameroon Federal Republic. Following this union, the former French Cameroun was renamed East Cameroon and the Southern Cameroons the federated state of West Cameroon. Eleven years later, the Federation was abolished and replaced with a unitary system of government --the United Republic of Cameroon. The focus of this study is on the former British trust territory of the Southern Cameroons. The following brief historical sketch is intended to provide background and perspective for the discussion in the rest of the study. Readers interested in more detailed historical analyses of Cameroon's political development should consult the various works dealing with the subject.[1]

The Council of the League of Nations on July 20, 1922, divided the former German Kamerun into British and French mandates with four-fifths of the territory going to the French. The remaining one-fifth under British mandate consisted of two small parts: Northern Cameroons which came to be administered by Northern Nigeria, and Southern Cameroons. The latter between 1922 and 1949 was variously called the "Cameroon Province" or "Southern Cameroons" and was placed first under the administrative control of the Nigerian Southern Provinces, then of the Eastern Provinces, and finally of the Eastern Region. Under this arrangement, the Cameroon Province became an integral part of the political history and development of the British Colony and Protectorate of Nigeria --now the Republic of Nigeria. From 1949 to 1954 the Southern Cameroons was divided for administrative purposes into a Cameroons Province and a Bamenda Province, both administered by the Eastern Region.

The 1954 Nigerian constitution, which outlined the framework for a federal Nigeria, also recognized for the first time the "Southern Cameroons" as an identifiable political unit.[2] This recognition led to the granting of a limited degree of self-government to this area as a "quasi-federal" territory within the Federation of Nigeria. In 1958, the Southern Cameroons attained full regional status, placing it on parity with the other regions in the federation. Scarcely one year later, elections were held for the now enlarged Southern Cameroons House of Assembly. The major campaign issue was the future status of the region in light of the imminent independence of Nigeria from Britain scheduled for October 1960. Campaigning for continued association with Nigeria were the Kamerun National Congress (KNC) led by E.M.L. Endeley and the Kamerun Peoples Party (KPP) led by P. M. Kale. They were opposed by Foncha's Kamerun National Democratic Party (KNDP) and the One Kamerun Party (O.K.) led by Nde Ntumazah, which championed the reunification cause in the Southern Cameroons. The K.N.D.P. won a clear and decisive majority in the new House and with this mandate from the people opened up negotiations with representatives of the Cameroon Republic on the reunification issue. These negotiations culminated in the United Nations' supervised plebiscite held in February 1961 in which the reunification alternative won by more than a two-to-one margin over the continued association with Nigeria option.

This study will examine how widespread the feeling of "we are all Cameroonians" is by focusing attention on English-speaking Cameroonians. The latter, by a majority of votes cast in the plebiscite, opted in October of 1961 to assume a new citizenship and be governed under new institutions and leaders. In examining the political culture of English-speaking Cameroon, I am particularly interested in the role environment plays in shaping and influencing individual and collective orientations toward the national government. I shall seek answers to the following questions:

How do rural peasants view government? How different are their views from those held by urban residents? To what extent are Cameroonians aware of the existence of government? Do they view government as important in their daily lives? Does it stand for things they value most? What are their expectations and experiences? How informed are Cameroonians about government policies and programs? Are they favorably disposed toward their government, its policies and programs? How knowledgeable is the average Cameroonian of his/her national leaders? How do Cameroonians from different ethnic groups relate to each other? To what extent are they committed to living together as a community of brothers and sisters? An attempt will be made to answer these questions in the chapters to come.

This book is organized into seven chapters. The first chapter attempts to formulate a theoretical framework within which the relationship between environment, ethnicity and political orientations may be analyzed. Chapter Two provides a socio-ethnographic context and outlines the criteria employed in selecting the units of analysis is this study. The contrasts and similarities among Cameroon's ethnic groups on a broad range of traditional values and institutions is the subject of Chapter Three. Chapter Four examines the impact of environmental change on ethnic group values. The fifth chapter focuses attention on the impact of environment upon the political identity system, i.e., the extent to which Cameroonians identify with each other and with the political state. In Chapter Six this impact is examined in the context of the rule and belief systems, i.e., the extent to which elite political values and goals coincide with those subscribed to by the Cameroonian masses. The concluding chapter is a summary, and an attempt to provide a profile of the political culture of Anglophone Cameroon.

Note to the Reader

Students unfamiliar with Cameroon history are often perplexed by the various names that have been employed to identify the country over the last fifty years. To avoid any confusion, a few words about my choice of terminology are in order. I use the German spelling, "Kamerun" when discussing the period of the German protectorate. For the mandate and trusteeship periods, the prefix "French" or "British" preceding the term "Cameroon" is employed to identify the mandates and subsequent trust territories. When I use "Southern Cameroons" I refer only to that section of the British-administered trust that later reunited with the Cameroun Republic in 1961. For the period of the Federal Republic of Cameroon, I use "West Cameroon" to refer to the former Southern Cameroons and "East Cameroon" to refer to the former Cameroun Republic. Following the establishment of the unitary system and abolishment of the two federated states, my choice of usage is "English-speaking" or "Anglophone" Cameroon for former West Cameroon and "French-speaking" or "Francophone" Cameroon for former East Cameroon. Throughout this study, the use of the term "Cameroon" without any qualifying prefix refers to the whole country.

Footnotes

1. The political development of the Southern Cameroons is ably discussed in Edwin Ardener, "The Political History of Cameroon," The World Today, Vol. 18, No. 8 (August 1962), pp. 341-350; Victor T. LeVine, "A Contribution to the Political History of Cameroon," ABBIA (Yaounde) No. 24, January-April 1970, pp. 65-90 and LeVine, The Cameroons from Mandate to Independence. Berkeley & Los Angeles: University of California Press, 1964, especially chapter 8; P. M. Kale, Political Evolution in the Cameroons. Buea: Government Printer, 1964; and Willard R. Johnson, The Cameroon Federation: Political Integration in a Fragmentary Society, Princeton: Princeton University Press, 1970.

2. See James S. Coleman, Nigeria: Background to Nationalism. Berkeley & Los Angeles: University of California Press, 1963, pp. 371-373.

1
Political Culture, Ethnicity, and Environment: An Overview

This study of the mass political culture of Anglophone Cameroon has attempted to do two things: first, to test empirically the relationship between environmental change, ethnicity and citizens' political orientations toward the Cameroon state; and second, to make the beginnings of a case for the rejection of the notion of "tribalism" (or sense of attachment and loyalty to an ethnic group) as the factor inhibiting the growth of a sense of national consciousness and identity among Cameroonians in particular and the peoples of Africa in general. These objectives are based on four major assumptions: (1) that attachment to ethnic group values--tribalism, so-called--holds true for the majority of people living in poly-ethnic societies; (2) that these values are held onto by ethnic man regardless of environmental variations; i.e., ethnic man remains ethnic man whether domiciled in a rural village or urban center; (3) that in spite of a sense of ethnic group attachment and loyalty the majority of people are still capable of positively identifying with national political culture values; i.e., tribesmen can also be patriotic citizens; and (4) that a lack of positive identification with the nation state results from perceptions people have of the regime conditioned largely by environmental influences.

This chapter will examine the relationship between political culture, ethnicity, and environment.

The Concept of Political Culture

The growth of political culture studies in the last two decades has been so rapid that any study which sets out to examine this subject within a comparative framework cannot hope to satisfy those who look for a neat dissection and summation of the range of issues it subsumes. Given the boundless accretion of data, the complexity of the subject, and the exigencies imposed by space, an analysis such as this, intended as a prefatory statement, cannot avoid limiting discussion only to the essential dimensions of political culture.

The concept of political culture has an old and impressive history in political science literature, although some students consider it a modern invention.[1] Its predigree can in fact be traced to the writings of Montesquieu and before him Aristotle and Plato. It is treated as a concept of recent vintage only because political culture has replaced the older concept of national character. Contemporary political culture studies are to a large extent the outgrowth of classical studies on differences in national character and on the psycho-cultural analysis of peoples, as found in the works of anthropologists such as Mead, Benedict and Gorer.[2] Political culture replaced national character in political science lexicon when it was reintroduced by Gabriel Almond in 1956. Almost a decade later a seminal work, <u>The Civic Culture</u>, authored by Almond and Sidney Verba further helped give this concept currency and legitimacy.

What after all do we mean by a nation's political culture, and why do we study it? Scholars working within the systems-functionalist framework (notably Almond, Devine, Easton, and Verba) have tried to establish that system stability and persistence reflect the level of support and the kinds of demands a political system receives from its members? This interplay of member-support and demands is central to any understanding of the concept of political culture. More specifically, political culture is the sum total of the range of political beliefs, knowledge, and attitudes that members have toward their political system. In this sense, political culture represents widespread agreement among members of any political system on certain fundamental political values, beliefs, and concepts, such as liberty, democracy, equality, and rule of law.

But political culture is more than just agreed upon values; values may remain nothing more than metaphysical abstractions. Political culture contains values that motivate people to act (to make demands or give support, voluntarily or through coercion). It is, in a very important sense, prescriptive of "proper" behavior within the political arena; a guide book, so to speak, that spells out the "do's" and "don'ts" for members in the society. Viewed thus, political culture serves as a safety-valve which regulates the quality, quantity and intensity of political demands members make of, and the support they give to, their political system. It monitors the degree of mass participation (demands) such that the political system is not overburdened and/or its leaders unable to anticipate and respond effectively to the mass public.

Is it possible to have all the members of a political system agree to the same values and share similar beliefs? If not, how can we then talk of a national political culture? By a nation's political culture, one simply means the modal patterns of political orientations of the mass publics toward specified political objects. The term "modal" as Mayer reminds us is ". . . the adjectival form of the statistical concept of mode, a measure of central tendency--specifically, the most frequently occurring type, the most typical."[3] He goes on to say that to attribute "a certain characteristic to a society's character or culture is not to imply that all members of that society share that characteristic. Such an assertion simply means that a substantial majority of the members possess that attribute in question."[4] Thus, a nation's political culture refers only to those salient political values and attitudes shared by a substantial majority of its members. It is possible, then, to have several political cultures in any given nation. Those cultures which reflect the political values and orientations of minorities can be described as political sub-cultures or marginal cultures in contradistinction to the predominant political culture, i.e., that to which the majority of the mass publics subscribe.

As a concept, political culture has been defined in a number of ways by different scholars in diverse contexts, yet most agree that it refers to that "set of attitudes, beliefs, and sentiments that give order and meaning to a political process and that provide the underlying assumptions and rules that govern behavior in a system."[5] For Beer and Ulam, political culture refers to those aspects of a society's culture which are "concerned with how government ought to be conducted and what it should try to do."[6] A distinction is made between what is actually happening in politics and what people believe about those happenings. It is the latter set of beliefs which holds significance from the point of view of political culture.[7] Such beliefs may or may not be true, but as Mayer explains, "the crucial question for the purposes of explanation is not the validity of the perceptions, it is the content of the perceptions themselves."[8] For it is what a people believe, regardless of whether it is true or not, that predisposes them to act in a certain manner toward the national political system. These beliefs are generated as a reflection of political moods, political stereotypes, the spirit of public institutions, formal as well as informal rules of the political game, goals articulated by the political ideology, and so on, all of which constitute major dimensions of the political culture of a nation.[9] But political culture is not political ideology. The latter Almond defines as "the systematic and explicit formulation of a general orientation to politics, including explicit doctrinal structure characteristically borne by a minority of 'militants'."[10] Political culture, in contrast, is "the product of both the collective history of a political system and the life histories of the members of that system" and is "to the political system what culture is to the social system."[11]

Although a consensus exists among students of political culture as to its basic meaning, confusion abounds in the consideration of the dimensions of political culture relevant to the analysis of the political climate in the multiethnic polities of the Third World. In his study of Burmese political culture, Pye identifies three types of cultural values and attitudes having an influence on political behavior: (1) <u>technical skills and competencies</u>, i.e., the knowledge and skills which members of a society are explicitly taught in order to manage socio-economic and political life; (2) <u>motivational goals</u>, the types of goals the socialization process teaches as appropriate and legitimate objectives of personal motivation, and (3) <u>associational sentiments</u>, which determine the capacity of people to relate to each other.[12] Many empirical studies on political culture and socialization have focused on the first and second dimensions.[13]

It is from these major dimensions of political culture that theorists have fashioned a typological framework. The most celebrated typology of political culture is the Almond and Verba classification of <u>parochial</u>, <u>subject</u>, and <u>participant</u> political culture according to the degree of "participation" by citizens in the political system.[14] Three other cultures are identified in terms of the degree of congruence between political culture and political structure. These are: <u>allegiant culture</u>, characterized by positive orientations in cognitive, affective, and evaluative dimensions; <u>apathetic cultures</u>, characterized by indifferent attitudes in affection and evaluation; and <u>alienated culture</u>, characterized by negative attitudes in affection and evaluation. The pattern of distribution or mixture of political cultures has in turn led to another kind of classificatory system;[15] for example, a <u>unified</u> political culture;[16] or a <u>dominant</u> culture co-existing with various sub-cultures; a dichotomous culture as seen in elite and mass political culture in India;[17] a fragmented one as seen in Burma[18] and many poly-ethnic societies; traditional vs. modern political culture;[19] and finally, non-secularized vs. secularized political culture.[20]

Why Study Political Culture

Why do we need to study political culture? First of all, as Easton and Hess suggest, to sharpen our ". . . understanding and exploration of those factors that contribute to the stability of different types of political systems, their change over time, and the direction of their change; whether these systems are democratic or dictatorial, modern or traditional, industrial or agricultural. . . ."[21] Thus to understand the dynamics of change or immobility in any political system, one must come to grips with its political culture. Only through a study of a nation's political culture can the student begin to understand in a systematic non-stereotypical way the political life and institutions of a society. To understand, for instance, the strong emotive attachment Britons have for their royal family or why the Westminster system of democracy has worked so well in Britain but failed when transplanted elsewhere, knowledge of British political culture(s) is crucial.

We also study a nation's political culture in order to find out what it takes to be (and to make) a good citizen; the kinds of information to which people should be exposed if they are to become better informed about politics and highly motivated to participate actively in public affairs.

Although the pioneers of political culture studies have confidently asserted that "every political system is embedded in a particular pattern of orientations to political action"[22]-- meaning every political system has a political culture--this assertion becomes controversial when the focus is on the emergent states of Africa.

Expert commentaries have underscored the need for unifying political culture in the polyethnic African states, a political culture that will transcend the loyalties directed toward ethnic units. In the words of Apter and Coleman, two seasoned Africanists:

> The principal challenge to the leaders of the new states is one of creating a sense of common citizenship in which there are certain shared political values, a measure of common purpose, and a respect for political institutions and established authority. They confront not only the problem of consolidating and stabilizing the new society, but also the monumental task of mobilizing the human and natural resources of their country in pursuit of the goal of rapid modernization.
>
> Confronted with heterogeneous populations having varied interests and making conflicting demands, they must create a common political nationality, and the role of participant citizen must be identified with that nationality. They must meet challenges to public authority and internal security, not only by the use of those coercive and punitive measures employed by all governments faced with crisis, but, more importantly, they must inculcate a positive loyalty to the new nation and a respect for the laws of the government of that nation.[23]

Various attempts have been made to explain the lack of homogeneous political culture in these new states. These rationalizations can be reduced to three. The first type of explanation frequently advanced, the historical discontinuity position, argues that historical discontinuities brought about by European colonialism slowed the evolution of a hegemonic Afrocentric system of shared political values. A second category of explanation, the ethnic/tribalism argument, sees ethnic group loyalties competing with national loyalties with the result that the latter are seriously compromised. Finally, a third approach, the socialization discontinuity argument, examines the patterns of socialization within the various ethnic groups and concludes that people are socialized for participating in the local ethnic system as opposed to the larger national community. In the following pages, each of these approaches will be examined in detail with the objective of highlighting its major weaknesses. This study takes as a point of departure the cumulative limitations of these three approaches.

Departing from traditional American socialization studies with their emphasis on children's political attitudes, the focus here is on adult values and political attitudes, i.e., the individual with a clearly defined political self. This is not, however, a study in political socialization per se; rather, the process is assumed to be fairly complete since we are dealing with an essentially adult universe. The attempt here would be to isolate those factors which may have conditioned people's political orientations as a necessary first step in understanding the source of cleavages and consensus in national political cultures in the emergent states of Africa.

The Historical Discontinuity Argument[24]

This explanation is fairly simple and uncomplicated. Its proponents argue that the absence of widespread consensus on salient political values within the new states is the logical result of an uneven and disjointed political growth brought about by the imposition of western colonial domination. This approach emphasizes the newness of these nations, their institutions and political values. As one prominent scholar points out: "The new African governments are recruited from new men. . . . The relationship of the leader with his followers, of ministers with their colleagues, with bureaucrats, with the general public, are new relationships."[25] The belief that the whole colonial period was one long history-less period in the lives of the African peoples has adherents among many nationalists. Speaking for the Guinean experience, although he could be speaking for all of colonial Africa as well, Amilcar Cabral makes the following observation:

> We consider that when imperialism arrived in Guinea, it made us leave history--our history. We agree that history in our country is the result of class struggle, but we have our own class struggles in our own country; the moment imperialism arrived and colonialism arrived, it made us leave our history and enter another history. Obviously we agree that class struggle has continued, but it has continued in a very different way; our whole people is struggling against the ruling class of the imperialist countries and this gives a completely different aspect to the historical evolution of our country.[26]

An examination of the history of colonialism will show that in theory and even more so in practice, the colonial overlord had no intention of promoting a sense of national community within the nations that were colonized. In fact, the colonial philosophy stressed the importance of the vertical ties with the metropole rather than horizontal bonds among the peripheralized colonized people themselves. The latter relationships are essential ingredients for the development of any sense of national identity.

As a result of the primacy given to metropolitan values and institutions, the political structures and values that gave the colonized pockets shape were essentially derived from the colonial universe. To the extent that we talk of a political culture, we mean alien political values that were transplanted from Europe and super-imposed on an indigenous system of values and institutions, values held there by the sheer force of the commanding colonial presence. Where a homogeneous political cultural base existed, it was driven underground since its development would have served as a challenge to the principle of vertical political integration to the metropolitan political system. In a sense then, colonial imposition effectively arrested the development of indigenous political cultures and institutions. This has resulted in gaps between pre-colonial and colonial African and also between colonial and post-colonial Africa.

The historical discontinuity argument is not without its critics, who point out that there is more historical continuity in African political development than is given credit.[27] As Tignor states:

> While I do not want to deny the validity of these views, I would like to suggest that contemporary analyses of African politics have not paid sufficient attention to pre-independence legacies-- pre-colonial and especially colonial inheritances. The colonial system resulted in the implanting of political behaviour in local communities. It left a legacy of action and attitudes which has been hard to supplant.[28]

Tignor suggests that these parallels between colonial and independent Africa may even constitute continuities between the two periods not only at the attitudinal level but also at the level of institutions. Tignor limits his study to the local government level which he considers "acted as a purposeful and efficient extension to the colonial government." Examining the chieftaincy institution, one is struck by the impressive continuity in office by chiefs (whether traditionally appointed or by colonial fiat). These agents of the colonial and later post-colonial bureaucracy tended to stay in power for long periods and in turn prepared the way for their successors. This would suggest that at the micro-local governmental level, there has been a modicum of institutional continuity between the colonial and post-colonial periods, enough to invalidate the theme of newness that many commentators quickly assign to the emergent nations.

While Tignor's exception is well-taken, it only explains <u>residual</u> continuities between colonial and post-colonial Africa at the local level. It fails to challenge the central proposition of the discontinuity model, that colonialism destroyed, or failed to leave behind, symbols and institutions at the national center which commanded the allegiance of a broad cross-section of the new citizens. My main objection to the discontinuity model is that it begs some very important questions. By tying the absence of political culture in the new states to the historical discontinuities caused by colonialism, this view assumes that it is <u>primarily</u> and <u>ultimately</u> the colonial factor that accounts for the absence of a sense of shared political culture values. But for this factor, the argument logically continues, these nations would by now have fashioned their own brand of political culture. This view, of course, assumes that prior to the colonial intervention politico-cultural homogeneity existed within these new societies which supported a strong feeling of common identity and nationality. The assumption may be correct but it is still a moot point.

The historical model is weak on another ground. It presupposes that traditional cultures are so rigid that they cannot resist the impact of colonialism.[29] On the contrary, there is evidence to suggest that many African cultures did resist colonial domination and their institutions were resilient enough to cope with and adapt to the new experience. This was partly due to the dynamic nature of these institutions and partly due to the deliberate attempts by the colonizing powers to systematically incorporate indigenous structures into the colonial administrative framework. This is evidenced in the policy of Indirect Rule which involved government at the local level employing principally indigenous institutions. This seems to suggest that the imposition of alien domination on traditional African societies did not necessarily result in a radical and irreversible transformation of values and institutional infrastructure. Again, this reinforces Tignor's contention that there is a strong thread of continuity linking pre- and post-colonial Africa, at least at the level of local government.

Essentially, the historical explanation amounts to no more than a description of colonial rule without really explaining the underlying factors (some of which may have nothing to do with colonialism) which have inhibited the growth of national political cultures in the emergent nations. I am in agreement with Merton that an empirical description of a fact is no adequate substitute for its theoretical explanation.[30] We must go beyond merely describing what colonialism did, to discovering what was in Africa prior to the arrival of colonialism. The value systems of the various population groups in these plural nation-states need to be critically examined with the objective of ascertaining whether they ever shared common political culture values, and to what extent these were destroyed by the colonial imposition. Bearing in mind that African societies were by no means static, immutable points in space and would therefore have changed one way or the other even without the presence of the colonial factor, it would be equally meaningful to examine how the cumulative impact of the twentieth century might have affected people's predispositions toward the nation-state. This, of course, would entail a comparative analysis, as I have done here, of population groups residing in localities which have been differently exposed to the contemporary tidal wave of social change and thus objectively manifest behavioral attitudes and orientations that are not necessarily similar.

Whereas the first explanation limits itself to those historical factors that may have affected the growth and eventual emergence of political culture, the next two approaches address themselves to the issue of value congruence or lack of it at the mass level. They differ from each other, further, with respect to the interpretation and definition of the major valuational forces militating against the sense of common national identity. One approach emphasizes the content of one solitary value cluster, namely tribalism, and considers this as the centrifugal force directing people's loyalties away from the national polity. The second approach stresses the processes through which certain political values are transmitted by different ethno-cultural groups to their carriers. An understanding of these socialization processes will enhance one's understanding of the difficulties they pose for the appearance of a national political culture. Let us take each approach in turn.

Ethnicity/Tribalism Argument

In a lucid discussion of tribalism, Professor Mafeje raised the following questions:

> Few authors have been able to write on Africa without making constant reference to 'tribalism.' Could this be the distinguishing feature of the continent? Or is it merely a reflection of the system of perceptions of those who write on Africa, and of their African 'converts'? Objective reality is very difficult to disentangle from subjective perception, almost in the same way as concepts in the social sciences are hard to purify of all ideological connotations. Might not African history, written, not by Europeans but by Africans themselves, have employed different concepts and told a different story? If so, what would have been the theoretical explanation?[31]

Mafeje goes on to argue that European colonialism in the process of restructuring African reality produced "certain blinkers or ideological predispositions which made it difficult for those associated with the system to view these societies [meaning African] in any other light."[32] Out of this recreated African reality emerged the ideology of "tribalism." Indeed, Africa remains the only continent where tribalism has been elevated to the status of a scientific paradigm and the ultimate source from which all explanations, justifications, and rationalizations of its sociopolitical reality are derived. An African coup d'etat, for instance, is described not so much in terms of the ranks of the officers who led it, as in terms of their tribal origins. Analyses of the competing liberation movements in Africa devote more space to their tribal following and less attention to their more important ideological differences on the nature of state power and how it should be used to resolve the continent's problems.

An examination of the many attempts by scholars and political leaders to explain the absence of national political cultures as well as other aspects of African social relations still finds them invoking tribes and tribalism as the fundamental contradiction in Africa. This bias has become quite entrenched at the expense of other more serious societal divisions such as class differentiations and class conflicts, generational tensions, rural-urban differences and so on, which are either ignored or blithely relegated to the level of residual contradictions. However, progressive Third World scholars such as Stavenhagen have challenged, in his words, "The importance attributed by ethnologists to cultural elements of . . . populations [which] has long concealed the nature of the socio-economic structures in which these populations are integrated."[33] Without in any way minimizing the importance of ethnicity in African socio-political relations, I agree with Shivji that ethnic consciousness itself "needs to be explained rather than be made an independent but divisive variable" (emphasis in original).[34]

But the romantic notion that African tribesmen are by nature incapable of becoming patriots of their new civic states still persists, enjoying wide currency in both popular magazines and serious scholarly journals. It has generally been held that the "tribe" in poly-ethnic African states constitutes a threat of enormous magnitude to national integration, and those primordial attachments generated by it invariably contribute to the disintegration of the polity. This view, shared by many Western scholars and Western-trained Africans, finds ethnic group cleavages so intractable that they serve not only to undermine the stability of the political community but also to prevent the emergence of broadly based political cultures in these new nations.

It is a view that has been popularized by Geertz, who is convinced of an imminent looming headlong clash between ethnic group loyalties, on the one hand, and those that are beamed toward the nation, on the other.[35] Both are set on a collision course. According to him, primordial tribal sentiments and attachments threaten the existence and political integrity of the emergent nations precisely because they contain a more ". . . ominous and deeply threatening quality than most of the other, also very serious and intractable problems that the new nations face. Here we have not just competing loyalties but competing loyalties of the same general order, on the same level of integration."[36] While Geertz falls short of calling for the forcible suppression of tribal loyalties by a leviathan state, he nonetheless makes it clear that unless these loyalties are domesticated, the emergence of a national political culture (what he calls civic sentiments) will remain a distant prospect.

In a similar vein, Nobel Laureate W. Arthur Lewis argues that antagonisms which result from these sentiments cannot be overcome by arguments and economic concessions, precisely because they are "not based on disputes about principles or interests. Hence [they are] the most difficult of all political problems."[37] This claim has been disputed by other students of African politics, and I shall return to it later.

Although Europeans formulated the ideology of tribalism, they have not been the only ones guilty of promoting it. Africans, unfortunately, have been fellow travellers. National leaders and many intellectuals have been held captive by the myopic view that regards tribalism and national loyalty as two mutually exclusive forces, with the former being dysfunctional a propos national integration.

Many of the continent's leaders have uncritically and foolishly defined the end product of the integrative process as a homogeneous political community in which ethnic group attachments must be completely obliterated. In a recent study of political development in Cameroon, French political scientist Bayart found that the country's ruling elite embraces a model of development which sees a contradiction between modernity on the one hand and the traditional political values and institutions of the extant ethnic groups on the other.[38] 'Tribalism' is condemned in all its forms and particularist loyalties are systematically suppressed, ostensibly in the interest of national consciousness. The Law of 12 June 1967 banned "any associations exhibiting an exclusively tribal or clan character" meaning "(a) any association which claims to admit as members only those coming from a named clan or tribe; (b) any association which, without altogether excluding those from other clans or tribes, in fact pursues an objective contrary to national unity."[39] Bayart concludes that as a result of the Cameroon government's cultural policy, one finds that:

> At the popular level the exigencies of practical politics are setting Cameroonians in conflict with their customary values and artistic expressions, or

at least are de-vitalizing these traditions. The state schools systematically discredit the vernacular languages--which do nevertheless transmit a global cultural vision; thus the child is torn between his own milieu and the political system.[40]

This Jacobin approach of constructing national unity through the systematic suppression of primordial attachments--in particular, ethnic and regional--obfuscates, in my estimation, the real forces impeding the growth of national consciousness in Cameroon. The campaign against ethnicity/tribalism, the cornerstone of the government's cultural policy, is in keeping with the regime's attempts to destroy potential sources of opposition which could be organized around ethnic associations.[41] But while tribalism/ethnicity is exorcised, available evidence suggests that it remains an important criterion for appointment to high office in Cameroon. The regime in effect engages in a double standard. In forming the cabinet every effort is made to balance it ethnically; yet before the masses these same leaders preach against ethnicity and in fact wish it away.

On the surface, this policy of using ethnic origin as a major criterion for appointing ministers is intended to ensure that political power is properly distributed among the diverse ethnic groups within Cameroon. With over 200 ethnic groups in the country, the ethnic arithmetic formula is seen as the best method for maintaining a delicate ethnic balance, reduce potential communal cleavages, and in the long run pre-empt any ethnically-backed challenges to the central authority. Yet when we examine dispassionately how this formula works in practice we find that the consequences are quite the opposite of what was intended. The policy has been subjected to widespread abuse to the point where it has helped instead to fuel ethnic suspicions and exacerbate inter-ethnic hostilities. Secondly, the policy has also worked to undermine the government's announced program of planned and balanced development.

The resort to the ethnic arithmetic formula as a means of maintaining some semblance of power has not meant an attenuation of ethnic differences; instead, these have blossomed. The policy has led to a practice where entire ministries, departments within ministries, para-statal organizations, etc. have been transformed into prebendary structures to reward members of the minister's ethnic group. In each ministry, preferential treatment in hiring and promotion is usually given to members of the minister's ethnic group. Applicants from other ethnic groups are considered only after the pool of candidates from the minister or department head's tribe has been exhausted. And in many instances, qualified candidates are denied appointments in preference for unqualified ethnic members.

A second problem with the ethnic balance formula as practiced in Cameroon is that it encourages a form of laissez-faire development that can best be characterized as "helter-skelter." That is, development projects are located in areas where they are least needed or can be least economically justified. The prime consideration in deciding where critical infrastructural development should be undertaken appears to be the ethnic origin of the minister. The government has recently built a major international airport in Garoua even though traffic at the Douala International airport is far from congested. Garoua of course is the home of Cameroon's president Ahidjo. To take another example, Nguti is a backwater village of no economic consequence which would have remained this way but for the fact that its representative on the cabinet, Nzo Ekangaki used his enormous influence to get an airport and major mission-run hospital built in this village of less than 3000 people. Yet Kumba, a short distance away, the largest urban center in Anglophone Cameroon and a burgeoning commercial city is not served by an airport and what passes for its hospital is only a hospital in name. The airport in Nguti was used intermittently when Ekangaki was in power (as a minister and later when he became administrative secretary-general of the O.A.U.) and now hardly any aircrafts land there. Vast sums of money went into the construction of this unused airfield which stands today as a reminder of how tax payers' money is misused by those in power all in the name of developing their ethnic communities. Or to take another example, Mbengwi, the home village of Solomon Tandeng Muna, one time Prime Minister of West Cameroon and Vice-President of the federation and now Speaker of the National Assembly, had street lights installed long before the streets of Bamenda, headquarters of the Northwest province and an important commercial center in the Grassfields, were electrified.

Overall, Ahidjo's ethnic policy only serves as a device for ethnic fragmentation and mass control drawing inspiration from the old Roman rule of divide et imperia. By tacitly promoting the idea that each member of the cabinet represents particular ethnic group interests and not the nation as a whole, the policy has succeeded in separating the mass of Cameroonians into hostile, competing ethnic groups. This is precisely what the ruling elite wants, since it allows for its leader, Ahidjo, to play the role of a deus ex machina who is constantly arbitrating among the quarreling and suspicious ethnic groups.

The policy also serves two other related purposes, both of which reinforce my preceding observation that ethnicity/tribalism is a tool employed by Cameroon's ruling elite to maintain its hold over the masses. First, the use of ethnic origin as a criterion for ministerial appointment transforms this factor into a narcotic for lulling the masses into a false sense of security and belief that they do participate in and can influence important decisions and policies through their own ethnic representatives on the cabinet. Second, when disparities in the distribution of economic resources coincide with an ethnic group, ethnic consciousness is exacerbated and likely to be channeled into violent attacks against the government. The formula of having each ethnic group represented in the cabinet helps to defuse such tensions since ethnic group complaints about the lack of socio-economic development in that region can be easily blamed on the cabinet representative from that ethnic group. He/she becomes the sacrificial lamb whose quick expulsion from the cabinet is interpreted as a sign of the government's commitment to ensure that the fruits of economic progress are distributed to all segments of the population. It also ensures that ethnic group anger is directed not at the collective national leadership but at the unfortunate cabinet representative who is simply a tool of convenience. In all of this, Cameroon's president and his policies are never criticized. His reputation as well as the integrity of his ruling party remain unassailed precisely because the ethnic arithmetic formula makes it possible to shift the blame for programmatic failures away from the collective leadership and to pin it squarely on the shoulders of the individual ethnic leader.[42]

Thanks to this formula, the masses believe they do participate in state affairs, even if indirectly, and this keeps alive the pretense of democracy in Cameroon. At the same time frequent Stalinist-type purges in the cabinet give the lie to the myth of a permanent leadership ensconced in office for over two decades unwilling to bring in new faces. Critics are disarmed and the masses are fooled into the belief that new blood is always brought in to rejuvenate the system. As Bayart argues, the fear of organized opposition to Cameroon's almost two decades of de facto one-party rule appears to be the justification for the government's offensive against particularistic loyalties and attachments. But from the point of view of genuine national consciousness and identity, this approach suffers because it rests on a faulty ideological premise: the notion that tribalism/ethnicity is a lingering and an embarrassing historical anachronism which has no raison d'etre in a modern Cameroon society. Therefore its suppression is made the precondition for the emergence of a new homogeneous Cameroon culture to replace the parochial cultures of the various ethnic groups.

This approach sees the relationship between ethnicity and national loyalties as a zero-sum game; an either/or proposition. I, however, find this position too rigid. Because it is so linear and uni-directional, it ends up creating an unnecessary and invidious dichotomy between ethnic group membership, on the one hand, and citizenship in the national community, on the other. At the micro-level, it makes the individual out as either a tribalist or a patriot but never both. At the macro-level, a nation's political culture is either civic (modern/homogeneous) or parochial (tribal/traditional/heterogeneous), again, never a mix of the two. What emerges from this poorly conceptualized framework is a dilectical relationship between ethnic attachments and national loyalties characterized by an inevitable struggle. The stage is then set not for a dynamic interaction between these two phenomena where both co-exist in a symbiotic relationship; rather, as if in a class struggle, one of the two must go. Simply put, it is as if to say that being a Bafaw and a Cameroonian at the same time is an unsupportable proposition.

This is not to minimize the formidable task of transforming Bafaws, Banyang, Metas into Cameroonians, of instilling in them a sense of Cameroonness which overshadows and in fact transcends their subordinate parochial loyalties to the ethnic group. It is a task which was accomplished by the older nations of Europe and North America only after several centuries and under circumstances much more favorable than is the case anywhere in Africa today. And yet even in Europe the task is far from complete; witness the fratricidal struggle in Northern Ireland, and the assorted separatist squabbles in Belgium, Canada, and Spain to mention only the more famous cases of western instability brought about by primordial attachments.

But the prominence given to tribalism/ethnicity as a disintegrative force and the antithesis of national consciousness is misleading at another level. In focusing attention on ethnic differentiation and consciousness as the fundamental contradiction in African socio-political relations, proponents of this view have wittingly or unwittingly glossed over the question of class divisions and class struggles as equally important factors in understanding how Africans relate to one another and to their states.[43] For too long African nationalists and others have put forth the view that African societies are 'classless,' and that class analysis has no validity or utility for the study of African politics. A 1965 Kenya Government White Paper on "African Socialism and its Application to Planning in Kenya" boldly and confidently asserts that:

> The sharp class divisions that once existed in Europe have no place in African socialism and no parallel in African society. <u>No class problem arose in the traditional African society and none exists today among Africans.</u> (emphasis added)[44]

Similar views about the non-existence of class divisions in pre- and post-colonial Africa have been advanced by other African leaders.[45] This, despite overwhelming evidence to the contrary. The myth of a classless African society has proved hard to dispel. The astonishing persistence of this myth, according to Kenneth Grundy, can be explained by the fact that it has been employed by Africa's ruling elite to justify the dictatorship of the one-party state, to explain and defend the now discredited ideology of African Socialism, and, probably most important of all, to rationalize, justify, and consolidate its dominant position in society.[46] In the process ethnicity was introduced into the analysis of socio-political relations as an ideological smokescreen and a convenient scapegoat upon which to blame the failure of the integrative revolution. Miller and others in contesting the claim of a classless African society recommend we view ethnic "loyalties as potential sources of tension which may be actuated by perceived inequalities and thus may also, theoretically at least, be avoided."[47] Drawing admiringly on Stavenhagen's studies on the social relations of Indians and Ladinos in southeastern Mexico, Shivji directs us to reverse the anthropologist's ethnicity-bound approach to African socio-political relations, and instead, to "make the place occupied by the actors in the social production process, the centre of analysis."[48] We have here the first clear attempt to move beyond the ethnic character of peoples to their relations to the productive forces as a basis for analysis. Thus the answer to the question of how dysfunctional and destabilizing a force ethnicity/tribalism is will follow from an analysis of the nature of African relations among themselves and between them and their states executed within the context of the whole socioeconomic structure. Such an analysis will reveal, I submit, that (1) ethnicity/tribalism is not necessarily dysfunctional and (2) that in many instances it has been used as an excuse to divert attention from the more realistic approach which implicitly recognizes the place of class divisions and class conflicts in African sociopolitical relations.

The contention here is that ethnic loyalties and attachments (or tribalism so called) can exist pari passu with national loyalties and that tribesmen can be patriots. To begin with the ethnic group and the loyalties it generates are permanent features of contemporary African societies and as an integral part of the continent's social dynamics they need to be properly analyzed and understood against a broader background in order to avoid falling victim to the view of them as inherently dysfunctional. Let me push ahead with this line of argument since it is here that I disagree fundamentally with the tribalism vs. national identify dichotomy.

A proper understanding of the phenomenon of tribalism has proved frustratingly elusive because there is no formal consensus among its users as to what it exactly represents. Not even among anthropologists, for whom tribalism has had such a special fascination, is there agreement on what it means. As one of them correctly observed, the term is so slippery and emotively charged that "it frequently arouses emotions which are so violent and so contradictory that they confuse clear thinking."[49] Perhaps part of the ambiguity surrounding the definitions attributed to the term lies in Gulliver's observation that an examination of tribe and tribalism involves a wide range of variables in an equally wide range of social contexts. Consequently, they take on different meanings depending on the contexts, and these in turn dictate the range of characteristics that are to be included in the meaning given to them.[50] In short, the notion of tribalism varies with time and situation.

La Fontaine[51] and others isolate three shades of meaning given to the concept of "tribalism." First, tribalism is characterized as the clinging to traditional life as opposed to an acceptance of modernity among people who are exposed to rapid cultural change. Tribalism here connotes atavism. It means a strong attachment to particularistic values and traditions as opposed to universalistic values necessary in the modern contemporary world. Second, tribalism has been equated with the notion of nepotism or political corruption. It is used here to deplore those actions which tend to leave behind the unmistakable impression that the distribution of power, status, and amenities in the modern African society operates along lines defined by particularistic ties of blood and kinship as opposed to more Westen universalistic criteria. Finally, tribalism can mean the emotions of solidarity aroused by leaders within certain ethnic groups who, as Mafeje appears to agree, invoke "tribal ideology in order to maintain a power position, not in the tribal area, but in the modern capital city, and whose ultimate aim is to undermine and exploit the supposed tribesmen"[52] as happened in Southern Cameroons immediately following the United Nations supervised plebscite of 1961. Disappointed by the results which showed the overwhelming majority of Southern Cameroonians electing to reunify with the Cameroun Republic, Kpe leaders of the C.P.N.C. (the party that had campaigned for continued association with Nigeria) E.M.L. Endeley and Motomby-Woleta summoned over 6,000 Kpe to the slopes of Mount Cameroon and talked them into agreeing to the following resolutions which were to be sent to the United Nations: (1) the administration of the Kpe according to their unanimous vote during the plebiscite; (2) the sending of a Kpe delegation to state its case for integration with Nigeria; and (3) a recognition of the fact that the Balondo, Bakossi, Bafaw are related to the Kpe and should therefore be administered with the Kpe.[53] The summons to the slopes of Mount Cameroon was in accordance with an ancient Kpe custom in which the supreme council of Kpe clan chiefs, the <u>Molongo</u>, was convoked in times of stress and war to make binding decisions on the whole ethnic group. But this time the <u>Molongo</u> was exploited by some tribal leaders who, having lost an important election, sought to re-establish their hegemony by appealing to the primordial and xenophobic instincts of fellow ethnics. What this indicates is that the "solidarity derived from common membership in a tribe, as expressed in certain cherished values"[54] can be exploited by unscrupulous political leaders to play off one group against another, or one collection of groups against another.

A closer look at La Fonatine's differentiation of the concept of "tribalism" reveals a broad streak of negative connotations attached to the terminology.[55] Tribalism is either the inability of Africans to embrace modernity, or an ideology of political coercion, manipulation and exploitation of the mass of Africans by their greedy and ambitious tribal-cum-national leaders, or the criterion for limited political recruitment and participation in the national reward system. There is nothing good about tribalism because it either pits the masses against their leaders, one group against another, or traditional values against innovative ones. These various interpretations of tribalism link up with what William Graham Sumner long ago identified as ethnocentrism: "the technical name for (the) view of things in which one group is the center of everything and all others are scaled and rated with reference to it . . . (in which) each group nourishes its own pride and vanity, boasts itself superior, exalts its own divinities, and looks down with contempt on outsiders."[56] Or what Robert Merton refers to as chauvinism: "the extreme blind, and often bellicose extolling of one's group, status, or collectivity."[57] This hubristic affirmation and extreme glorification of an ethnic group, accompanied by a belief, implicit or explicit, in its cultural superiority and hence its inherent right to rule over other ethnic groups is a <u>consequence</u> and not an essential component of tribalism. It developed under particular social and historical conditions which must be identified and explicated if this phenomenon is to be placed in its proper perspective.

That ethnic loyalties have been exploited by Africa's ruling class to further its own special interests, deplorable though this is, does not make these primordial attachments candidates for extinction. Neither should patriotism be discouraged because it has been used in its extreme jingoistic form to justify imperialism and, in the hands of the Nazis, to advance the doctrine of white Aryan supremacy. The problem is not ethnic loyalties or patriotism <u>per se</u> but the conditions which have given rise to it, and the manner in which these profound human emotions have been put to use, in particular, when these have been used as the rallying cry to arouse some of our basest instincts. A proper and sympathetic analysis of the phenomenon of tribalism, especially as it relates to the issue of transcendent national loyalty, must begin with an analysis of the sociohistorical conditions that have given it refuge.

An exegetical exercise of this sort must begin by confronting head-on this very simple yet somewhat hard to accept reality: Africa is a continent of people who belong to tribes (or nationalities or ethnic groups). And by tribe, one simply means a group of people who conceive of themselves as being alike by virtue of their shared values, common heritage, real or fictitious, and who are so regarded by others. Such a group must be biologically and valuationally self-perpetuating through the processes of procreation and socialization, must share common cultural values and organizations, communicate through a mutually intelligible language, may or may not share the same ecological domain (i.e., Maine's notion of local contiguity is not a crucial definitional criterion) and, its members should identify themselves and be identified by others in such a way that they form a category distinguishable from other ethnic categories. Following Edel, I shall refer to the warm and close ties members have toward their ethnic groups as tribalism or ethnic identity or ethnicity or ethnic loyalty.[58]

For the mass of Africans, expressions of tribal attachments and identifications are no more than the manifestations of group pride, dignity and achievement. It is pride and dignity in a way of life that has sustained countless generations of people. It is pride in the traditions and values that sum up a culture group and in many ways define the genius (past and present) of its culture-carriers. It is these culture groups (or ethnic parts) that in turn give Africa its totality, i.e., its civilization. For the African civilization is a mosaic of its ethnic components. Senghor seems to describe this better with his gift for words:

> Our fatherland is the inheritance which our ancestors have transmitted to us;

> land, blood, a language, or at least
> dialect, manners, customs, folk lore,
> art, in a word culture rooted in the
> soil and the race . . . <u>the fatherland
> is the land of the Serer, the Malinke,
> the Sonrai, the Mossi, the Baule, the
> Fon.</u> (Emphasis added)[59]

Note that for Senghor, the Senegalese fatherland is the aggregation of its ethnic units; so too we conceive of the African <u>patrie</u>--the ultimate pan-African community.

Ethnic group pride is usually objectified in dress, music, names, language, and so on. When so expressed they attest to a people's desire to maintain and preserve their cultural originality and individuality without prejudice to those sentiments which also bind them to the larger political community of the nation-state. There is nothing peculiarly African about this since this phenomenon can justifiably be generalized as one which is characteristic of multiethnic societies. Ethnic pride in the United States, for instance, did not begin with "Black Power" and the "I-am Black-and-Proud" slogans of the early sixties nor has it been confined only to the darker complected people of this multiethnic configuration. Its paternity is shared by almost all the ethnic groups represented in American society.

In societies marked by ethnic pluralism, ethnicity becomes the response to, and the ideological instrument (often times effective) for combatting the revolution of rising expectations. As Paul Mercier points out, "Tribalism is a series of defensive reactions which can quickly disappear when the facts of inequality disappear."[60] Ethnicity finds expression in the political arena where the struggle for scarce economic resources is usually waged. In the ensuing contest for economic and political power ethnic group loyalty becomes politicized but not in the sense that La Fontaine and Mafeje talk of tribal politicization. I am talking of politicization in the classic sense as resulting from the competition for scarce goods and services and for power and status which takes place in every modern polity. In the struggle for "who gets what, when, and how," people organize themselves into optimal groups in order to compete effectively for their share of political and economic rewards and then to preserve and protect them once achieved.

Pressure or interest groups that are so organized linger on to the extent that they remain effective as agents for articulating and aggregating the demands of their members. In many of the multiethnic African states, some groups of people are denied, or believe they are denied, full participation in the political process as well as access to the fruits of economic progress, because they happen to belong to a particular ethnic, racial, religious, or regional group. Where this is the case, it is not unusual that pressure groups organized to protest against this perceived inequitable distribution system will be differentiated along ethnic, racial, religious, or whatever primordial criteria, which have been used in the first instance to discriminate against their clients. The experience of the pluralist United States of America reveals very strikingly how oppressed minority ethnic groups (if not all, at least most) effectively employed their ethnic distinctiveness as the focal point for regroupment and realignment of forces in their bid for economic and political power.[61]

The African experience is also rich with examples of ethnic and regional groups that combined their forces as a prelude toward greater political participation within the larger political system.[62] The heterogeneous nature of most African societies sets the stage for conflicts in values and interests among the different ethnic groups. However, some ethnic groups have been able through a combination of several factors (size, geographic location, advantage in educated manpower, favored treatment from the departing colonial power, etc.) to establish hegemony over others.[63] These groups successfully preempt for themselves choice command positions and a disproportionate share of economic and other privileges in the country. Confronted with such a situation the dispossessed ethnic groups respond by organizing themselves into political movements whose primary objective is to claim for their communities a fair share of national power, status and material benefits. Taking place here is what Anber drew our attention to with respect to the Ibo "problem" in Nigeria where tribal loyalties were developed and politicized because of the nature and context of modernization.[64]

As Anber observed in the Nigerian situation, unbalanced modernization can lead to inter-ethnic conflicts and domestic instability. Thus, where there has been a higher level of socio-economic and political advancement in one ethnic sector of the national polity without corresponding modernization among the other ethnic segments ethnic cleavages are exacerbated, become very pronounced and politicized. Two things unusually happen. First, the economically dispossessed ethnic groups resort to defining the boundaries of the state system as coterminous with those of the politically and economically dominant ethnic group(s). That is, the state is viewed as the chasse gardee of the ruling ethnic group(s) and hostility usually reserved for the exploiting ethnic group(s) is now extended to the national polity. This sets the stage for a clash between state and ethnic group loyalties. The state is denied the loyalties it would normally have commanded from a cross-section of the populace because it is now closely identified with a particular ethnic group or collection of ethnic groups. This was the case during the First Nigerian Republic where depending on which ethnic group one belonged to, the federal government was viewed variously as under the domination of the Hausa-Fulani from the north, or the Yoruba from the West, or the Ibo from the East. Thus people identified with, or were alienated from the central government--and by extension the Nigerian state--depending on their perceptions as to which of the three major ethnic groups was dominant.[65]

Second, to the extent that some ethnic groups be-lieve they are less favored, are being victimized and deprived of meaningful political participation and equal opportunity of access to the nation's economic and social privileges, they will appeal to particularistic sentiments in their bid to challenge the balance of power in society. Since the political movements-cum-pressure groups that emerge from this nascent politicization of demands represent specific ethnic groups, criteria for recruitment into and participation within them are primarily ascriptive. It is my contention that these political organizations will continue to maintain an ethnic base insofar as the collective demands of their constituents appear not to have been resolved satisfactorily by the power brokers at the national level. So too will these ethnically anchored organizations continue to appeal to ethnic ties as long as their ethnicity is felt to be the major reason why equal opportunities and access to instruments of political power have been denied their members. Clearly then, ethnic cleavages and societal fragmentation will plague Africa for a long time to come until gross social inequalities and economic imbalances are corrected. Attempts at legislating ethnic groups out of existence will only prove futile and illusory.[66]

It is remarkable that many scholars who have commented on the putative disruptive features of ethnic identification in Africa fail to take into consideration that in most cases the phenomenon of tribalism is nothing more than a reaction to the unfair distribution of benefits and services within a nation-state. Ethnic cleavages simply reflect this differential access to economic resources and political power enjoyed by ethnic groups where some ethnic groups and/or regions come out more equal and more favored than others. While overtly the struggle for resources like employment, wages, housing, education and so on is between and among ethnic groups (and not between political parties differentiated on ideological lines as in many West European countries), this is simply not because Africans think in exclusively ethnic terms or define their worldview in very parochial language. That this struggle takes on ethnic overtones does not only confirm Sklar's observation that in Africa intense passions tend to flow easily into tribalistic channels. More importantly, it brings out clearly the fact that in poly-ethnic societies people react differently to the stresses and strains that accompany the modernization revolution and the resultant struggle for economic resources and political power. As Wriggins pointed out in the case of Sri Lanka, the revolution of modernization can cause a disruption in the equation between education and opportunity.[67] That is, economic development and growth may not keep pace with expanding educational opportunities, resulting in high unemployment among a fairly well educated cadre. When this takes place in a political system where political and economic spoils are allocated on the basis of kinship ties, job opportunity becomes synonymous with belonging to the "right" group(s). Confronted with such a reality, an educated but unemployed mass of people quickly ignore their wider loyalty to the nation, replacing it with a loyalty that comes from belonging to a particular ethnic group. The reason for this is obvious, since for them the ethnic group is now considered as their last hope for upward mobility. Only by politicizing their groups and using them to wrest political control can they begin to enjoy the benefits of belonging to a nation.

Ethnicity/tribalism can also serve as a rationalization of the relations between ethnic groups within an economic context. For example, nationalism in the British Cameroons was marked by hostility toward the Nigerians, particularly the Ibos[68] who entered the territory in large numbers after 1945. They settled in the coastal urban centers and prospered as businessmen, civil servants, small retailers, tailors, shoemakers, and laborers in the Cameroon Development Corporation plantations. They constituted what Shivji calls a "commercial bourgeoisie."[69] In 1958,

Nigerians--the majority of whom were Ibos--constituted over 30 per cent of the plantation work force. By 1961, they constituted 12 per cent of the civil servants staffing the government departments. Nigerians accounted for nearly 25 per cent of the positions in the federal government services operating in Southern Cameroons, nearly a quarter of the positions with the ports authorities, one-third of those with post and telegraph offices, one-half of those with custom services, and three-fourths of those in the technical services. Nigerians, particularly Ibos also controlled 85 per cent of the commercial establishments and most of the African-run transportation services in the Southern Cameroons.[70] This commercial dominance of the Ibos was particularly felt in, though not confined exclusively to, the coastal urban centers of Buea, Kumba, Muyuka, Tiko, and Victoria. The Ibophobia that surfaced during the nationalist phase in Southern Cameroons is not, as some commentators have noted, simply xenophobia toward Nigerians in general and Ibos in particular because of their "alien-ness."[71] Admittedly, some political leaders, notably the pro-unificationists led by Foncha, encouraged this xenophobist sentiment and made political capital out of it by emphasizing the putative cultural differences between Nigerians and Cameroonians: "Cameroonians are not Nigerians!" was the theme that carried them on to victory in the reunification plebiscite.[72]

The Ibophobia which swept Southern Cameroons during the reunification fever had much to do with the context in which the mass of Cameroonians and the Ibo immigrants interacted and the dominant relation which ensued from this interaction. This context was economic, and the dominant relation between the Cameroonian masses and the Ibos was commercial. The Cameroonian met the latter mainly as a producer of minor consequence and a consumer. For the Ibo in Southern Cameroons was the trader, the broker, and the creditor who dominated the territory's commercial life. The immigrant confronted the Cameroonian peasant and worker in an antagonistic production relationship determined by the Ibo dominance of the commercial sector. The Ibophobia that served as a prop for Southern Cameroon nationalism was derived from this sphere of production relations which largely determined the fundamental relationship between the two communities. It would be misleading to explain Cameroonian hostility to the Ibos as an emanation of culture or ethnicity; the origins were economic. To the Cameroonian masses, the Ibos represented the exploiting class; thus, their essential relationship was that between exploiter and exploited. It is this factor, in my view, that conditioned Cameroonian predispositions toward the Ibos. But this hostility toward the Ibo was not confined to the Cameroons. In 1946, rioting broke out between the Efik and Ibo in Calabar provoked by the long standing domination of the internal economy of Calabar by the Ibos who were strangers to the city. According to Ndem:

> The role of the Ibo in the internal economy of Calabar, a town of close proximity to Ibo territory is of profound significance. At first their main articles of trade consisted of stock-fish and clothing materials which they bought from European stores. <u>They became the middlemen thus ousting the natives from their historic preserve</u>. As peddlars they penetrated every corner of Efik plantation, making friends and enemies as they went along. Before the end of last war their economic interests had widened; stockfish and clothing materials were to them too narrow a compass. New grounds had to be broken and extended. And to the surprise and annoyance of the indigenous natives the Ibo plunged, without reservation, into the selling of such consumption goods as yams, garri, crayfish, fresh and smoked fish, including all sorts of spices and greens. All these, with the exception of the first two, yam and garri, were, and are

> still to the natives, the preserves of their women-folk. . . . When the Calabar-Mamfe road was being built the majority of the labourers were Ibo. This gave them a vantage point to establish contacts with the local people. The Ekoi, whom the Ibo who subsequently arrived found a willing clientele. Soon the traders have established an Ibo settlement; farming is undertaken as an ancillary activity. The local hunters instead of carrying their kill to Calabar as they hitherto had done now sell to the Ibo who will smoke the meat and retail it to Efik housewives at prices considered exhorbitant if not prohibitive (my emphasis).[73]

The Ibo displacement of the indigenous Efik from their historic preserve followed by the former's ascendancy as the dominant economic force in Calabar clearly indicates that the two communities confronted each other in an antagonistic production relationship, a relationship which was assymmetrical and to the disadvantage of the autochthonous Efik. In stereotyping the Ibos as "pushy," "avaricious," "crude," and other such negative imagery, the Efik were in fact giving vent to their anger and frustration at their economic inferiority vis-a-vis the more successful Ibo. The conflict which arose in this and other such situations (the intense Ibophobia unleashed in Southern Cameroons, for example) was the consequence of one group becoming "convinced that the terms of exchange are becoming unfair, either because the other group is alleged to be making an unduly large profit [as in the case of the sale of smoked meat in Calabar quoted above], or because it is actually usurping the place of the first (as in the case of the Efik women food-sellers). In all of these cases cultural stereotypes can readily be brought into play, but it should be noted, <u>they are essentially expressing conflicts of economic interests</u>" (my emphasis).[74]

Indeed when the struggle for these essentially economic interests abates, interethnic relations take on a character of warmth, understanding, and cooperation. West Cameroonian reaction to the Nigerian civil war is illustrative of this tendency. When the Ibos became involved in the bitter fratricidial struggle with General Gowon's troops to carve a new Biafran state out of the crumbling Nigerian federation, the outpour of public sympathy for their cause was surprisingly overwhelming in West Cameroon.[75] So powerful were these pro-Biafran sentiments that when at the end of hostilities Gowon made a triumphant state visit to Cameroon he confined his stay to the French-speaking sector. It is remarkable that the same West Cameroonians who a decade earlier had reviled the Ibo presence in their midst now embraced and supported their cause, even when such support was against official government policy which was unswervingly pro-Gowon.[76] The plight of the Ibo and their persecution under Hausa/Fulani hegemony struck a responsive chord among West Cameroonians (who themselves were chafing under the same form of domination since 1961) eliciting powerful human feelings of brotherhood that clearly transcended narrow ethnic distinctions. Ten years earlier, these feelings could not exist when the context within which Ibos and West Cameroonians interacted was characterized by a struggle to maximize each community's "essential" economic interests; a context in which the Ibos' dominant position in the territory's economy made them scapegoats and easy targets for directing pent up anger and hostility long festering under the West Cameroonian collective surface.

I have indicated in the foregoing discussion that ethnicity can be interpreted as an expression of ethnic group pride and not simply as an atavistic stance against the forces of modernity and change. It can also be used as a basis for organizing into political movements for the express purpose of bargaining for power, status and amenities in the political marketplace on behalf of groups that have by design or accident been excluded from full participation in the political system on the basis of their ethnicity. In neither of these two formulations do I consider tribalism (i.e. sense of ethnic group attachment and loyalty) as inherently dysfunctional or a deterrent for the emergence of a full blown national political culture. This then constitutes my first criticism of the tribalism vs. national loyalty dichotomy.

Secondly, I reject the view that ethnic group loyalties and national loyalties are mutually exclusive and therefore exhaustive, because this denies the possible existence of overlapping group memberships and by extension cross-cutting loyalties. This rejection is sustained by findings derived from studies on multiple memberships and loyalties in other nation-states.[77] Richard Rose and Robert Ward have shown for England and Japan respectively that a nation can have a political culture which combines both traditional elements and modern values.[78] Even in those Western countries where mutually antagonistic subcultures are present, the emergence of broadly based political cultures has not been held back because the people were incapable of transferring loyalties from the primary local community to the national one. This has been the experience of the Netherlands, Ireland, Switzerland and Belgium.[79]

My final criticism of this monistic approach hinges on the belief that it advances a very simplistic, culture-bound explanation of a problem that is far too complex and in need of far more refined explanatory tools. Indeed, by narrowing the explanatory focus to one solitary variable, ethnicity, it inhibits the search for other variables. But above all, it ignores or is unaware of some compelling evidence drawn from empirical studies which seem to indicate that other factors inherent in the socio-political make-up of a nation do affect degree of political participation and in the long run, the type of political culture that eventually emerges. The Five-Nation Study conducted by Almond and Verba found that the political cultures of France, Italy and Mexico were heterogeneous as opposed to the homogeneous civic political cultures of Great Britain and the United States. Examination revealed that the former political cultures were fragmented into subcultures which are embedded in various role structures, such as political parties, communication media, and so forth. A common feature of such fragmented political cultures, the authors found, was the tendency for subcultural loyalties to reinforce or parallel each other. Catholics will vote for Catholic-oriented parties, belong to Catholic labor unions, read Catholic newspapers, send their children to Catholic schools, in short participate in an existential network that is determined primarily by this subcultural identity. As Kavanaugh notes, it is this mutual reinforcement of social, religious, and political loyalties at the micro level that heightens the antagonism between subcultures at the macro-national level.[80]

The finding suggests that political cultural fragmentation exists in other parts of the world and that this is not a function solely of a failure to rise above parochial _tribal_ loyalties and attachments. Fragmentation and cleavages become evident _only_ when important role structures in a society address themselves to essentially parochial audiences, and thus reinforce primordial attachments. This, we submit, is not the case in the majority of the African societies. There are no labor unions that are exclusively ethnic-based and few such parties. Their absence, therefore, means that ethnic parochial loyalties are denied, at the national level, those important political structures and agencies which might have helped in solidifying ethno-cultural distinctiveness and in the long run severely fragment the nascent political culture.

The example of the political party might high light the point just raised. Studies have shown that in the new nations of Africa, the role-structure that has been most vulnerable to ethnic co-optation and penetration has been the political party.[81] But the party (with few exceptions) as any student of African affairs very well knows, is a recent phenomenon in that continent and therefore lacks the historical continuity that its European counterpart enjoys. As a result, the loyalties and attachments that it generates lack the very important ingredient of time depth. African political leaders are veterans in the art of "carpet crossing"--a desire always to team up with the political party that seems assured of success. Party allegiances are changed indiscriminately and with relative ease because ties to any one party are tenuous at best, and non-existent at worst. Unlike the average European partisan, party ties are not deeply rooted in family history or tradition. For the African party militant, political prejudices are static since they are hardly transferred, as in the American case over generations from parent to offspring as voting studies have consistently established. The absence of this factor leads one to believe that watertight ingroup/outgroup dichotomies based on political affiliations have not developed or are in their incipient stages. Thus, the non-institutionalization of ethnic particularisms at the national center makes it difficult to talk of ethnic group-oriented labor unions, schools, churches and so forth in the same breath that one would talk of such religious-dominated institutions in France and Italy, for example.

The point I am trying to make here is that the type of "tribalism" that could prove divisive from the point of view of national integration is that which is sheltered at the national center and constantly being reinforced at all levels of society by role structures that are themselves "tribally" determined. Unless it can be shown that this is the case for the majority of African polities, constant reference to "tribalism" would amount to no more than reification of the concept. More importantly, however, is the theoretical vacuity of the concept of "tribalism" in the broader framework of social science research. It is ideologically-laden with Eurocentrism such that it impedes serious comparative cross-cultural and cross-national analysis.[82] The point has been commented upon by Sklar while addressing himself to the problem of violence and instability in Africa:

> In all underdeveloped countries where the traumas of secularization are strong, the potential for violence is great. In Africa, violent passions flow easily into tribalistic channels. <u>It is not very meaningful to say that a particular nation has been disrupted by tribalism.</u> <u>Political science should seek deep to find the root causes of tension and violence.</u> (Emphasis added.)[83]

Sklar's stricture applies equally to those social scientists who seek the easy way to explain the absence of political cultures in the emergent African states. The fundamental objective of scientific inquiry is to develop and test general rules and statements that would be applicable beyond the boundaries of any single society. This cannot be fulfilled if we meekly accept concepts that are culture-bound. Tribalism is one such concept.

Inconsistencies in Patterns of Socialization Argument

The "tribalist" approach sketched out the African as a one-dimensional person who must decide whether he intends to remain forever a "tribal" man or a citizen participating in the new experience. Other serious scholars have sought to explain the African dilemma by drawing on the rich body of data on childhood socialization studies in America.[84] It is generally accepted among students of political socialization that the absence of a uniform set of political orientations among citizens of a given national political system can be attributed to the discontinuities, inconsistencies, and value incongruences resulting from the different socialization processes each individual undergoes in his lifetime.[85] As one student puts it, "where the socialization process results in disparities between what is learned in childhood and the experiences of adult contact with the political process, the political system suffers some strain."[86] Relating this to Africa, Robert Levine points out that in the new nations there is considerable discontinuity between the political orientations of the citizens and the prevailing political values of the new civic state. This is so because childhood socialization prepared the individual only for participation in the local ethnic community, not the national community. Since these political values and orientations acquired as a child persist into adulthood, it becomes extremely difficult for most people to shift from the local ethnic to the national political scene.[87] Another view holds that aside from the content, i.e., the political values learned in childhood, variations in political socialization may occur as a result of the relative gaps between pre-adult and adult experiences, when the nature of the political process varies.[88]

As to the most important socializing agent, Levine suggests in his study of the Nuer and Gusii (two East African segmentary ethnic groups) that in order to understand and predict the contemporary political behavior of African peoples who lived in stateless societies prior to Western contact "one must take account of the traditional political values involved in their local authority systems particularly since such values continued to be internalized by new generations after their society has come under the administration of the modern nation-state."[89] Levine and Apter,[90] in their various studies on African political systems, also found that people reacted differently to the nation-state depending on the type of traditional political system into which they were socialized. Thus, a person from a stateless society is able to relate to the new nation by transferring certain political values learned from the family to the new reference group. Apter and Levine suggest that variations in national political orientations can be explained as a function of the differences in ethno-cultural group values and structural organizations.

Although the Apter/Levine position has some shortcomings (which will be discussed later) its attempt to explain political culture through an examination of the political values (and processes by which these are communicated to new members) of the ethnic groups is a welcome relief from the two previous approaches already discussed. One of the assumptions of this study is derived from the Apter/Levine formulations: that the ethnic system remains one of the most important socializing agencies for most Africans in general, and Cameroonians in particular; and the experiences picked up from the socialization received there may not necessarily be in conflict with the modernizing political values of the new nation-state. In other words, certain ethnic political values could be supportive of regime values, such that experiences shaped in the ethnic community do not cause the individual to reject a priori the political values of the overarching political system. An individual may cling to his ethnic group loyalties and identifications independently of those loyalties he directs toward the national political community. It may be that other existential factors not ethnically grounded may have a contributory impact on his national loyalties; therefore, the focus of study must go beyond an analysis of ethnic group values and methods of political socialization to a consideration of what these other factors might be.

The Apter/Levine approach takes as its point of departure the proposition that political orientations derived from ethnic group traditions will have a continuing impact on the individual's political behavior at the national level. It then proceeds to analyze the content of these traditions, and the processes through which they are transmitted, within a comparative framework. In their various studies Levine and Apter take into account the colonial impact on values, especially the local authority system which Levine saw as ". . . compounded of traditional political patterns, forms introduced during colonial administration, and changes wrought under pressure of contemporary economic conditions."[91] In short, the general orientation is to consider the ethnic system and the values it encloses not as a static but as a dynamic system responding to change.

Although Levine and Apter have stressed the comparative approach in all their studies, their observations have been limited to comparing the behavior and authority patterns of people from essentially similar ethnic systems. Levine, for example, studied the contemporary political behavior of two East African ethnic groups--the Nuer of the Southern Sudan and the Gusii of southwestern Kenya. These two groups come from the same culture area, and are similar in social structure, being traditionally acephalous groups differentiated into segmentary patrilineages as the major form of socio-political grouping, with agriculture and animal husbandry as the basic mode of production. Apter, on the other hand, was interested in how traditional societies that are hierarchically organized respond to innovation and modern values associated with change. He compared the Buganda kingdom of East Africa with the Ashanti confederation in West Africa. Although he differentiated between the two on the grounds that one was hierarchical while the other (Ashanti) was a pyramidal system, the distinction is not sharp enough to regard them as fundamentally two different systems. This limitation to similar ethnic systems narrowed considerably their comparative range.

Furthermore, no attempt was made to observe behavior across several localities, that is, to take into consideration the impact of environment e.g., rural-urban differences on political values. It would appear that Levine confined his study to patterns of authority among rural families.[92] Thus, his generalizations about the impact of authority patterns on the political outlook of the peoples are qualified by the fact that they apply only to persons living in rural areas. Again, this methodological limitation undermines the comparative force of these superb pioneering studies.

An attempt has been made in this study to avoid some of the major weaknesses of the approaches just discussed. Political values and behavior are compared for the two systems and also across three types of environmental localities--rural villages, peri-urban plantation camps and urban centers. Using the approach of controlling background factors by specification, the colonial influence is held constant in such a way that it has identical value for the three groups. This is treated in detail in the next chapter.

Theoretical Framework

The view taken here is that political orientation is as much the result of responses to environmental stimuli as it is of political socialization and ethnicity. In short, the specific geographic location (village, town, or city) of an individual or of groups of people influences their political values and behavior. The conventional viewpoint held by students of political socialization interprets the antecedents of political orientations in pedagogic terms. Most studies assume that political behavior develops largely through a learning process.[93] Thus, the focus has usually been directed toward an examination of certain major institutions in society (family, school, peer group, etc.) deemed central in the transmission of political values and attitudes to members.[94]

Valid as this assumption is, it fails to underscore the importance of non-pedagogical factors in the acquisition of political orientation. More to the point, it leaves unanswered the question: how much does environment influence political behavior? Therefore, this study tested the hypothesis that individual and group conformity to patterned political values and behavior varies with exposure to environmental influences. That is, variations in geographic location are accompanied by parallel contrasts in political orientation, resulting in different patterns of political attitudes toward the nation by urban and rural residents.

This analysis will present some of the observations that have been made respecting the putative difference between rural and urban communities and their populations. The distinction between rural and urban behavior and the debate over the distinction's validity is an old one indeed. Its roots reach back to Maine, Tonnies, and Durkheim, all of whom contributed important dichotomies of societal characeristics.[95] Others have carried on this tradition.[96] Venerated as this dichotomy came to be for some social scientists[97] it has nevertheless generated much adverse criticism from the academic community.[98]

In attempting to draw "causal" links between locality and manifest political attitudes, one ventures into territory that has only been partly explored. The problem has been noted and commented upon by several scholars.[99] The evidence, still fragmentary and not quite representative of the universe of political systems, indicates that significant differences exist between rural and urban people with respect to their national political sentiments.

In a study of Italian political culture, LaPalombara notes the strong impact that traditional structures and values have on the political orientations of rural Italians. In a similar vein Banfield's investigation of the behavior of villagers in a southern Italian village uncovered a strong attachment to the family and the kin group. So extreme was this "amoral familism" among Montenegrians that it severely undermined any sense of community or national identity. Both studies conclude that the majority of rural southern Italians still remain firmly tied to the family, to affective, diffuse, and particularistic standards in contrast to the more affectively neutral, specific, and universalistic standards found among urban northerners.[100] Frey's study of the political orientations of Turkish peasants confirms the findings of LaPalombara and Banfield. Frey also found that rural village Turks had a lower incidence of nationalistic sentiments than their urban compatriots, and even village youths seemed to be notably less oriented toward the nation than their urban peers attending public Lycee-level schools.

The foregoing examples suggest that there is some basis for arguing that environmental factors do affect peoples' attitudes and values. The term "environment"[101] (and its substitutes, "geographical location," "locality," etc.) will be used here to represent the context within which ethnic values and political orientations are examined. It will be used in much the same way that system-functionalists, especially Easton, utilize the concept of "system." In the context of this study, however, environment is not viewed as an artificial mental construct called into play solely for the purpose of reducing complex reality into manageable parts for analysis. Common sense impels us to argue that the lines that separate rural countryside from urban centers especially in the Third World are real and concrete. These lines are real in the sense that they separate two localities which occupy opposite extremes on a spatio-temporal continuum; two localities representing different levels of socio-economic development, different stages and periods in time and space.

The view has been articulated by many that a person making the journey from the countryside to the city is undertaking a trip that cuts across time and space.[102] For in historical and sociological terms, the gap between countryside and city is so vast that it reflects their differential rate of social progress, historical situation, level of development, mode of production, social values and structures, ethos, etc.--in a nutshell, those tangible and intangible aspects of life and society that constitute culture. This gap is abundantly clear in Cameroon, where 71.5 per cent of the population lives in rural areas and only 28.5 per cent in the urban centers. Yet as the following figures suggest, the fruits of socio-economic development are more evident in the areas with the least population, i.e., cities and towns. The 1976 Census reveals that 85 per cent of the children from 6 to 14 years of age living in urban centers are in school as opposed to 61 per cent in the rural sector; only 8.3 per cent of the rural population has access to pipe-borne water in contrast to 58 per cent in the urban centers; less than 1 per cent of the rural population uses electricity as against 22.6 per cent in the cities and towns; almost four-fifths of the urban population live in houses with corrugated iron roofs or tiles against 36.2 per cent in rural villages; and only 1 out of every 10 rural resident lives in modern housing complexes compared to 1 out of every 3 in the urban centers. For students of political culture the important question is whether the sharp differences in material resources that these figures suggest exist between town and countryside influence the manner in which residents from these two types of localities view the national government.

My view is that political knowledge, beliefs and opinions about the political system are strongly influenced by one's objective location in society. For the difference between one environment and another may be the difference in who gets to go to school, learn to read and write and be able to read newspapers containing information about the government, get a job and earn enough money to buy a radio from which to listen to news broadcasts, buy better clothes, eat well, sleep in cleaner and bigger homes; have access to hospitals, walk on paved roads and so forth. In short, one type of locality may provide wider opportunities for its population to gain access to human and material comforts which will in the long run influence its political outlook. One locality may preempt for its population a disproportionate share of goods and services provided by the state at the expense of other localities and their populations. Political socialization aside, it would seem that localities which enjoy certain advantages over others with respect to basic economic and political rewards will be more favorably disposed to the political system (which made such bountiful gifts possible in the first place). The reverse should hold for localities that have no access to the national spoils system. That is, the more distantly removed, figuratively speaking, a locality is from the centers of political power, the lower its rank on the hierarchy of national priorities; the fewer economic benefits it receives and, therefore, the less favorably disposed its populations will be toward the political system. Such a population will be characterized by a low sense of political knowledge and opinions about the national political system.

Because economic growth and political modernization are clearly far more advanced in Cameroon's urban centers than in the rural periphery, I am hypothesizing that the majority of residents in the former localities will be more favorably disposed toward the national regime than the latter population group. In political culture terms, urban residents in contradistinction to rural folk will or should subscribe to political orientations that are favorable to the national political system. They will or ought to be, generally speaking, more politically informed and aware than rural folk; have a higher level of political <u>savoir faire</u>, a stronger attachment to the nation (its institutions and leaders), and a higher sense of national community identity. The reverse of these will characterize rural village folk. I am saying then that the aggregative effects of environmental location will lead to urban residents being more in favor of and sympathetic to the regime than rural people.

It must be emphasized that rural/urban differences (and their corresponding impact on political culture values) cannot be understood solely in terms of the amenities enjoyed by their respective populations. To limit the factors distinguishing these two localities purely on the observable variations in their levels of socio-economic development would be ignoring the fact that there are indeed some villages, rare though they may be, that can be considered more developed than some towns (if we reduce our definition of development to nothing more than the relative abundance of social amenities in any given locality). While material differences constitute an important cluster of variables for demarcating town and countryside, they do not capture the total reality.

It is of course safe to say that a person who bites the hand that feeds him is really not exercising good judgment. One would therefore expect residents from relatively developed and modernized sectors of society to be favorably disposed toward their benefactors--the national regime. Although this close and positive identification of the masses (or a segment of them) with the larger national political system is an important political culture attribute, it constitutes only one part of the matrix. For there is also a complementary side to national identity--that which relates to the feeling and sense of community shared by members of the same nation. Does variation in levels of modernization within different localities also explain variations in levels of community identification? Or are there any other factors competing against a shared sense of group identity?

At first glance, it would appear that variations in levels of modernization defined in terms of the rural/urban dichotomy only help in weakening nascent bonds of fellowship felt by members of a state. That is, those members of the population whose localities are not favored by amenities will naturally be resentful of their compatriots who are blessed with many. Instead of a sense of one common identity emerging several identity systems surface, all defined in terms of socio-economic criteria. Accordingly, fellowship is defined in terms of the "haves" in contrast to the "have nots."

Without underestimating the negative impact on perceptions to feelings of community brought about by differences in the socio-economic status of the localities in which individuals reside, a case can still be made for understanding the whole question of common national identity by showing that towns are still different from rural areas even on criteria other than their differential levels of socio-economic development. If we view the expression of a common national consciousness as the consequence of a process which seeks to bring together people from diverse social and cultural backgrounds, then we are confronted with two very important questions: (1) can it be said that some localities are in a position to accelerate this process while others retard it? (2) can we explain the acceleration or retardation of this process as reflective of the differences between countryside and urban centers? My answer to these questions is that environmental differences are central to an understanding of variations in levels of community identity.

Feelings of common national identity express an orientation (or a complex of orientations) which can grow only if exposed to the right climate. These orientations must be nurtured via the process of socialization or resocialization within certain types of institutions and agencies designed with the express objective of turning out people who share a sense of common nationality. Institutions such as the military, youth brigades, schools, and increasingly in Africa, the single party, which draw their membership from a cross-section of the population, discharge this task. Even a superficial familiarity with Africa in general and Cameroon in particular would leave one in no doubt as to where these types of institutions and agencies are concentrated: as a rule, in the urban areas. Thus the distribution of those institutions that serve to resocialize citizens for participation in the new national experience can be employed as an index for demarcating town and countryside. In terms of opportunities to participate within these agencies and institutions town residents are clearly more advantageously placed than rural people. It is therefore fair to assume that because town residents are exposed to institutions that teach and reinforce community values, they will manifest a higher level of community feelings than will rural residents.

In poly-ethnic societies the process of developing strong feelings of national identification (among other political culture values) depends a great deal on how well national institutions open up opportunities for social mobility and interaction. The question of community identification is still an unanswered one until people have been able to develop attitudes that are consistent with the objectives of the new socialization agencies. This is ultimately a matter of how wide or how limited opportunities are for inter-ethnic contact and communication. Because rural areas are almost always ethnically homogeneous, they do not provide the same opportunities as the ethnically heterogeneous towns for close interethnic contacts which ultimately lead to the building of strong interpersonal and interethnic friendship networks. These networks constitute the very foundation of any long and lasting sense of common national identity.

The multiethnic character of urban centers leads me to expect that their residents will be better placed than people from ethnically homogeneous rural areas to participate in friendship and occupational networks that cut across ethnic boundaries. In the long run urban based dwellers should manifest a stronger sense of community identity than rural residents.

In summary then, the position taken here is that the differences between rural districts and urban centers are of such a fundamental nature as to cause their respective populations to subscribe to different political orientations. Although the design will examine three types of localities, villages, plantation camps and towns, the peri-urban camps and towns will be regarded as polar opposites of rural villages. However, plantation camps will be considered different from towns in the sense that the latter have developed through a form of laissez-faire urbanization as opposed to the forced urbanization of the former.

Hypotheses to be Tested

Research is more than a fact-gathering activity, as Cohen advises:

> There is . . . no genuine progress in scientific insight through the Baconian method of accumulating empirical facts without hypotheses or anticipation of nature. Without some guiding idea we do not know what facts to gather. Without something to prove, we cannot determine what is relevant and what is irrelevant.[103]

I endorse this prescription of the scientific enterprise as the relationship between empirical observations within a conceptual frame of reference, consequently I shall now state the research hypotheses that form the background to this study.

There are two central hypotheses in this study: the ethnic value consistency hypothesis and the environmental location difference hypothesis.

A. <u>The Ethnic Group Value Consistency Hypothesis</u>--This hypothesis holds that variations in geographical location do not produce concomitant changes in the values subscribed to by persons from different ethnic systems. Reformulated into a null hypothesis, it now reads:

> THERE WILL BE SIGNIFICANT DIFFERENCES BETWEEN RURAL AND URBAN RESIDENTS FROM DISSIMILAR TRADITIONAL SYSTEMS WITH RESPECT TO THEIR ATTACHMENT TO ETHNIC GROUP VALUES.

B. The Environmental Difference Hypothesis--
In the theoretical framework I postulated that environmental location significantly affected political orientations. That is to say, the extent to which individuals and groups conform to patterned political values and expectations varies with the extent to which they are exposed to varying environmental influences. The null hypothesis now reads:

> THERE WILL BE NO SIGNIFICANT DIFFERENCE BETWEEN PERSONS LOCATED IN THE COUNTRYSIDE FROM PERSONS LIVING IN URBAN LOCATIONS WITH RESPECT TO POLITICAL ORIENTATIONS.

This hypothesis is broken down for testing as follows:

i. Rural village residents will tend to be different from labor camp and town dwellers with respect to political culture values;
ii. Labor camp residents will tend to be different from village and town residents with respect to political culture values;
iii. Town residents will tend to be different from village and labor camp residents with respect to political culture values;
iv. Rural village residents will have a lower sense of identification with the national political system than camp residents;
v. Labor camp residents will have a higher sense of identification with the nation than village residents but a lower sense compared to town residents;
vi. Town residents will have a higher sense of identification with the national political system than both village and camp residents;
vii. Rural residents will have a lower sense of national community identity than camp and town residents; conversely, residents

from camps and towns will have a high sense of community identity.

Footnotes

1. See Young C. Kim, "The Concept of Political Culture in Comparative Politics," Journal of Politics, 26, 2 (May, 1964).
2. Margaret Mead, "The Study of National Character," in Daniel Lerner and Harold D. Lasswell, eds., The Policy Sciences, Stanford: Stanford U. Press, 1951, and "National Character" in International Symposium on Anthropology, New York. Anthropology Today: An Encyclopedic Inventory (ed.) A. L. Kroeber, Chicago: University of Chicago Press, 1952; Ruth Benedict, The Chrysanthemum and the Sword: Patterns of Japanese Culture Boston: Little, Brown and Company, 1946 and Patterns of Culture. Boston: Little, Brown and Company, 1958; G. Gorer, The American People: A Study on National Character New York: W. W. Norton, 1948; "National Character: Theory and Practice," in M. Mead and R. Metraux (eds.), The Study of Culture at a Distance Chicago: University of Chicago Press, 1953; and Exploring English Character. New York: Norton, 1955.
3. Lawrence Mayer, Comparative Political Inquiry Homewood, Illinois: Dorsey Press, 1972, p. 163.
4. Ibid., p. 163.
5. Lucian W. Pye, "Personality and Changing Values" in his Aspects of Political Development. Boston: Little, Brown, and Company, 1966, p. 104.
6. S. A. Beer and B. A. Ulam, eds. Patterns of Government. New York: Random House, 1968, Chapter 3: Political Culture.
7. Sidney Verba, "Germany: The Remaking of Political Culture," in Lucian W. Pye and Sidney Verba, eds.; Political Culture and Political Development. Princeton: Princeton U. Press, 1965, p. 516.
8. Mayer, op. cit.
9. Richard E. Dawson and Kenneth Prewitt, Political Socialization. Boston: Little, Brown, and Company, 1969, p. 29.
10. Almond, "Comparative Political Systems," Journal of Politics, 18, 3 (August 1956), p. 397.

11. Lucian W. Pye, "Personality and Changing Values," in his *Aspects of Political Development*, op. cit., p. 105.

12. Lucian W. Pye, *Politics, Personality, and Nation-Building: Burma's Search for Identity*. New Haven: Yale University Press, 1962, pp. 48-49.

13. See, for instance, R. W. Wilson, *Learning to be Chinese: The Political Socialization of Children in Taiwan* Cambridge, Mass.: M.I.T. Press, 1970; Lucian W. Pye, *The Spirit of Chinese Politics: A Psychological Study of the Authority Crisis in Political Development*. Cambridge, Massachusetts: M.I.T. Press, 1968; Richard Fagen, *The Transformation of Political Culture in Cuba*, Stanford: Stanford U. Press, 1969.

14. Almond and Verba, *The Civic Culture*, op. cit.

15. A. Brown, "Introduction" in A. Brown and J. Gray, eds., *Political Culture and Political Change in Communist States*. New York: Holmes and Meier, 1977.

16. T. Ishida, *The Political Culture of Japan: Conformity and Competition*. Tokyo; Tokyo University Press, 1970.

17. L. Rudolf and S. H. Rudolf, *The Modernity of Tradition Political Development in India*. Chicago: University of Chicago Press, 1967.

18. Pye, *Politics, Personality, and Nation-Building*, op. cit.

19. Samuel P. Huntington and J. I. Dominguez, "Political Development," in Fred I. Greenstein and N. W. Polsby, eds., *Macropolitical Theory, Handbook of Political Science*, Vol. III. Menlo Park, California: 1975.

20. Gabriel Almond and G. Bingham Powell, Jr., *Comparative Polity: A Developmental Approach*. Boston: Little, Brown and Company, 1966.

21. David Easton & R. D. Hess, "The Child's Political World," *Public Opinion Quarterly*, XXIV (1960), p. 636.

22. Gabriel Almond, "Comparative Political Systems," *Journal of Politics*, op. cit., p. 396.

23. David E. Apter and James S. Coleman in American Society of Pan-African Culture, eds., Pan-Africanism Reconsidered, Berkeley, Calif.: University of California Press, 1962, p. 96.

24. It would be an exercise in futility trying to trace out the formulations of this approach to any one particular scholar or group of scholars. For in actuality, the approach is one taken by almost every student of Africa who seeks to provide explanations for the transitional problems Africans have been faced with since the withdrawal of the colonial presence. It is customary to take the colonial fact as a point of departure (and for some the first and ultimate cause of all African problems) when analysing the problems confronting contemporary Africa.

25. Lucy Mair, The New Nations Chicago: University of Chicago Press, 1963 p. 123, cited in Tignor, "Colonial Chiefs in Chiefless Societies," Journal of Modern African Studies, Vol. 9, No. 3 (1971), p. 339. See also Arnold Rivkin, ed., Nations by Design: Institution Building in Africa. New York: Anchor, 1968.

26. Amilcar Cabral, Revolution in Guinea. New York: Monthly Review Press, 1970, p. 56.

27. Issa Shivji for one disagrees with Cabral and points out that "throughout the colonial period different sections of the people in one way or another were engaged in making history: by their anti-colonial struggles, peaceful and violent." The view that the colonial peoples returned to history only after independence is unacceptable since they continued to make history throughout the colonial phase. Issa Shivji, Class Struggle in Tanzania (New York: Monthly Review Press, 1976), pp. 55-56.

28. Robert L. Tignor, op. cit., pp. 339-340.

29. I am grateful to Professor Remi Clignet who brought this point to my attention in a personal memorandum.

30. Robert Merton, "A Paradigm for the Study of the Sociology of Knowledge," in Paul F. Lazarsfeld and Morris Rosenberg, eds., The Language of Social Research, New York: The Free Press, 1955, p. 502.

31. Archie Mafeje, "The Ideology of 'Tribalism'," *Journal of Modern African Studies*, Vol. 9, No. 2 (August, 1971), pp. 253-261.
32. *Ibid.*, p. 253.
33. Rodolfo Stavenhagen, "Classes, Colonialism, and Acculturation," in J. A. Kahl, ed., *Comparative Perspective on Stratification: Mexico, Great Britain, Japan*. Boston: Little, Brown, and Company 1968, p. 31.
34. Issa G. Shivji, *Class Struggles in Tanzania*, op. cit. p. 41. Cf. Cynthia H. Enloe, *Ethnic Conflict and Political Development*. Boston: Little, Brown and Company, 1973.
35. Clifford Geertz, "The Integrative Revolution, Primordial Sentiments and Civic Politics in the New States," in Geertz, ed., *Old Societies and New States*. New York: The Free Press, 1963.
36. *Ibid.*, p. 111.
37. W. Arthur Lewis, *Politics in West Africa* (London, 1965) p. 66 quoted in Robert A. Miller, "Elite Formation in Africa: Class, Culture, and Coherence," *Journal of Modern African Studies*, 12, 4 (1974), pp. 537-38.
38. See J.-F. Bayart, "One-Party Government and Political Development in Cameroon," in Ndiva Kofele-Kale, ed., *An African Experiment in Nation-Building: The Bilingual Cameroon Republic Since Reunification*. Boulder, Colorado: Westview Press, 1980, pp. 159-187.
39. *Ibid.*, p. 163.
40. *Ibid.*, p. 169.
41. *Ibid.*
42. So seriously have ministers taken their role as ambassadors for their respective ethnic groups that one minister, no longer in the cabinet, is rumored to have compiled a master list of all his ethnic people in institutions of higher learning both in Cameroon and abroad. As each one graduated, so goes the folklore, he/she was immediately given an appointment in the gentleman's ministry. It mattered little that the person's qualifications were better suited for another ministry as square pegs were forced into round holes. Few Cameroonians are fooled by the government's public pronouncements on the evils

of tribalism and nepotism. They know better. Unfortunately, it is the whole country that ends up losing in the long run from this mad scramble by cabinet officers to get the most for their ethnic groups.

43. There have been some notable exceptions to this tendency to analyse African social relations exclusively in ethnic and cultural terms. See Kenneth W. Grundy, "The 'Class Struggle' in Africa: An Examination of Conflicting Theories," The Journal of Modern African Studies, 2, 3 (1964), pp. 379-93; Frantz Fanon, The Wretched of the Earth (New York: Grove Press, 1967); Martin L. Kilson, Jr. "Nationalism and Social Classes in British West Africa," Journal of Politics, XX, 2, (May, 1958), pp. 368-87; Robert A. Miller, "Elite Formation in Africa: Class, Culture, and Coherence," op. cit., pp. 521-542; Issa G. Shivji, Class Struggles in Tanzania (New York: Monthly Review Press, 1976); Kwame Nkrumah, Class Struggle in Africa (N.Y.: International Publishers, 1970); Igor Kopytoff, "Socialism and Traditional African Societies," in William H. Friedland and Carl G. Rosberg, Jr., eds.; African Socialism. Stanford: Stanford University Press, 1964, pp. 53-62.

44. Reprinted in Paul E. Sigmund, ed., The Ideologies of the Developing Nations. New York: Praeger Publishers, 1967, p. 275.

45. See, for instance, Leopold Sedar Senghor, On African Socialism New York: Praeger, 1964; Kwame Nkrumah, Consciencism. New York: Monthly Review Press, 1970; Julius Nyerere, "Ujamaa: The Basis of African Socialism," in Friedland and Rosberg, eds., African Socialism, op. cit., pp. 238-247. Nkrumah was to change his views on the classless nature of African society and to acknowledge the existence of class divisions and class conflicts in Africa. See his Class Struggle in Africa, op. cit.

46. Kenneth Grundy, op. cit.

47. Robert Miller, op. cit., p. 538.

48. Shivji, op. cit. In the United States, the trend is to view socioeconomic status as the single most important social background influence on levels of participation behavior. This has

resulted in a de-emphasis of other social background factors like personality and ethnicity. Verba and Nie, for example, in their recent work on participation, refer to the relationship between socioeconomic status and participation as the "Standard SES Model" and make only passing reference to ethnicity. See Sidney Verba and Norman H. Nie, Participation in America. New York: Harper and Row, 1972. While Verba and Nie perhaps remain the foremost proponents of the socioeconomic status model others have also argued that differences in the level of participation between American ethnic groups are merely the result of their socioeconomic differences. See, for instance, Lester W. Milbrath, Political Participation, Chicago: Rand McNally, 1965; Milbrath and M. L. Goel, Political Participation. Chicago: Rand McNally, 1972; also Milton M. Gordon, Assimilation in American Life, New York: Oxford University Press, 1964.

49. Michael Twaddle, "Tribalism in Eastern Uganda," in P. H. Gulliver, Tradition and Transition in East Africa. London: Routledge and Kegan Paul, 1969, p. 193.

50. P. H. Gulliver, "Introduction," in Gulliver, ed., Tradition and Transition, op. cit., p. 19.

51. J. S. La Fontaine, "Tribalism among the Gisu: An Anthropological Approach," in P. H. Gulliver, op. cit., pp. 177-192.

52. Mafeje, op. cit., pp. 258-259.

53. Willard Johnson, op. cit., p. 165.

54. May Edel's definition is cited in Twaddle, op. cit., p. 193.

55. W. J. Argyle, "European Nationalism and African Tribalism," in P. H. Gulliver, op. cit., pp. 412-58; Father O'Connell claims that the term "tribalism" as employed everywhere in West Africa is given a pejorative twist" to designate the sentiments and ambitions of those who urge the maximising of the influence of a particular nation within the state to the detriment of other groups and to the injury of political unity." O'Connell, "Senghor Nkrumah and Azikiwe: Unity and Diversity in the West African State," The

Nigerian Journal of Economic and Social Studies, Vol. 5, No. 1 (March, 1963), p. 81.

56. William Graham Sumner, *Folkways*. Boston: Ginn & Company, 1907, p. 13 cited in Robert K. Merton, *The Sociology of Science*. Chicago: University of Chicago Press, 1973, pp. 108-109.

57. Robert K. Merton, op. cit., p. 109 ff.

58. May Edel, op. cit., p. 193.

59. Paul Mercier, "On the Meaning of 'Tribalism' in Black Africa," in Pierre van den Berghe, ed., *Africa: Social Problems of Change and Conflict*. San Francisco: Chandler, 1965, p. 695.

60. Leopold Sedar Senghor, *Report on the Principles and Programme of the Party* (English translation), Paris: Presence Africaine, 1959, p. 15.

61. For a recent and lucid discussion of this phenomenon in the American urban context, see Ulf Hannerz, "Ethnicity and Opportunity in Urban America," in Abner Cohen, ed., *Urban Ethnicity*, London: Tavistock Publications, 1974, pp. 37-76; the literature on American ethnic groups as interest groups engaged in struggle with other groups for resources in the political and economic market place is quite vast: Joseph Lopreato, *Italian Americans*. New York: Random House, 1970; Humbert S. Nelli, *Italians in Chicago, 1880-1930: A Study in Ethnic Mobility*. New York: Oxford University Press, 1970; Donald R. Cressey, *Theft of the Nation: The Structure and Operations of Organized Crime in America*. New York: Harper & Row, 1969; Gerald D. Suttles, *The Social Order of the Slum: Ethnicity and Territory in the Inner City*. Chicago: University of Chicago Press, 1968; Caroline F. Klare, *Greenwich Village 1920-1930: A Comment on American Civilization in the Post-War Years*. New York: Harper and Row, 1965; Nathan Glazer and Daniel Patrick Moynihan, *Beyond the Melting Pot*. Cambridge, Massachusetts: MIT Press, 1963; St. Clair Drake and Horace R. Cayton, *Black Metropolis: A Study of Negro Life in a Northern City*. New York: Harper and Row, 1962; Kenneth Allsop, *The Bootleggers* London: Hutchinson, 1961; Daniel Bell, *The End of Ideology: On the Exhaustion of Political Ideas in the Fifties*. New York:

Collier Books, 1961; Maldwyn Allen Jones, American Immigration, Chicago: University of Chicago Press, 1960; Henry Pelling, American Labor. Chicago: University of Chicago Press, 1960; Oscar Handlin, The Uprooted: The Epic Story of the Great Migrations that made the American People. Boston: Little, Brown and Company, 1952; William Foote Whyte, Street Corner Society: The Social Structure of an Italian Slum. Chicago: University of Chicago Press, 1943; and Harvey Zorbaugh, The Gold Coast and the Slum. Chicago: University of Chicago Press, 1939. This selection, by no means, exhausts the universe of studies on America's ethnic groups.

62. See, for example, Abner Cohen, Custom and Politics in Urban Africa: A Study of Hausa Migrants in Yoruba Towns. Berkeley and Los Angeles: University of California Press, 1969, for a lucid discussion of how a migrant minority group, the Hausa, employed their ethnicity as an inspirational source for political organization in Ibadan, Nigeria.

63. In Cameroon, for example, the Bantu-speaking groups, notably Duala, Kpe and Bassa, whose long and intensive contact with Europeans caused an early attainment of literacy were for a long time over-represented in the various colonial and post-colonial bureaucrcy as well as those occupations which required extensive intellectual formation. Another Cameroonian example of ethnic group hegemony resulting from natural and historical reasons is the case of the northern population (the dominant Islamized Fulani and the dominated Kirdi) whose numerical superiority has been translated into considerable political power. For close to two decades, leaders from the dominant Fulani have presided over the politics of Cameroon.

64. Paul Anber, op. cit.; see also Audrey Chapman Smock, "The N.C.N.C. and Ethnic Unions in Biafra," JMAS, Vol. 7, No. 1 (1969), pp. 21-34; Howard Wolpe, "Port Harcourt: Ibo Politics in Microcosm," JMAS, Vol. 7, No. 3 (1969), pp. 469-93; Donald Rothchild, "Ethnic Inequalities in Kenya,"

JMAS, Vol. 7, No. 4 (1969), pp. 689-711; are representative articles on the politicization of ethnic cleavages.

65. See K. W. J. Post and Michael Vickers, Structure and Conflict in Nigeria, 1960-65. London: Heinemann Educational Books, Ltd., 1973.

66. The persistence of ethnicity as a factor in political behavior has been documented in the post-industrial United States. See Michael Parenti, "Ethnic Politics and Persistence of Ethnic Identification" American Political Science Review, LXI, 3 (September 1967), pp. 717-26; George Antunes and Charles M. Gaitz, "Ethnicity and Participation: A Study of Mexican Americans, Blacks, and Whites." American Journal of Sociology, 80 (1975), pp. 1192-1211; Andrew M. Greeley, "Political Participation Among Ethnic Groups in the United States: A Preliminary Reconnaissance," American Journal of Sociology, 80 (1974), pp. 170-204; Edward O. Laumann, Bonds of Pluralism. New York: Wiley, 1973; Gerhard Lenski, The Religious Factor. Garden City, New York: Doubleday, 1961; and Dale C. Nelson, "Ethnicity and Socioeconomic Status as Sources of Participation: The Case for Ethnic Political Culture," American Political Science Review, Vol. 73, No. 4 (December 1979), pp. 1024-1038.

67. Howard W. Wriggins, "Impediments to Unity in New Nations," in Jason Finkle and Richard W. Gable, eds., Political Development and Social Change. New York: John Wiley and Sons, Inc., 1966, pp. 563-572.

68. M. Z. Njeuma, The Origins of Pan-Cameroonism. Buea: Government Printer, 1964.

69. Shivji, Class Struggle in Tanzania, op. cit., pp. 45 ff. Edwin Ardener, Shirley Ardener and W. A. Warmington, Plantation and Village in the Cameroons: Some Economic and Social Studies (Oxford: Oxford University Press, N.I.S.E.R., 1960) remains the only major study of the economic history of English-speaking Cameroon. No one has attempted to do for this sector of the country what Richard A. Joseph has done for the French-speaking sector, that is, an analysis of the evolution of socio-economic divisions and

their impact on political development, particularly during the nationalist phase which in French speaking Cameroon involved an armed struggle. The reader is referred to his excellent Radical Nationalism in Cameroun (Oxford: Oxford University Press, 1977).

70. Sir Sydney Philipson, Report on the Financial, Economic and Administrative Consequences to Southern Cameroons of Separation from the Federation of Nigeria (Buea: Prime Minister's Office, 1959) in Willard R. Johnson, The Cameroon Federation op. cit., pp. 93-94.

71. See Johnson, Ibid., p. 147; and Edwin Ardener, "The Nature of the Reunification of Cameroon," in Arthur Hazlewood, ed., African Integration and Disintegration: Case Studies in Economic and Political Union. London: Oxford University Press, 1967, p. 297.

72. The reunification movement has been ably discussed by Claude Welch, Dream of Unity: Pan-Africanism and Political Unification in West Africa. Ithaca, N.Y.: Cornell University Press, 1966; Willard R. Johnson The Cameroon Federation, op. cit.; and Bongfen Chem-Langhee and Martin Z. Njeuma, "The Pan-Kamerun Movement, 1949-1961," in Ndiva Kofele-Kale, ed., An African Experiment in Nation-Building, op. cit., pp. 25- 64.

73. Eyo B. E. Ndem, Ibos in Contemporary Nigerian Politics. Onitsha: Etudo Ltd., 1961, pp. 17-18 quoted in K.W.J. Post and Michael Vickers, Structure and Conflict in Nigeria 1960-65. London: Heinemann Educational Books, Ltd., 1973, p. 31.

74. Post & Vickers, p. 32.

75. The author was born in Lagos, Nigeria and years later attended King's College, Lagos where he met and made friends with many Ibos, some of whom played an active role in the Biafran secessionist struggle. Over the years the author has maintained contact with these colleagues and has also had numerous personal interviews with ranking officers of the Biafran army as well as top level policy-makers of this short-lived state. They all confirm my observations about the widespread sympathy for their cause in West Cameroon.

A number of them also mentioned the role West Cameroon played as a clandestine conduit for arms and other essential material to the Biafran frontlines. For very obvious reasons, I would prefer to keep the identity of my sources under wraps. I have urged a number of them to pen down their memoirs, if and when these become a reality then the full story will perforce be revealed.

76. The Cameroon government was understandably concerned with these widespread pro-Biafran sentiments in West Cameroon. The prevailing belief within the O.A.U. fraternity (with the notable exception of Gabon, Tanzania, Zambia, and Ivory Coast) was that a successful Biafra would serve as a source of inspiration and encouragement for secession among the many restless and oppressed nationalities that are still captives within the artificial states that European colonialism bequeathed to Africans before their hasty exit from the continent. West Cameroonians who were becoming increasingly restless, frustrated, and disappointed over the broken promises of reunification were seen as a prime candidate for a secessionist attempt. The reaction of Cameroon's President Ahidjo to these fears is instructive. At a press conference in Bamenda, West Cameroon, Ahidjo made the following comments:

> En ce qui me concerne, tant que je serai à la tête du Cameroun, il ne sera jamais question de reconnaitre un Etat sécessioniste du Nigeria. . . . Cette position, on l' a critiquée en dehors du Cameroun et même au Cameroun; on m'a prêté . . . des excuses en disant [que] si le président ne reconnaît pas le Biafra. . . . C'est parce qu'il a peur pour son pays qui est si divers, qui a deux Etats [dont] le Cameroun occidental qui est anglophone. . . . Il n'y a pas de tentative de sécession, au Cameroun, et je n'ai pas peur une espèce de sécession, quelle <u>qu'elle</u> soit au Cameroun. Et même si j'avais peur,

> j'estime que ce serait une peur saine car tout chef d'Etat sain d'esprit et degine de ce nom ne peut admettre qu'une partie de son pays fasse secession.

Conference de presse de S. E. El Hadj Ahmadou Ahidjo, 8 mai 1969--Bamenda, mimeo, p. 9 cited in Jacques Benjamin, Les Camerounais occidentaux. Montreal: Les Presses de l'Universite de Montreal, 1972, pp. 162-163.

77. See various studies discussed in Lucian Pye and Sidney Verba, eds., Political Culture and Political Development. Princeton: Princeton University Press, 1965.

78. Richard Rose, Politics in England, London: Faber and Faber Ltd., 1964.

79. Dennis Kavanagh, Political Culture, London: MacMillan Press, 1972.

80. Ibid.

81. See James S. Coleman, Nigeria: Background to Nationalism. Political party development in Cameroon is a case in point. Prior to independence there were, at one time or another, almost 100 political organizations in the country, almost all of which associated with particular ethnic groups. See Victor T. Le Vine, The Cameroons From Mandate to Independence, op. cit. Johnson also points out that every major political party in Cameroon had an ethnic base from which diffuse support was drawn even after the participation base had been broadened to include other ethnic groups. Willard Johnson, op. cit.

82. Mafeje, op. cit.

83. Richard Sklar, "Political Science and National Integration--A Radical Approach," Journal of Modern African Studies, Vol. 5, No. 1 (May, 1967), p. 6.

84. Specifically the pioneering efforts by Professor Robert Levine: "The Internalization of Political Values in Stateless Societies," Human Organization, XIX, 2 (Summer 1960) and "The Role of the Stimulus-generalization hypotheses," Behavioral Science, V (1960); and "Political Socialization and Culture Change," in Clifford W.

Geertz, ed., <u>Old Societies and New States</u>, op. cit.

85. Dawson and Prewitt, <u>op. cit.</u>, pp. 81-97.
86. Patterson, <u>op. cit.</u>, p. 193.
87. Levine, 1960, p. 51.
88. Patterson, <u>op. cit.</u>, p. 193.
89. Levine, 1960, p. 51.
90. David Apter, "The Role of Traditionalism in the Political Modernization of Ghana and Uganda," <u>World Politics</u>, 13 (October, 1960) pp. 45-68; Levine, 1960, <u>op. cit.</u>
91. Robert Levine, "Political Socialization and Culture Change," in Clifford Geertz, <u>op. cit.</u>, pp. 289-90.
92. <u>Ibid.</u>
93. Kenneth P. Langton, <u>Political Socialization</u> (New York: Oxford University Press, 1969), pp. 8-16.
94. David Easton and R. D. Hess, "Youth and the Political System," in S. M. Lipset and Leo Lowenthal, eds., <u>Culture and Social Character</u>. New York: The Free Press of Glencoe, 1961, pp. 226-251; R. D. Hess and Judith V. Torney, <u>The Development of Political Attitudes in a Fragmentary Society</u>, Princeton: Princeton University Press, 1970; Kent M. Jennings and Kenneth P. Langton, "Political Socialization and the High School Civics Curriculum," <u>The American Political Science Review</u>, 67 (September 1968) pp. 852-867; and Jennings and Langton, "Mother versus Father: The Formation of Political Orientations among Young Americans," <u>Journal of Politics</u>, 31 (May 1969) pp. 329-358.
95. Henry Maine, <u>Ancient Law</u>. London: J. Murray, 1961; Ferdinand Tonnies, "Gemeinschaft and Gessellschaft," (1st ed., 1887), trans. and ed. Charles P. Loomis, <u>Fundamental Concepts of Sociology</u>. N. Y.: American Book Company, 1940; Emile Durkheim, <u>The Division of Labour in Society</u>, trans. George Simpson. New York: Macmillan Company, 1933.
96. Robert Redfield, <u>Tepoztlan: A Mexican Village</u> Chicago: University of Chicago Press, 1930 and "The Folk Society," American Journal of Sociology, 52 (January 1942) pp. 293-308; Louis

Wirth, "Urbanism as a Way of Life," _American Journal of Sociology_, 44 (January 1938) pp. 1-24.

97. Ibid.

98. George Murdock, "Review of the Folk Culture of Yucatan," _American Anthropologist_, 45 (January-March) 1943, pp. 133-136; Melville J. Herskovits, _Man and His Works_. New York: Alfred A. Knopf, 1948, esp. pp. 604-7; Oscar Lewis, _Life in a Mexican Village: Tepoxtlan Revisited_. Urbana: University of Illinois Press, 1951; and Horace Miner, "The Folk-Urban Continuum." _American Sociological Review_, 17, October 1952.

99. Edward C. Banfield, _The Moral Basis of a Backward Society_. Glencoe, Illinois: The Free Press, 1962; Joseph LaPalombara, "Italy: Fragmentation, Isolation and Alienation," in Lucian W. Pye and Sidney Verba (eds.), _Political Culture and Political Development_. Princeton: Princeton University Press, 1965; pp. 282-329; Dankwart A. Rustow, "Turkey: The Modernity of Tradition," in Pye and Verba, _op. cit._ pp. 171-198; Frederick W. Frey, "Socialization to National Identification Among Turkish Peasants," _Journal of Politics_, 4, November 1968; and Fredrick W. Hayward," _Rural Africana_, 18 (Fall 1972) pp. 40-59; and "A Reassessment of Conventional Wisdom About the Informed Public: National Political Information in Ghana," _American Political Science Review_ Vol. 70 (1976) pp. 433-451.

100. The emphasis here is on the higher order of parochialism typical of rural people when contrasted to urban residents. Italian political culture is generally fragmented, isolative and alienative and these profiles, though fairly widespread, are certainly more pronounced in the rural south than the urban, industrialized north. For a contrary view, see Fred Hayward, _op. cit._ who disputes the claim that rural people are not politically sophisticated about national affairs.

101. The Upper Voltan historian, Ki-Zerbo expounds on this theme in very forceful language in his essay appearing in Apter and Coleman, eds., _Pan-Africanism Reconsidered_, _op. cit._

102. This definition is influenced by Anthony Leeds' use of the term "locality." See his "Locality Power in Relation of Supralocal Power Institutions," in Aidan Southall, ed., Urban Anthropology: Cross-Cultural Studies in Urbanization. New York: Oxford University Press, 1973, pp. 15-41.

103. M. Cohen, A Preface to Logic, New York: Meridian, 1956, p. 148, cited in Fred Kerlinger, Foundations of Behavioral Research. New York: Holt, Rinehart and Winston, Inc., 1964, p. 18.

2
The Socio-Ethnographic Context for this Study

The setting for this study on political culture is the English-speaking section of the United Republic of Cameroon. The study proper was conducted in the coastal region of Cameroon, along the narrow strip of plain near Victoria, in parts of the West Coast, and in the Tiko plain and the villages lying on the slopes of Mount Cameroon. The area covered lies between 1,500 feet and 3,000 feet above sea level. It is an area of great vegetational and climatic variation. On the one extreme are the hot and usually humid towns of Victoria and Tiko, surrounded by dense rain forest; and on the other extreme is Buea, perched at an altitude of 3,000 feet above sea level, along the slopes of the volcanic Mount Cameroon, the beneficiary of a grassland-type vegetation[1] and a temperature several degrees cooler than Victoria's. The coastal region was selected for three reasons. First, this area initially felt the impact of predator Western European culture. As a result of this long historical contact, a widely held belief was spawned that the indigenous coastal ethnic groups (Kpe-Mboko, Isuwu, Duala, etc.) have become so Europeanized that they no longer identify with their traditional customs and institutions. Quite a few Cameroonians and non-Cameroonians familiar with the country's history would undoubtedly share one anthropologist's assessment of the coastal Kpe as "the most Europeanized tribe of British Cameroons,"[2] or put differently, the most "detribalized" ethnic group.

If, in fact, the coastal groups were the first to feel the impact of European customs they most certainly were not the last. For European influence, it should be pointed out, was not entirely confined to the coast. Missionary activities and the gradual spread of the colonial blanket to cover the hinterland inevitably meant European encroachment into traditional life in areas far removed from the coast. And while the process of colonial expansion continued, large numbers of hinterland people were migrating to the "detribalized" "Europeanized" coastal areas. The significance of the hinterland-to-coast migration lies in the fact that many of the migrants eventually returned to their rural communities after having spent some time on the coast. They took back with them new ideas and values picked up from the "Europeanized" coast. While the colonial bulldozer was busy doing away with (either purposefully or inadvertently) traditional values and customs, the ubiquitous coastal 'been-to' was also contributing in his own way to the breakdown of indigenous customs as he sought to share the new values learned in the coast with his rural brethren.

Clearly then, no portion of the Cameroonian landscape escaped the European bulldozer (in the form of traders, explorers, missionaries, soldiers or colonizers) and no extant ethnic group has succeeded in maintaining its purity. By conducting the study in the coast, it was possible then to control for the colonial factor, since one was essentially studying a homogeneous universe. The research design sought to co-opt the European exposure variable by holding it constant for all the ethnic groups studied, a method Parsons and Nadel have described as control of background factors by specification.[3] In defining the universe as a victim of "Europeanization", this necessarily reduced the predictive or explanatory power of the European factor. People from the hinterland areas have lived in the coast for over fifty years, have interacted with the coastal groups and have, like them, been exposed to occidental values and institutions.

A second reason for selecting the coast had to do with the presence of a large immigrant group from other parts of the country living in the urban centers of the coast. Under the various colonial administrations a number of important towns were developed on the coast to serve as administrative (e.g., Buea) or economic and commercial

centers (e.g., Tiko and Victoria). Urbanization
and industrialization came first to the coast and
these proved to be the magnet attracting hinterland groups to this area. It can be said of these
coastal towns that they are truly cosmopolitan in
the limited sense that they contain a cross-section of the Cameroonian population. This cannot
be said without some reservations of such non-
coastal towns like Bamenda, Bafoussam or Garoua--
which are fairly large urban centers but ethnically
homogeneous.

The presence of plantations on the coast was
a third factor prompting the selection of this area
for the field study. Opportunities for trade triggered off the first European 'scramble' for the
Cameroon coast and the discovery of the rich allu-
vial volcanic soil which could support an agro-
industrial complex resulted in settlement[4] and
colonization. Beginning with the German colonial
administration around the end of the nineteenth
century, large parcels of fertile land were expro-
priated without compensation to the autochtonous
coastal groups (especially the Kpe and Duala).
These lands were developed into huge plantations
for the production of commercial crops for export
to Europe.[5] The Kpe and other neighboring peoples
who were first conscripted to work in these plantations were not enough to satisfy labor demands,
so more workers were recruited from among the hinterland ethnic groups, from the French Cameroon,
neighboring Nigeria and even as far afield as Li-
beria, and German Togoland. Today, these coastal
towns and the surrounding plantation camps support
a large number of immigrants from other parts of
Cameroon.

Selection of Environmental Locations: Towns,
Labor Camps, and Rural Villages

Urban Center/Towns--

The town was one type of locality selected in
order to observe the relationship between ethnic

group values and variations in national orientations. Most of the major towns in English-speaking Cameroon are located on the coast, and the reasons for this are clear:

> Cameroon's first contacts with the West were along the coast, and it was natural that the early coastal trading centers should have been the nuclei around which Cameroon's first urban centers grew. The burgeoning coastal towns, as nexuses of the Western exchange economy fostered the growth of trade and, in the process, created an elite based on nontraditional values . . . and thereby hastened the breakdown of traditional social structures.[6]

Urban centers have been regarded by many as the focal point of cultural exchange and the bastion of a nontraditional, literate, upwardly mobile elite. The view that most social and economic changes begin among the urban bourgeoisie, then spread downward to the traditionally inarticulate classes and then outward to the countryside is taken very seriously by some scholars.[7] Speaking about the primate cities of Asia, Hoselitz says; "Their intermediate position between East and West, their contact with old markets of commodities and ideas, their lack of many traditional bonds make them into eminently suitable vehicles for the introduction of new ideas and techniques."[8] A brief description of the towns selected follows.

Towns: The three coastal towns selected, Buea (population 24,584), Tiko (population 20,000) and Victoria (population 27,016) can hardly be described as urbanized when compared to Douala (population 458,426) or Yaounde (population 313,706)[9] but their importance in Anglophone Cameroon is well earned. Buea, capital of the South-West Province (formerly capital of the defunct federated state of West Cameroon) has always been the headquarters of one administration or another dating back to 1885 when Puttkamer and Krabbes raised the German flag there.[10] From then on every successive colonial and post-colonial government has located its administrative capital in this small quiet town. Located on the slopes of Mount Cameroon (Fako as the Kpe call it) at a height of 3,000 feet above sea-level with an excellent climate influenced by the proximity to Fako, Buea is also the ancestral home of the Kpe ethnic group (who make up one of the three ethnic units studied in this research). The name Buea is a colonial corruption of Gbea from the Kpe word ligbea.[11]

Buea has always exercised an ascendancy over the Kpe villages based partly on the fact that it was here that one of the most successful resistances to German colonial penetration in Cameroon was launched;[12] a fact which inflated the stature of the Buea Kpe in the eyes of other Kpe. It became conventional thereafter to regard the village chief of Buea as the paramount chief of all Kpe people. When effective colonial administration was established in Cameroon, the chief of Buea was given a special place of honor in keeping with Kpe tradition. Under the British, he was installed as District Head, responsible to the colonial administration within the context of the policy of Indirect Rule. Buea also owes its importance to the role it has played in the annals of English-speaking Cameroon politics; for it was here and in the other coastal towns that some of the personalities who were to dominate the political stage for a considerable period emerged. It was here also that the stage was set for the enactment of some of the most important events in the country's political history.[13] Lastly, the importance of Buea in the overall socio-economic development of Cameroon is derived also from its centrality in the agro-industrial complex of the southern area, the ramifications and consequences of which have already been discussed at length in several excellent studies.[14]

Tiko, the second town singled out, has historically been a trading town and the point of contact between coast and interior. Tiko is derived from a Kpe word '<u>tikoa</u>' meaning 'to exchange' or 'barter.' Folklore states that the original inhabitants of Tiko were fishermen (since Tiko is a seashore town) who on designated days would bring their fish to exchange for farm products brought in by people from the interior; Tiko derived its name from this form of '<u>Tikoa</u>' barter.[15] From a small trading mart, Tiko later developed into an important commercial center. It lies in the Tiko plain, the area in which the most intensive commercial activity under the C.D.C. is carried out. It has a large immigrant population made up mostly of plantation workers from all over Cameroon and traders from the southern states of Nigeria.

Until recently, Tiko was the only port in the country with facilities for ocean-going steamers serving as a gateway to the Cameroon Development Corporation's products and most of the timber exported from former West Cameroon. With the opening of a direct road link between Douala and the agriculture areas of the former West Cameroon, the port of Tiko declined in importance, as products for export are now being diverted to the ports of Douala and Bonaberi. With an estimated population of 48,000 people, Tiko is one of the largest and most heterogeneous of the English-speaking coastal towns, and thus, for the purposes of a study designed to observe behavior in a multiethnic setting, a very important town.

<u>Victoria</u> was founded in 1858 by missionaries of the Baptist Society led by the Reverend Alfred Saker and historically is the first permanent European settlement in Cameroon.[16] An important political center beginning in 1894 when it became the capital of a <u>Bezirk</u> or District in the German Kamerun Protectorate, it is now the home of the Senior Divisional Officer of Fako (formerly Victoria) Division.

Victoria has had a very long history as a commercial town dating back to the early trade contacts between its people and the Portuguese, a trading history which in fact antedates the coming of the missionaries. The political changes that Cameroon has gone through in the last 15 years have taken their toll on the commercial importance of Victoria; the town has now been eclipsed by Douala, the nation's business capital. Victoria's once busy port has definitely taken a back seat in the export trade. However, C.D.C. operations are still being carried out in Victoria and the Corporation's head office is located in Bota, a residential suburb. It is hoped that with the recent discovery of petroleum along the coast of which Victoria forms a contiguous part, along with the election promises by the government to open a deep sea harbor as well as a refinery, this town will once again find itself basking in the economic limelight it has traditionally enjoyed over the years.

    A description of Victoria without mention of its people would be analogous to a discussion of Indian reservations without reference to those who live there. Victoria is not a Kpe town and was not settled prior to the arrival of the missionaries. It has, however, since 1858, been the home of a small Creole group, descendants of the original two hundred or so loyal families that accompanied Alfred Saker to Victoria when he was compelled by the Spanish government to terminate his missionary activities on the island of Fernando Po. These families were manumitted slaves brought in from Freetown or those en route to the New World and subsequently liberated by the British man'o'war. The Creole group intermarried with the Isuwu, Wovea and other Kpe-Mboko peoples and gradually lost their distinctiveness. Their greatest gift to the people of Cameroon is <u>cos' pidgin</u>-- the lingua franca of the country. Although <u>cos' pidgin</u> began as a language of trade between the Europeans and the coastal people and later became the only vehicle of communication between the colonial administrators and the nonliterate subject people, its subsequent popularization all over Cameroon was the work of Saker's Creole group. They came to Cameroon speaking no other language than Creole which they used to communicate with the indigenous people in the course of their missionary and other activities. In addition to the Creole people of Victoria, the town is also the home of generations of hinterland people, many of whom know no other home than Victoria.

Rural Villages--

We initially saw rural villages in the light of Redfield's formulation, i.e., an ideal type of folk society and the polar opposite of urban society. Redfield found his folk-type society exhibiting the following characteristics:

> Such a society is small, isolated, non-literate, and homogeneous, with a strong sense of group solidarity. The ways of living are conventionalized into that coherent system which we call "a culture." Behavior is traditional, spontaneous, uncritical, and personal; there is no legislation or habit of experiment and reflection for intellectual ends. Kinship, its relationships and institutions, are the type categories of experience and the familial group is the unit of action. The sacred prevails over the secular; the economy is one of status rather than of market.[16]

For Redfield, the folk society was essentially removed from the main currents of modern influence, static and still luxuriating in its traditional purity. But the concept of folk society cannot be taken too literally since for Redfield it is "an ideal type"; a "mental construct"; "No known society precisely corresponds to . . . ." The concept is created "only because through it we may hope to understand reality. Its function is to suggest aspects of real societies which deserve study, and especially to suggest hypotheses as to what, under certain defined conditions, may be generally true about society."[17]

Within the Cameroon context, the effects of cross-cultural contact over a long period, especially in the coast where this study was conducted, have had a substantial impact on traditional values and institutions. Few villages, if any, have escaped untouched and undisturbed not only the effects of inter-ethnic contact but of European winds of change. Writing about traditional Banyang society, Ruel observed that the high incidence of Banyang migrating to the coastal urban centers and plantations has resulted in the introduction of new ideas, aims, and values by the 'coastal been-to's; new lifestyles, not all of which are necessarily consonant with traditional Banyang values. "It would be impossible," Ruel contends, "to remain long in a Banyang village, however isolated, without very quickly becoming aware of the influence of the south."[18] For "south," read the cumulative experience of the Cameroon people with foreign western values and customs, the forces of modernity and change, and the picture becomes clearer.

The Banyang experience can be replicated in the rest of Cameroon. Mention has already been made of the impact of the West on the coastal areas and the legacies inherited from this relationship; of the long history of hinterland migration to the southern coastal towns and villages creating a situation where immigrants now outnumber indigenes within their towns and villages. Some of the demographic and sociological problems attendant upon this massive influx of non-native settlers on native land have been well-documented.[19] The Bakweri Land Problem—brought about by the huge alienation of Kpe lands by Government and the land squeeze faced by the Kpe as immigrant settlers took effective occupation of the remaining available areas—received official recognition in the late 1940s.[20]

The sociological problems resulting from the contact of non-native settlers with indigenous coastal people has for a long time captured the interest of Ardener. He, for instance, explained the problem of Kpe marital instability as a consequence of the presence of immigrants in the plantation camps.[21] However, no large scale study has been attempted on the changes in the values and belief systems of coastal villages with substantial immigrant population. We do know that the presence of plantations within Kpe "country" has affected village life in four significant ways: (1) There has been a diminution of rural population as all the young and able-bodied men drift to the plantations in search of gainful employment. This factor in itself unleashes a chain reaction. (2) As the young people leave the villages, only the old and infirm are left behind and the process of developing the villages is retarded as a result. (3) With the young ones in the plantations, non-native settlers move in to take effective occupation of village lands encountering very little resistance from the old folks; and (4) according to Ardener, the high divorce rates among the Kpe can be traced to the presence of non-native settlers in the plantation camps who with their relatively high income are able to provide a higher standard of living for their women and so end up enticing the women away from their poorer Kpe menfolk.[22]

What we do not know is how immigrant settlers from other parts of Cameroon have affected the values and beliefs of the Kpe people among whom they have lived for several generations and how these visitors have in turn been affected by the values of the host culture. Neither do we know for certain the extent to which rural villages in general have changed genotypically and the concomitant changes in the phenotypic postures of its inhabitants. To what extent has the introduction of urban values into villages by those who have had opportunities to live in urban centers contributed toward the weakening of rural values and institutions? Whatever the answer, in more ways than one rural villages represent one polar extreme on a continuum that places urban centers at the other extreme; as such village life can be characterized as qualitatively different from urban way of life.[23] This view draws support from the findings of various studies conducted among or involving rural folk which indicate that, comparatively speaking, village folk hold on to orientations that are fundamentally different from those held by urban residents. Frey, for instance, found the Turkish village peasant to be less oriented toward the nation than the more urbanized Turk.[24] Almond and Verba found a sense of parochialism and a feeling of alienation to be rampant among the less educated and lower class Mexicans and Italians who were essentially village folk.[25] "Amoral familism" is how Banfield characterized the political culture of the less developed southern Italian villages where his study was conducted.[26] The consensus then is that villages still maintain certain values, lifestyles, and behavior patterns not usually found in the urban areas. It was my intention to investigate the relationship between domicile in a village and political orientation by examining three types of village settings--a coastal village(s) where the population was exclusively made up of Kpe people; a second village in the forest region where the major population group was Banyang, and a third village made up of Grassfields people. The last two are located in the hinterland. Such a spread would not only permit one to make fairly solid generalizations about village political culture but also leave ample room to make comparisons between coastal and hinterland village folk political orientations.[27]

Plantation Camps/Labor Villages--

To test the underlying hypothesis that environment (meaning place of domicile) contributes in the shaping of man's experience and through this his perceptions and dispositions, the peri-urban plantation camps were included in the research design, in contrast to rural villages and urban centers. It was the intention of this study to find out if plantation camps, as an integral part of an agro-industrial institutional complex, would carry with them a distinctive industrial subculture different from the traditional "cultures" from which they drew their labor force, and from the urban "cultures" that surrounded them. Secondly, the intention was to investigate the extent to which this industrial/plantation culture did affect the political orientations of its carriers. A previous study of the plantation camp system found camps to be active seedbeds for the growth of a sense of community.[28] Ardener and others in this study take note of a community of feeling among the workers that transcended local ethnic identity. They explain this phenomenon as a function of the high level of communication and contact among the different ethnic groups and of the fact that no one group has been able to dominate the plantation labor force or immigrant body as a whole.

For Ardener then, the absence of superordinate-subordinate distinctions based upon ethnic differences produced little or no friction and thus reinforced the high sense of community identity held by the plantation workers. For instance, when asked whether they would prefer to live in camps or work in gangs with only persons of their own ethnic group, an overwhelming 80 per cent of the plantation respondents preferred working and/or living with people from other ethnic groups. Briefly stated, our interests in plantation camps can be formulated into a question: How different are these camps from villages and urban centers with respect to the political orientations subscribed to by their inhabitants?

One cannot discuss plantation camps and the lifestyles they permit or engender without dialectically relating these to the broader historical context of plantation industry in Cameroon. The rise of plantation camps coincide with the beginnings of plantation industry in Cameroon and are, as a matter of fact, the direct progeny of this agro-industrial institutional order. Therefore, what follows is a brief sketch of that history, a sketch not intended to reval those major studies that have been devoted exclusively to this subject.[29] The history of plantation agriculture in Cameroon may be divided into four broad historical periods: Period 1884-1914; 1914-1938; 1939-1959; and Post-Independence Period (1960-   ). Each will be discussed in the following pages.

The Period 1884-1914

This period coincides with the era of German colonial administration in Cameroon. Plantation agriculture was triggered by big German commercial interests out to cripple the infant trade between the indigenous coastal people and small-scale German traders. The problems involved in by-passing indigenous middlemen before getting to the valuable forest products and the difficulties in transporting products from the interior were factors that forced these giant firms to see the advantages of large plantations. These would grow a variety of export crops in greater quantities, much more efficiently utilizing the latest farming techniques and cheap local labor. Consequently, pressure was brought to bear on the German Imperial government and its local administration in Cameroon to provide free land for these large German business establishments to grow crops. Resist they did, but eventually the colonial authorities bowed to this pressure by annexing between four to five hundred square miles of fertile land on the slopes of Mount Cameroon, which was then parcelled out to private individuals or large companies (like the West Afrikanische Pflanzunsgesellschaft Victoria (WAPV) which owned over 40,000 acres of land). These large concessions of land were then developed into plantations growing crops like banana, rubber, palm nuts and tea.

To work the plantations, labor was initially recruited from the ethnic groups that were living contiguously with the plantations. As time went on, a series of labor shortages were experienced as a result of the high death rate of workers due to the unhealthy climate and poor working conditions. The labor shortage problem was resolved by importing workers from the hinterland ethnic groups beginning in 1896. These workers were initially provided housing by their owners on the estate and so began the first plantation camps. The movement of workers from the interior first started slowly but gradually increased to the point where finding housing for them in the plantation camps was proving difficult. Some workers and their families were allowed to spread into non-estate lands owned by the indigenous Kpe people. Some obtained the land legally by going through recognized traditional channels, others squatted, and yet others staked their claims oblivious of native rights of domain. The importing of labor from the hinterland soon became the policy of plantation owners and the movement of these immigrants into the ancestral lands of the indigenous people once started became an irreversible process.

The Period 1916-1938

The European War of 1914-18 put a temporary halt to German activities in Cameroon, and German estates were placed under the control of a Public Custodian. Under him production continued until 1925 when the Germans returned. After the war these estates were put up for sale in two public auctions in London by the victorious allied powers: Britain and France who had now inherited all German colonial holdings in Africa and were administering them as mandated territories of the League of Nations were the auctioneers. In the first auction of 1922, a ban was placed restricting ex-enemy nationals, i.e., Germans from bidding. As a result very few of the estates were sold, and so a second auction was held in 1924, this time lifting the ban on ex-enemy nationals from participating. The Germans bought back almost all their former property and by 1926 production was resumed in full swing and plantation development expanded apace in response to the postwar boom. With expanded production labor demand increased and the Germans reinstated the old policy of recruiting workers from the interior. Allowing for drops between 1929-1932, employment figures steadily rose and reached over 25,000 in 1938. Nigerians now began to form a significant part of the labor force. With the large influx of Grassland and Nigerian migrant workers the indigenous population was soon outnumbered both in the plantations and outlying villages. In 1927, for instance, of about 10,542 plantation workers in Victoria Division (where the bulk of the plantations were located), only 732 were indigenous to the Division.[30] Two decades later the immigrant population had grown to 25,515 against an indigenous population of 15,062; the plantation force stood at 19,005 of which 16,000 were immigrants.[31]

During the period under review various halfhearted efforts were made by plantation owners to improve the wage scale and the health and living conditions of the workers. In 1929 the plantations were made Labor Health Areas and the employers required by law to provide certain standards of housing accommodation, sanitation and medical care.

The Period 1939-1959

When hostilities began again in 1939 ushering in the Second World War, German-owned plantations reverted for a second time to the Custodian of Enemy Property who kept production going--even at a loss--until the end of the war. After the war and following a series of talks between the Colonial Office and the local administration in Nigeria, it was decided that the ex-enemy lands under the Custodian's jurisdiction should be purchased by the Governor of Nigeria (Ex-Enemy Lands--Cameroon--Ordinance 1946, No. 38). The Governor upon acquisition of these lands was to declare them Native Lands to be held and developed by him for the common good of all the inhabitants of the Cameroons Trust Territory under British mandate. A second ordinance provided for the establishment of a statutory corporation--The Cameroons Development Corporation (C.D.C.)--to whom the new acquired lands were to be leased on renewable sixty year leases "at a rent for the first thirty-five years calculated to reimburse the Governor, with interest, for the purchase price of the plantations (some 850,000 pounds sterling) and subsequently at a peppercorn rental."[32]

The 1946 Ordinance charged the Corporation with providing for the religious, educational, and general social welfare of its employees. The corporation was also responsible for providing suitable training opportunities for its native Cameroonian employees which would prepare them for promotion to managerial positions. The Corporation did its best in discharging the wide mandate granted it by the 1946 Ordinance and by the various directives that were later to come from the Southern Cameroons regional government. Within a short time the Corporation embarked on a program of new staff housing, construction of workshops, offices, roads, bridges, railways, and wharves. These capital development programs greatly enhanced the socio-economic infrastructure of the Southern Cameroons territory, making the Corporation one of the most important partners in national development. This fact which did not escape the watchful eyes of a 1952 United Nations Visiting Mission to the Cameroons, which noted with interest that: "It was sometimes difficult to draw a line in the Trust Territory between government services and the Corporation's duties and functions."[33]

Throughout the 1939-1959 period, the corporation was the largest employer besides the government. It began life in 1949 with about 15,500 workers on its payroll and by mid-1954 this number had climbed to 27,000. From then on, the Corporation experienced some very serious developmental setbacks and financial difficulties which forced it to cut back on the labor force and to scale down on some of the more ambitious development projects. At the end of 1959, the labor force stood at 16,300 which was still over one half of the employed persons in the Cameroons trust territory under United Kingdom administration.[34]

Post-Independence Period (1960-   )

The financial problems of the corporation continued into the new year, as a result of which the Southern Cameroons government was obliged to seek help from outside. This led to the takeover of the C.D.C. by the British Commonwealth (then Colonial) Development Corporation (Comdev) as managing agent with the right to appoint the General Manager and to retain half the ordinary seats on the Board of Directors. Following the reunification of the two Cameroons in 1961, the C.D.C. was subsequently taken over by the Federal Cameroon government in 1962-1963, without, of course severing the relationship with Comdev.

In spite of its many difficulties, the corporation at no time gave up its position as the dominant institution in the economic framework of English-speaking Cameroon. As Johnson notes, at the corporation's height it accounted for 65 per cent of export tonnage and 55 per cent of export earnings (excluding trees and lumber). However, by 1961, its export tonnage (excluding wood) had dropped to 44 per cent and export earnings to 28 per cent. The labor force of 17,286 was half the total paid labor of English-speaking Cameroon and the corporation was and still is the next largest employer besides the Cameroon government.[35] In 1972, the Cameroon Development Corporation operated 114 labor camps with an estimated population of over 30,000 (workers and their families), more than 20 per cent of the total population of the entire Fako Division.[36]

Inheriting the lands formerly owned by Germans, the C.D.C. improved on them and substantially increased their economic value. Ploughing back the profits into capital development projects, social and welfare programs that have benefited not only its workers but a broad section of the Cameroon population, the C.D.C. has been, as Bederman described it in his monograph, "A Partner in National Growth."

As a result of its long history of contact with the West, its existence a focal point of convergence for the many and diverse ethnic groups in Cameroon, and its fairly urbanized and economically developed centers, the coastal region proved an ideal site to test propositions on the effects of environment on ethnic group values and the political orientations of English-speaking Cameroonians.

Criteria for Selection of Ethnic Groups

One of the major objectives of this study was to shed light on the relationship between ethnicity and national orientations. To avoid the weakness of earlier studies which examined the orientations only of people from segmentary societies, it was necessary to select ethnic groups with different socio-political organizations. Fortunately for Cameroon, the ethnic map is one of diversity and complexity with ethnic groups whose socio-political structures range from hierarchical chiefdoms to segmentary societies of one variety or another.[37] Although the criteria employed for classifying the different ethnic or tribal groups in Anglophone Cameroon have caused wide disagreement among ethnographers, estimates suggest that there may be as many as 80 different ethnic units in this section of the country.[38] On the basis of linguistic criteria, these units are broadly classified into two major linguistic zones: a Bantu-speaking zone which includes all the peoples of Fako, Meme and Ndian Divisions (with the exception of the Korup and Efik of the western borders of Meme Division) who speak Bantu languages of the North-western Group.[39] The other major linguistic zone is the Bantoid-speaking one which includes the peoples of Manyu Division and the whole of the North-West Province, the "Grassland Belt."

MAP 2 MAJOR PLANTATIONS AND ADMINISTRATIVE AREAS, C. D. C., 1969.[a]

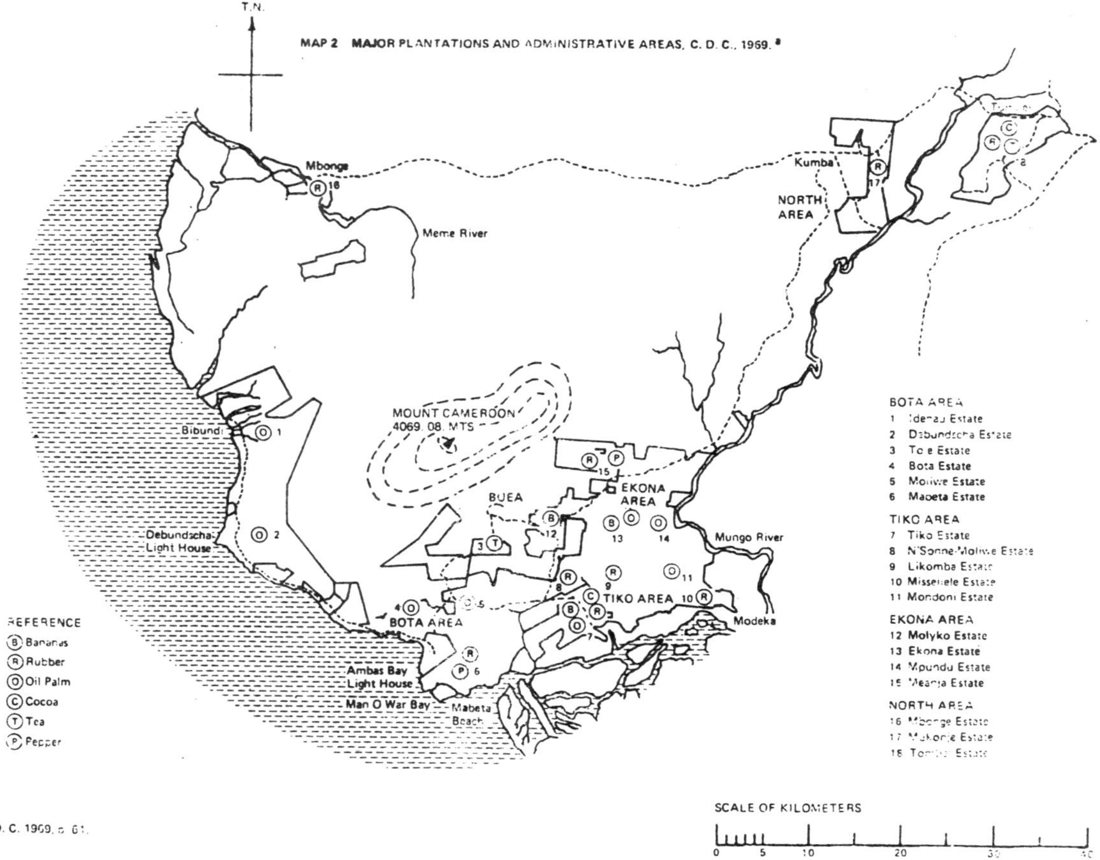

T.N.
Mbonge
Meme River
Kumba
NORTH AREA
MOUNT CAMEROON 4069. 08. MTS
Bibundi
Debundscha Light House
BUEA
EKONA AREA
Mungo River
TIKO AREA
BOTA AREA
Modeka
Ambas Bay Light House
Man O War Bay
Mabeta Beach
REFERENCE
B Bananas
R Rubber
O Oil Palm
C Cocoa
T Tea
P Pepper
BOTA AREA
1 Idenau Estate
2 Debundscha Estate
3 Tole Estate
4 Bota Estate
5 Moliwe Estate
6 Mabeta Estate
TIKO AREA
7 Tiko Estate
8 N'Sonne-Moliwe Estate
9 Likomba Estate
10 Missellele Estate
11 Mondoni Estate
EKONA AREA
12 Molyko Estate
13 Ekona Estate
14 Mpundu Estate
15 Meanja Estate
NORTH AREA
16 Mbonge Estate
17 Mukonje Estate
18 Tombel Estate
SCALE OF KILOMETERS
0 5 10 20 30 40

[a] C. D. C. 1969, p. 61.

Three ethnic groups were selected--two with segmentary structures and the other a collection of centralized chiefdoms. Of the two acephalous groups, one was Bantu-speaking (the Kpe) and the other Bantoid-speaking (Banyang) located in Manyu Division, mid-way between the coastal south and the grassland north. The third group came from the "Grassland Belt" and is designated in this study by the unfortunate word "Grassfield." Each of these groups had a sizable population residing in the coastal region with large numbers of them working in the plantations run by the Cameroon Development Corporation.

Ethnographic descriptions of the three ethnic groups investigated will be presented later in this section. Here a fuller discussion of the selection procedure and the logic behind it will be undertaken. The 'model' for the research took as its inspiration the Przeworski and Teune Most Different Systems Design.[40] Central to this design is the proposition that observable human behavior can be adequately explained at several levels, e.g., individual or group or community or nation. The design therefore tries to explain variations in observable behavior using intra-systemic variables and shifting to system-wide variables when within-system factors fail to effect the highest reduction in variance. The central objective of the most different systems design is to eliminate factors that separate social systems within which observations are made.

This study was interested in explaining variations in national political orientations, operating on the assumption that factors other than ethnic primordial considerations prevent the crystallization of a civic political culture in the developing nations of Africa in general and Cameroon specifically. In the context of the most different systems design, this means that if the majority of respondents from the three different ethnic groups manifests similar patterns of orientations toward the Cameroon state, then those factors which distinguish these ethnic units should not be considered in the explanation of variations in their political orientations. If, on the other hand, variations in national orientations among members from the different ethnic units disappear when factors such as education, occupation, exposure to mass media, etc., are controlled for, then the differences among these ethnic groups other than the above-mentioned variables are unimportant in explaining their national orientations.

The objective of this design is to provide variables that promise to offer the highest reduction in variance and by extension the highest yield in prediction to account for the pattern of behavior being observed. It approaches this goal by first rejecting systemic differences as explanators for individual behavior and only resorting to them when other non-systemic variables have failed to explain the variance.

The most different systems design operates on two very important assumptions: (1) that social "systems" selected for any comparative research be as different as possible from each other (I shall refer to this as the assumption of heterogeneity); and, (2) that a comparative study must take as its point of departure the elimination empirically, i.e., holding constant, of those systemic factors which are irrelevant to the explanation of the studied behavior (I shall call this the assumption of homogeneity).

The assumption of heterogeneity--

If individuals from social systems that are organically and otherwise different end up sharing similar behavioral characteristics, then those aspects distinguishing their systems have very low explanatory power, if any at all, in describing their behavior. The three ethnic groups selected in this study were different in at least four very important aspects: (i) traditional socio-political organizations; (ii) location; (iii) size;

and (iv) political importance in the larger context of national politics. The "Grassfield" who are organized into powerful kingdoms are located in the northern section of the area studied, some two hundred miles removed from the coast; they are very populous with over 60 per cent of the entire population of English-speaking Cameroon, and they are politically very significant. A predominantly Grassfield political party, the K.N.D.P., took over the reins of government in English-speaking Cameroon in 1959 and later championed the successful fight for reunification with its neighbor to the east. The only two Vice-Presidents of the Cameroon federation have come from the Grassfield; so too have other important cabinet ministers and key members in the National Assembly and the CNU political bureau.

The next ethnic group in this study is the Banyang, who occupy the forest region of Cameroon and can be considered halfway between the coastal Kpe and the hinterland Grassfield. The Banyang are numerically a minority and are organized into segmentary village councils with very powerful secret associations. Coming from one of the most impoverished and physically isolated Divisions, the Banyang have a long history of migration to the coastal regions for economic reasons. Over the years this group has made impressive strides in education and politics. The last of the ethnic groups is the coastal Kpe, who, like the Banyang are organized along segmentary lines but who lack any powerful secret associations that are responsible for major decisions affecting the group. The Kpe are a minority (less than 50,000 people) long considered the cream of Anglophone Cameroon ethnic groups whose strategic coastal location brought them into early contact with modern westernizing influence. Having founded the nationalist movement in this section of the country, the Kpe intelligentsia enjoyed almost two decades of unrivaled political hegemony which was later taken away from them by the Grassfield.

I considered these three groups sufficiently different from each other to have met the requirements spelled out by the assumption of heterogeneity of the most different systems design. These differences can be summed up as follows: (1) linguistic criteria; the two major linguistic zones in English-speaking Cameroon, the Bantus (Kpe) and Bantoids (Banyang and Grassfield) are represented; (2) traditional socio-political organization was varied by including segmentary (Banyang and Kpe) and centralized chiefdoms (Grassfield); (3) size, this ranges from the very populous Grassfield on the one hand to the minority Banyang and Kpe on the other; (4) location; a coastal "detribalized" Kpe as well as two ethnic groups that are geographically far removed from the "westernized" coast; (5) political and economic influence; the politically "have been" Kpe were joined in this analysis by the enterprising and upwardly mobile Banyang and the politically and economically well-placed Grassfield.

The assumption of homogeneity--

The logic of the most different systems design requires that samples of individuals (whose behavior is to be observed) should be drawn from a homogeneous population, since the assumption is that systemic factors are irrelevant as explanators for variations in observed behavior. The goal then becomes one of testing (in order to confirm or falsify), step by step, this proposition in the course of cross-systemic investigation. To accomplish this goal two factors had to be held constant in this study: (i) exposure to westernizing values as a result of long contact with these forces; and (ii) exposure to other modernizing values as a result of living for a number of years in communities that are ethnically heterogeneous. Since the Kpe ethnic group is located on the coast and has had a long history of contact with westernizing forces, it was necessary to show that the other two ethnic groups have shared somewhat in this experience in order for the study sample to have met the criterion of a homogeneous population.

This same potential shortcoming held for the second factor; unless factors connected with exposure to multiethnic urban centers could be held constant it would be difficult to explain that these may not have been the reason some ethnic groups hold on to a certain type of national orientation. Both sets of factors were eliminated in the following manner: (1) the entire urban sample was drawn from the <u>coastal</u> towns of Buea, Tiko, and Victoria. A requirement for inclusion was that all individuals to be interviewed must have spent at least ten years in the coast (since the Kpe are native to the coast this rule did not apply to them). While a period of ten years does not compare to the decade of contact the Kpe have had with Western values and institutions, it was still felt that a 20-year old immigrant who has resided on the coast for at least a decade at the time this study was conducted would not be too different from a Kpe youth of a comparable age with respect to exposure to westernizing values; (2) the three ethnic groups were divided into three communities: villages, plantation camps, and towns. The last two are multiethnic. This division made it possible to determine whether observed differences in political orientations (after controlling for other non-systemic factors) are due to environmental location, i.e., the fact that some people have lived their entire lives in plantation camps or villages, a determination which would have proved difficult to make had the sample been comprised only of people from only one type of locality. The entire indigenous and immigrant urban sample was drawn from the coastal multi-ethnic plantation camps and towns, i.e., a fairly homogeneous universe.

Description of the Ethnic Groups Compared in this Study*

The Grassfields

In this study the Tikar, Chamba and Widekum ethnic congeries have been called, for lack of a better term, Grassfield.[41] This arbitrary reclassification can be justified on two grounds: first, these three clusters of people share certain common features in their political, economic, and social organizations. This is apart from the fact of local contiguity, since they all live in close proximity to each other on the Bamenda highlands. Without exception, all these groups are organized into chiefdoms of varying size. Throughout the areas occupied by these groups, men's associations are an important feature of their social and political organization. They are all highly hierarchical and stratified with a ranking social and title-holding system, and all possess the important regulatory society, the Kwifoyn. Throughout the area, the kinship systems are similar (with the exception of the Wum and Kom groups which are matrilineal); they are all patrilineal, and the basis for social organization is the localized patrilineage.[42] Secondly, as an identity group, when they leave their highland settlements and venture out to other parts of Cameroon (usually southward to the coast) other ethnic groups refer to them as Grassfields (or Grasslanders or Graffi). This designation has gained widespread acceptance and Grassfield people generally regard themselves as different from the Banyang and coastal Kpe. There is, therefore, a

---

*Following conventional practice the descriptions of the ethnic groups is done in the ethnographic present without prejudice to the fact that each of them have undergone major transformations in culture and organizational forms over the years. No major attempt was made to spell out the various changes that these groups have undergone as this would be beyond the scope of the study. Each of the ethnic subsystems has had to adapt to changing circumstances but each still maintains its raison d'être and that is what counts in this study.

clear-cut in-group/out-group dichotomy. The Grassfields then should be seen as a distinct ethnic group arising from the coastal urban social situation.[43]

Location: The Western Grassfields (which includes the three ethnic congeries and all the other groups in the Bamenda highland) occupy the administrative divisions of Bui, Donga-Mantum, Menchum, Mezam and Momo[44] which in 1976 had a total population of 980,531 (almost 60 per cent of the population of English-speaking Cameroon) including about 18,360 Fulani. These five divisions previously formed part of the short-lived Bamenda Province, one of the two provinces of the British-administered Cameroon trusteeship territory (the other province was designated Cameroons Province).

History and Traditions of Origin:[45] Traditions of migration and settlement are often difficult to collect because as Kaberry discovered, these traditions are usually less concerned with the origins of peoples and more interested in the histories of dynasties, chiefdoms, offices, and institutions.[46] The attempt to present a collective history of the origins of each of these groups under study is further complicated by the fact that where such histories exist, they are usually fragmentary and largely personal recollections that emerge haphazard and contradictory. Briefly, the Widekum (made up of five clans: Moghamo, Memeno, Ngemba, Ngie and Ngwaw) claim to have emigrated some two hundred years ago from the fringes of the Congo and settled first at Widekum and later at a place called Gowin. The Tikar moved into the Bamenda highland from the northeast around the Lake Chad region as a result of Fulani and Chamba pressure, some three hundred years ago. The most recent wave of migration into Bamenda was the Chamba; horseborne, they invaded this area as they were in turn being pushed out of their original enclaves by Fulani warriors.[47]

A detailed description of each of these groups would distract from the focus of this study. Instead a representative group from this cluster--the Bafut--will be described in some depth.

Bafut: A Tikar Chiefdom[48]

Bafut is one of the Tikar ethnic groups that make up that congeries. Administratively, it is part of Mezam Division. In addition to Bafut, there are six other villages that make up the Bafut chiefdom (Babanki, Babanki-Tungo, Bafreng, Bambui, Bamemdankwe and Bambili). Each of the seven villages has its own chief and is autonomous, but the Fon of Bafut is recognized as the paramount chief. The history of the migration of the Bafut people traces a westerly movement from Ndop and then a westward expansion into Banso hills. A conquest state, the Bafut have a history of minor wars and affrays in which they harried or absorbed the semi-forest Widekum peoples.[49]

Bafut contact with Europe began in 1889 following the arrival of the intrepid German explorer Zintgraff. For refusing to permit German penetration farther inland, the Bafut were subjected to a punitive expedition sent out in 1895 which, among other things, burned down the Fon's palace and forced his temporary exile. In 1904, the Basel Mission was founded in Bafut, beginning a long history of mission involvement and penetration of the Grassfields.

Political System

The Bafut political community is an elaborate hierarchical system at the top of which is the Fon--the spiritual, executive, legislative and political leader of his people. He is assisted in the execution of his many functions by two of his brothers whom he appoints to act as chiefs of staff following his accession to the Fonship. The subalterns are empowered to act in the Fon's absence.

Clearly the most important political institution in the Fon's political organization is the Council of Elders, comprising his two lieutenants and a group of twelve nobles (bukum).[50] The council serves as an advisory board for the Fon, assisting him in formulating policy and helping to draw up religious and judicial decisions. All the councillors belong to a secret society called the Kweyifon. Appointment to the Council of Elders is for life, and upon the death of a councillor a successor is raised from the ranks of the bukum by the Council with the approval of the Fon. The Council of Elders is headed by the tabekweyifon, who is at the same time 'Prime Minister' and Head Priest: "As chief executor of the Fon's orders, he has a great deal of secular and spiritual authority reinforced by the powerful Kweyifon secret society which he heads."[51] His religious importance is evidenced by the secrecy and elaborate ritual that shrouds his person.

The Fon and his Council of Elders govern through delegation of powers. The villages are sub-divided into quarters, each headed by a quarterhead, tanukuro. The quarterhead is the Fon's representative in that quarter; he represents the quarter at central headquarters and transmits information, announcements, and orders from there to his quarter. In addition, his functions include supplying and organizing people from his quarter for community projects such as road-building, working in the Fon's compound and/or clearing his farms. The quarterhead is also empowered to collect an annual poll tax from the male adults in his quarter.

Bafut has been described as a "highly organized society with a developed political system, which at this point may be termed a benevolent dictatorship."[52] The considerable power which has been delegated to a nobility raised by service from commoner ranks seems very beneficial and useful in controlling nepotism and in keeping government distributed among a wider group than the royal family alone.[53] This authoritarian Bafut political structure, it has been argued, has persisted over the years due to the widespread belief in traditional supernatural forces and an acceptance by the governed that governorship was a divine right. However, the steady encroachment of Christianity into Bafut society threatens to destroy this factor of religious reinforcement of secular authoritarian power. Even more ominous is the growing suspicion among the governed that the Fon is of blood and flesh and not a divinity. In the words of Ritzenthaler and Ritzenthaler "elements such as (these) . . . are the seeds of destruction which portend a dubious future for the petty kingdoms, not only at Bafut, but throughout the Bamenda area. The disappearance of such kingdoms and powerful chiefs from the acculturated coastal region points up the fate in store for those in the highlands."[54] These fears are justified in the light of Cameroon history. To the extent that the "westernization" of the coast resulted in the erosion and destruction of indigenous institutions, the Ritzenthalers are correct, though it should be pointed out that the coastal groups have historically developed outside the framework of centralized chiefdoms or kingdoms. The powerful chiefs the Ritzenthalers are referring to were in fact European creations and their disappearance is strongly associated with the decline of support given them by their European creators.[55]

Conflict Resolution: The system for conflict resolution among the Bafut is an extension of the political realm. The Fon with the aid of his Council of Elders performs the judicial duties of judging and sentencing on all criminal cases. With the advent of British Indirect rule and the introduction of the Native Authority Court system, the judicial powers of the Fon and Council were severely curtailed. From previously adjudicating on all civil and criminal offences, the Fon's jurisdiction is now confined to hearing cases concerning boundary disputes, bride price, and petty thievery. His judicial powers are further limited since his decisions can still be appealed in the civil and criminal courts.

Succession and Inheritance: Succession to Fonship is not by primogeniture. The Fon usually chooses his successor from among his sons aided by the bukum. Personal qualities are a factor, since selection is not automatic but on the basis of qualifications and abilities. The same principle is followed in property inheritance. Whoever has been appointed successor inherits the deceased name, the compound, all his wives and property as well as the entire responsibility for the estate. Where a head of lineage dies without a son as successor, his brother will appoint one of their sons as the new head. But a lineage head never inherits the property of any deceased male members of his lineage. He, however, is responsible for the care of any older wives, while the younger ones are inherited by the deceased's successor.

Kinship System: Like the majority of Tikar kingdoms, Bafut are patrilocal and patrilineal. The lineage is composed of all the people descended from a common male ancestor and marriage between its members is strictly forbidden. The avunculate is also practised among the Bafut.[56] Boys and girls have close relationships with their mother's brothers. It is important to note that in Bafut while both paternal and maternal uncles are treated with great respect, it is the mother's senior brother who receives the bulk of attention from his sister's children.[57]

Age Sets: The Bafut have no tradition of age groups but men's associations are an important feature of social organization. The most important male association is the manjong (or mandjong or mandjon) society to which all adult males automatically belong. The manjong is organized by quarters and in the olden days functioned as a powerful military organization; this role, however, has waned with the cessation of interstate wars.

Manjong men were selected on the basis of their strength and bravery and formed a core of reservists ready to take part in military duties. The society now functions as a drinking club and for service at funerals to which they are sent by the Fon to help "cry the die" of a dead chief.

Associations: There are a number of secret societies for both titled persons and commoners in Bafut, all of which are an integral part of the political and religious organization of the kingdom. Membership is restricted to males and all the societies have closed meetings. By far the most important of these is the regulatory society Kweyifon (or Kwi'fo) from whose membership ranks princes are excluded: "Membership of it was so essential to advancement that princes would seek its permission to enter a son and start paying dues which would secure the son's membership when they died."[58] The Kweyifon is composed of noblemen who have been raised from the ranks of commoners through payment of required fees and as a result of honorable service to the Fon. It provides a pool of noblemen (bukum) from which the Fon's "privy councillors" (to borrow Chilver's and Kaberry's phrase) who make up his Council of Elders are drawn. The kweyifon is headed by the tabekweyifon, second only in importance to the Fon in the politico-religious hierarchy of the Bafut kingdom. As head of the kweyifon he is also prime minister and chief priest.

The Fon as a secular monarch rules the kingdom through the Kweyifon, which also considers the Fon as its son--"son of the Kweyifon." Theoretically, a Fon can be deposed or killed by the kweyifon when he oversteps his secular and spiritual authority. The Kweyifon serves in this respect as a check on the powers of a monarch who is regarded as a divinity. Thus, the Kweyifon is the only institution capable of interceding between the people and their ruler when the latter becomes too autocratic. Paradoxically the kweyifon is also subordinate to the Fon in the sense that it is he who appoints its members by virtue of his position as the supreme noble. A most interesting set-up emerges: the Fon appoints commoners, who have demonstrated their unflinching loyalty to him, to become noblemen and by right members of the kweyifon; the Fon who abuses his power and disregards the sage counsel of his kweyifon sooner or later confronts a kweyifon that has withdrawn its support from the Fon and dissociated itself from any decisions taken by him.

The Kpe

Location: One of the non-centralized coastal ethnic groups of Cameroon is the Kpe or Bakweri (as it later came to be called). Actually Kpe is a corruption of Vakpe (singular Mokpke). As an ethnic cluster, the Kpe are a congeries of people comprising the Kpe, Mboko, Isuwu and Wovea groups.[59] Together with the Duala-Limba and the Tanga-Yasa, the Kpe belong to the northwesterly branch of the Bantu-speaking peoples that straddles the entire coastal section of the United Cameroon Republic.[60] The roughly 50,000 Kpe are found living in over one hundred small villages scattered along the slopes of Mount Cameroon (Fako as the Kpe refer to it) with some of the groups (like the Isuwu and Wovea) farther down and south along the coast as well as on some off-shore islands.

History and Traditions of Origin: The Kpe like all the ethnic groups of the coastal Bantu have traditions of migrations, though not all from the same direction.[61] One colonial source traces the beginnings of the Kpe ethnic group "as the result of simple wanderings of small families or groups of families from their villages either voluntarily in search of land or compulsorily as a penalty for some infringement of traditional law and custom. The majority of these 'nomad bands' claim to have originated from the villages known as Bakwere (sic). In the Bambuko group, however, the villages of Batoke, Bakingili, Nsanje and Bibundi trace their origin directly from the Bambuko clan, and the villages of Bota . . . are said to have been founded by emigrants from Fernando

Po."62 Kpe generally claim to have originated from Mboko country by way of the northern side of the Cameroon Mountain.63 Tradition of origin claims that most of the Kpe villages developed fissiparously from a nucleus of about "fourteen villages which lie in a belt between 2,000 and 3,000 feet up the Cameroon Mountain, and that expansion has been generally north and south along the mountain, the greatest concentration being toward the southern and south-eastern foothills."64

Attempts to record with historical exactitude when the Kpe came to their present sites have been abortive. Ardener claims there was no European record of the Kpe proper before 1841 when they appear as "Bakwileh" in some reports by explorers and traders.65 Using genealogical records Ardener places the arrival of the Kpe at their present turf between 1750 and 1770.66 These dates are at best tentative given the record of Portuguese contact with coastal peoples as early as the middle of the fifteenth century.67 By 1493, the Portuguese had established settlements in Fernando Po and Sao Tome (both islands a little over twenty miles from the Cameroon coast). The Portuguese carried on a brisk trade with the coastal people (notably the Duala, Bulu and Isuwu) first in palm oil, palm kernels and ivory and later in slaves. The aforementioned coastal groups generally acted as brokers in the coastal trade, standing between the European traders and the indigenous producers. The produce sold to the Europeans was generally procured from the interior. Now, the present site where the Kpe are settled is roughly twenty miles from the Ambas Bay coast where the European factors were located. In those days it would have taken about a day's journey to cover the distance between Gbea and these marts. One way or the other Kpe must have been an important link in the coastal trade chain, as producers and/ or traders who collaborated with the Duala and Isuwu in their middleman role. The Kpe, could have been heading toward or might already have been established near their present settlement much earlier than Ardener suggests.

History of Western Contact: As already suggested in the preceding paragraph, the Kpe were among the other coastal groups that first came into contact with European merchants.[68] Along with the entry of European mercantile interests came missionary activity; the missionaries began their proselytizing mission along the coast by 1844.[69] Colonialism was introduced by the Germans some forty years after the London Baptist Mission led by Alfred Saker first established a bridgehead in Kpe-Mboko territory. German colonial expansion and domination was resisted for many years by the Kpe. In 1891 a German military expedition under Freiherr von Gravenreuth, which had been sent out to subdue the restless Kpe, was soundly defeated.[70] Three years later a larger and better equipped military expedition successfully subdued the Kpe, who lost their leader, Kuva Likenye, on the battlefront. The German defeat and the subsequent treatment meted out to the Kpe greatly affected and in many ways molded the collective attitude of Kpe people toward white rule.

For the sheer temerity of defeating the Germans, the Kpe had their villages burned down, and their new chief (who had succeeded the departed warrior, Kuva) exiled to Duala (which was then the capital of the German Kamerun Protectorate). Their land was also alienated and they themselves were resettled in 'native' reserves. To cap it all, the alienated lands were turned into plantations for which the Kpe were conscripted to work-- without pay![71] The development of plantation agriculture also brought in an avalanche of workers from upcountry. Originally recruited by plantation owners and later by the German government, the new immigrants were initially housed on the plantations themselves but as their numbers increased (relatives joined them, attracted by the increased opportunities for participation in the market economy) the immigrants gradually spread into traditional strongholds where scarce land was generally supplied to them for a pepper corn rental. Today, as a result, the Kpe are outnumbered by the immigrant population in both the plantation camps and towns. For instance, Ardener's 1955 estimates placed the number of immigrants in 'native' areas at about 35,000; in 1959 Victoria Division (now subsumed under Fako Division), home base of the Kpe, had a population of 85,000 persons of whom 66,000 were immigrants.[72] Today, there are an estimated 17 immigrants to every native-born person in Fako Division and nearly 4 immigrants to every native Kpe in the native areas alone.

Political System: A major characteristic of acephalous societies is the absence of an elaborate system of centralized authority where political power is concentrated in a chief or king. The basic political unit of the Kpe political structure is the village, i.e., the extended family. The extended family usually began with the nuclear family and "as the sons grew to manhood and married, they left the parental roof and either wandered away to found new villages or established themselves in the neighborhood."[73] So the family expanded into a number of persons all linked by close ties of blood, acknowledging descent from a common ancestor, and thus evolved the extended family.[74] Two theories have been offered to explain why and when the extened family broke up to form another. One theory is derived from the fact of internal disintegratation or the process of fission while the other seeks to explain the phenomenon in terms of the fusion or absorption process. Fission takes place when a social unit becomes too large and unwieldly such that loyalty to the leader becomes diffuse or divided causing one faction to break away to form a totally different social unit. This must have happened to many Kpe villages. As the new break-away villages developed, their numbers were usually swollen by fresh bands of 'nomads' who "preferred to share in the harvest sown by others rather than hack a living for themselves from the primeval forest."[75]

And here fusion began. The fresh bands of settlers would be given land and gradually absorbed into the extant settlements until eventually they claimed blood relationship with the original inhabitants.

Government in Kpe village is theoretically the administrative system of the extended family, writ large, with the family of the founder of the village by the most senior branch in the patrilineal line taking precedence.[76] Age and descent from the family of the founder are the two most crucial pre-requisites for leadership. In each village, the oldest man and descendant of the founder is the acknowledged head of the village-- de facto and de jure. The oldest man, in one student's words, was "the oracle and patriarch who presided over the spiritual and temporal welfare of his flock. In the old pagan days it was his duty to sacrifice to the family gods and the respect paid to him was due partly to this power of communion with the deities and partly to his exceptional experience of the world."[77]

Jealously proud of their independence, the Kpe do not confer autocratic powers on their ruler. He is just a village head (sang'a mboa-- literally head of country) who is in effect the leader of the body of elders, Vambaki (singular mombaki.) The sang'a mboa is ". . . no autocrat and his judgments or orders were never given except in collaboration with other family elders; but at every meeting he was the acknowledged president and even if his physical or mental facilities were failing, his presence was considered essential for the discussion of any matter of importance."[78] Theoretically, village government is borne by the extended family as an administrative unit but in actual practice, day-to-day administration is carried out by a council composed of the village patriarchs, which swells during matters of general interest to a mass meeting New England style.

Conflict Resolution: When not deciding political issues, the sang'a mboa and his vambaki, assisted by other responsible men in the village, devise and execute laws and legal decisions. Conflict resolution is based on the principle of trial by acclamation where the entire community sitting as a collective group-judge listens to cases and passes judgments. Ardener states that "laws are generally enforceable by public opinion, if they really represent the wishes of the majority."[79] Where the author of a crime is in doubt or unwitnessed, an oath or ordeal is usually administered to the suspect in an effort to force a confession.[80]

<u>Succession and Inheritance</u>: Succession and inheritance are not strictly by primogeniture. Ardener states: "In theory, succession to the chieftaincy falls to the eldest son of the deceased, but this is not automatic, the new chief being elected by a body of <u>vambaki</u> will take into account age and personal qualities and in practice many chiefs are brothers or younger sons of their predecessors."[81] The following persons are in principle disabarred from the lines of succession: (1) persons with disabling infirmities and (2) maternal relatives.

As a rule, property is inherited by the eldest son of the deceased or his oldest surviving brothers where the deceased has no sons or his sons are young. Women do not inherit, as they are technically part of the property to be inherited. Property is usually divided among close patri- and matri-lineal kin of the deceased. Variations to the rule of inheritance from father to son, or if there is no son, the deceased's oldest surviving brothers, exist. Where a man has no sons or brothers (or even when he has living brothers) he may specifically request that his sister's son inherit his property. A man can also will his property to his daughter, if he has no sons and she in her turn, in the absence of any male issue, can will her property to her daughter. Ardener summarizes the inheritance pattern as follows: "the most acceptable heir is the eldest son; in default of a son, normally a brother (but by arrangement before death even a sister's son); in default of a brother, a sister's son or a daughter."[82]

Kinship System: Kinship relationships play an important role in Kpe social life. The Kpe have a double descent kinship system with patrilineal links being more dominant in most aspects of life: "Virilocal marriage leads to formal stress on the patrilineal links and only patrilineages are named and localized."[83] It has been mentioned elsewhere that village headship devolves on the oldest member of the senior branch of the founding patrilineage, making it possible for a whole village to be descended from one common patrilineal ancestor. While the stress is on patrilineal links, matrilineal affiliations are not ignored, since they are of great emotional and spiritual significance. Matrilineages come together on certain occasions especially during fertility rituals and for medical purposes. Husbands, however, have no role in their wives' matrilineage fertility rites. Marriage is prohibited between persons who can trace any degree of relationship, either matrilineally or patrilineally; so also is marriage prohibited between distant in-laws. A man cannot, therefore, marry two women from the same family. Great variations occur in the Kpe kinship system lending it a "certain looseness in texture"; for instance, ". . . while patrilineages provide the framework of the local unit, it is very common for men to live in the village of their mother or their mother's mother."[84]

Age Sets: Among the Kpe there are no elaborate rites de passage that signal the entry into adulthood; this stepwise introduction in different aspects of life provides the raison d'etre for age sets. The Kpe, therefore, stand in contrast to their Duala neighbors who prescribe definite rules and rites which boys between the ages of twelve and fifteen years are required to observe before being allowed to group themselves into age sets (mwemba). Though the term 'mwemba' exists in Kpe language, it merely translates to mean people who are approximately of the same age and it has no formal corporate existence as such. The Kpe in short have no system of age sets.

Other Associations: Kpe have no "secret associations" that have important roles to play in the decision-making process of the community. The only type of associations in existence are those that function primarily as recreational agencies. Men's associations are organized separately from women's. The important men's societies are Male and Nganya and for women Liengu and Malova.

The Banyang

The Banyang (singular Manyang)[85] occupy the central portion of the upper Cross River basin. The ethnic groups that border Banyang territory are the highland Tikar and Bangwa to the East; the Mbo group on the South-east; the Keaka group on the South and South-west; the Boki group on the West; the Anyang on the North-west and the Menka on the North. The Banyang form part of Manyu administrative Division of the South-West Province of the United Cameroon Republic. The 1953 census estimates gave the Banyang a population of 18,000 persons living within native lands and an additional 4,000 to 5,000 (about one fifth of the total population) living and working away from home in other parts of the country. Of these emigrants, the vast majority (87 per cent) are concentrated in the coast; of that number, between 54 percent and 60 per cent are employed in the coastal plantations of the Cameroon Development Corporation.[86]

History and Traditions of Origin: Before colonial rule, Banyang were not politically united as a people. They lived in scattered, separate settlements with the largest political units not exceeding 2,000 people and usually fewer. The Banyang are a classic example of an ethnic group that achieved corporate identity through the influence of the colonial factor. The origins of the Banyang people remain obscure; there is no tradition of common descent or a myth of common origin. One source speculates that similarity in name and speech leads to the natural assumption that there is an affinity with the Anyang, their neighbors on the northwest.[87] Another speculation as to Banyang origin considers the group as part of the Tikar or Mboum group which came down from Bornu and allegedly broke off from the Jukuns and later arrived at their present site by way of Dschang.[88] Banyang themselves insist that they have always occupied their present site since time immemorial.[89] Because they have no memory of a common descent or even of the inter-relationship of any of the eponymous ancestors, the concept of 'Banyangness' is derived from the commonality in customs and language.[90]

Any consideration of the Banyang as an ethnic group is based, therefore, on language and shared cultural patterns. The Banyang group is made up of fourteen clans which are divided into two major sub-groups, an Upper (Eastern) Banyang and a lower (Western) Banyang.[91] The dichotomy is based on certain differences in dialect and cultural values that exist between the two sub-groups. Geographically, Upper Banyang are closer to the Bangwa and highland Tikar chiefdoms, while Lower Banyang are closer to the Anyang and Ejagham. Each of the two sub-groups has been the victim of cultural diffusion as evidenced by the many cultural features borrowed from their respective neighbors. The language and culture of Lower Banyang is closer to those of the eastern Ejagham (Keaka) and there is mutual admiration between these two peoples. Some Lower Banyang institutions, especially secret associations and cult agencies, were acquired from the latter.[92] On the other hand, Upper Banyang have for a very long time practiced intermarriage with the neighboring Bangwa and have assimilated many other cultural symbols and products (for a period the official robes worn by their chiefs were Bangwa in origin) from this group.[93] Another area where the two sub-groups differ, even if only in degree, is in the values associated with village leadership. These differences notwithstanding, the Banyang (both Lower and Upper) in their relationship with out-groups hardly make the distinction between Lower and Upper but consider themselves as a distinct ethnic cluster.[94]

Early European Contact: Contact with the Europeans was not established until the last two decades of the nineteenth century. Count Eugene von Zintgrtaff, a hired explorer in the employ of the German colonial administration was probably the first European to gain entry into Banyang country in July 1888. He was closely followed by eager German traders and a series of military expeditions; but it was not until 1902 that the first civil administration was established at Ossindinge under Count Puckler-Limburg. Puckler was killed in 1904 by a section of Banyang who disapproved of his highhanded tactics. His assassination sparked off a military campaign by the Germans (similar in scale and degree of ruthlessness with the 1894 one against the Kpe of Buea) to punish the disobedient Banyang. Puckler-Limburg was replaced by Mansfield, a more understanding and relatively capable administrator who remained in charge of the district until it passed into British hands in 1916 following the defeat of the German reich.[95]

As everywhere else in Cameroon, the confrontation between Europe and Banyang was harsh and brutal; all in all, a most traumatic experience. Under the German administration (especially after the death of Puckler) a campaign of massive reorganization was undertaken as villages were transplanted from their original sites to new ones dictated by the German authorities. This was explained away as 'town-planning', but in actual fact the intention was to bring the 'natives' closer to the headquarters of German administration. For an understaffed colonial administration this proved to be the easiest method to keep the 'natives' under surveillance. While this proved advantageous to the colonial administration, for the Banyang, its implications were devastating. Traditional authority was seriously disturbed as villages were broken up and then amalgamated with other villages to form new entities; village heads not favorably disposed toward the German colonial administration were disposed and replaced by more malleable ones, euphemistically designated 'official chiefs' who were directly responsible to the German colonial administration. The new villages created by the Germans were then relocated to new sites and Banyang men and women conscripted to work in many construction projects undertaken by the colonial regime, notably in the plantations of the coast and railway construction. Under the British further changes were introduced which affected in no small way the general equilibrium of traditional Banyang society.

The Political System: Like the Kpe the Banyang have a segmentary organized society. Their political system has been described by one authority as a diffuse political community, i.e., a community where the centers of political power and authority are dispersed and not concentrated in one person. Central to Banyang political theory (Banyang conception of their political community in relation to the distribution of power and authority) is the concept of etok which is subject to three different interpretations. Etok could mean settlement, i.e., "a group of houses, a settlement or place of common residents."[96] A second translation renders etok as a 'community' or more precisely a 'residential community,' i.e. "a group of people who reside together and who by their common residence share a solidarity and have a common identity."[97] Thirdly, the concept of etok could also be used in a more restrictive sense to denote a body or group of persons who collectively represent the wider residential community (as defined in the second meaning). Ruel considers these three meanings of etok as constituting the epicenter of Banyang political theory.

Structurally the Banyang political community is divided into three main levels: a village section, a village, and a village group;[98] and each at its own level is represented by a body of leading and senior men "who by virtue of the fact that they do represent the group have the power to make authoritative decisions concerning it."[99] Each of these groups sitting corporately makes decisions and authoritatively carries them out with the political authority of an etok. There is an element of self-autonomy within each level of decision-making: "Each group (other than the largest) has limited political independence and in some contexts it has the power to act independently, but in other contexts it must accept the authority of the wider group in which it is merged," which is the etok at the village group level.[100] Ruel refers to this interplay of independence and dependence as the principle of 'phased autonomous action.' The presence of an over-arching political authority to which lesser political authorities owe 'allegiance' is a significant difference between the Kpe and Banyang political systems. The former do not accept the idea of a pontifex maximus in their theory of government. The body of vambaki in each village is the supreme decision-making organ subject to no other authority. At first glance, one may be tempted to equate the Banyang system with that of the Bafut; however, the resemblance is only superficial, as the two systems of government operate on entirely different principles. This will become apparent in the discussion that follows.

In describing the operational structure of Banyang political community, Ruel delineates two types of councils: (1) those councils that are coterminous with the three main levels of community organization: village section council, village council, and village group council; and (2) a more exclusive body which generally meets in camera that Ruel calls the 'inner council.' In practice, membership overlaps, as an elder could jointly hold membership in the village section council and the village group council. The inner council exists in all the three levels of community power structure but it is generally at the level of a village that the inner council is most effective. It is composed of the village leader who is also the most senior elder together with a number of other prominent elders ('persons of the community'), usually leaders of the various village sections that make up the village. The inner council closely resembles the cabinet in parliamentary government, charged with the formulation of policy and the coordination of "the interests and knowledge of the different leading members of its various sections and to give continuity to the governmental actions carried out at different levels."[101]

The Banyang leader (whether at the village section, village or village group level) has little personal authority, merely what he has derives from the support of the council of which he is merely the primus inter pares.[102] Like the acephalous Kpe, the Banyang have no concept of chieftaincy. Leadership is neither an innate right nor one of formal authority. A leader is essentially a representative of the people and his position is the collective property of the community subject to its control. But this relationship is not assymmetrical, for according to Ruel:

> Comunity leaders are by no means mere spokesmen of a group whose form or policy is beyond their power to influence. The reverse is in fact the case. While insisting upon the formal equality of all who are members of the community, Banyang also respect and acclaim those whose personal qualities of leadership serve to maintain and enhance the solidarity of the group. . . . So also it is said that 'a community cannot exist without someone at its head.'[103]

Conflict Resolution: The councils representing the different levels of the political community in matters judicial sit as a court. There are two types of cases usually brought before the council-cum-court setting as in: (1) cases of tort, i.e. interpersonal disputes, and (2) cases of offense against the community. The type of case and the predisposition of the complainant determine by and large which of the council-cum-court level adjudication will be sought. This is more so especially in interpersonal matters where the choice of judicial tribunal is left entirely to the discretion of the complainant.

As a general rule, three factors are usually considered before a decision is reached as to which of the court level is competent to try a case. The first of which is "the ease of convening the council and the degree of formal constraint which it is wished to bring to bear upon the defendant."[104] This varies with community-type groupings; at the lowest level, i.e. village section council, the degree of formality is less and convening the council is much easier. In addition, the fines that can be imposed on the guilty party are usually much lower. But at the next two higher levels (village and village group councils) the reverse is the case. Thus the higher the level of judicial body, the more difficult it is to convene its members, the higher the fines are that can be imposed, and the greater the degree of formality. A second factor that determines choice of court is the degree of publicity the case is likely to attract and the consequential effects on the solidarity of the group from which the plaintiff and defendant belong. Where the degree of publicity is likely to be great and small group solidarity threatened (in the sense that the group is obliged to abdicate control over its internal affairs due to a usurpation of it by a higher level) redress is sought in lower level councils. Put this way, a plaintiff from a village section who a priori elects a village court to try his case is implicitly questioning the competence and integrity of his section level as a judicial body which in the long run affects the sense of cohesiveness in the group. To avoid this, lower level councils are preferred in instances where a case can be settled within this jurisdiction. The third factor determining court selection has been alluded to in the first and that is the question of sanction. In the higher level councils sanctions are greater than in the lower level ones.

The judicial process is very flexible. Cases brought before a higher level court could always be sent back to a lower-level, where it is the 'appelate' judges' conviction that the latter court is in a better position to know the full facts of the case. Appeals are also allowed from one level to another and defendants not satisfied with a decision of a lower court can appeal the matter to the next level. There is, however, one major restraining factor. Since the councils are empowered by the people authoritatively to make decisions that are binding on all, a rejection of its judicial decisions is generally viewed as an act of insubordination or stubbornness. It is therefore the case that the "higher-level councils usually give some weight to the conclusions of a lower-level council and as a matter of principle would seem where possible to uphold them."[105]

Mention has already been made of types of crime as determinants of choice of tribunal for the working of due process: crimes of tort and crimes against the community. The Banyang approach to crimes against the community is radically different from traditional African jurisprudence with its emphasis on the element of arbitration and reconciliation. Community councils, therefore, react with some ruthlessness to any implied challenge of corporate authority and would impose the severest sanctions on those found guilty of crimes against the community.

Age Groups: The Banyang regard age groups as literally those born at the same time, i.e., within a few days of each other, or one or two months apart. Before adolescence, age mates are pointed out by parents to the children. Upon reaching adolescence, a group of coevals becomes formally organized and empowered to manage its own affairs independently, make its own laws, and punish any members who contravene them. The age group, it follows, only assumes corporate existence upon the attainment of adolescence by those children who were born about the same time.

Each age group is composed of three grades: the senior or front grade among whom the leader of the age group was chosen; the middle grade; and the backgrade. These age grades are based on age differences within the group, with the oldest members in the front grade and the youngest and newly initiated in the back grade. Age groups function primarily as recreational groups though they usually meet for functional purposes, like helping out a member on his farm in return for food and wine. Age groups operate on the basic norms of group solidarity and mutuality of relationship between co-members. Sharing and treating of each member as equals are the inherent operative principles. Group loyalties continue to operate throughout the life-span of its membership with meetings held occasionally until the last of the members have died out.

There are three important points concerning Banyang age groups: (1) the transferability of status among age groups from different villages. Although age groups are usually organized in each village, yet they operate a network of reciprocal relationships such that a stranger from a different village is always welcomed to a meeting of his equivalent age group in another village (and while participating in the meeting he still maintains the grade he occupies in his original age group); (2) age groups serve to rank all its members by age-status thus defining the relative seniority of any man to another. In a society where age is a major determinant of status and degree of formal respect one receives, this aspect of age groups is extremely significant; and (3) age groups provide a forum for general discussion and thus play a critical role in leadership socialization and preparation.[106]

Succession and Inheritance: The distinction between Upper and Lower Banyangs surfaces in the way each views the principles of succession and inheritance. In principle succession to village leadership is by nomination by the predecessor. There seems to be no special formality for nomination: the village head merely allows his views on the subject to be generally known and in Upper Banyang accompanies these on his death bed with a gift of leopard's skins, ivory and whatever may comprise the headman's regalia. It is on the question of inheritance that the split between Upper and Lower Banyang becomes obvious. In the latter group, the nominee is usually the choice. These rules serve merely as guidelines and in practice they are not strictly adhered to.

Associations: A variety of associations performing a number of different functions (political, economic, religious, social, etc.) exist among the Banyang. There are some whose activities and interests are local and therefore restrict themselves to a few villages or village groups while others extend throughout Banyang country. A distinction can be made between traditional associations (where traditional is defined as a historical and conceptual term) and 'modern' associations, where the latter are historically of recent origin formed in response to contemporary conditions. A key feature of traditional Banyang associations is their rules of secrecy which are designed to preserve in-group exclusiveness and also, one suspects, to lend an air of mystery to their proceedings. Associations are organized for members only, who pay fees, and accept the rules that govern their conduct for the duration of their membership. While committed to the satisfaction of the various needs of its membership, an association also has far-reaching authority over its membership, including the power to fine and punish recalcitrant members. As a rule outsiders are excluded from participating in activities of associations they do not belong to and are also not subject to the legal authority of these associations. However, there are some associations whose coercive authority extends beyond their own membership and in practice can and do fine and punish non-members who are offenders.

There are three very active and widespread traditional associations in Banyang with extensive command powers over non-members. These are: Basinjom, Tui, and Ngbe 'secret cults.' The Basinjom is a supernatural association whose main function is the detection and exposure of witchcraft. In the course of performing this function the entire community is subjected to its antics and it can summon any individual suspected of witchcraft to prove his/her innocence through the ordeal method. Tui is an association whose main function traditionally has been punishment by death for offenders of certain crimes. The Ngbe is both a recreational and a political association. In its political or governmental role, Ngbe operates as an authoritative body that protects the rights of individual members of the association or upholds community decisions originating from the community councils. Individual rights protected are those that relate to land and property. In its relations with the community, Ngbe is used as a megaphone (in its literal and metaphorical sense) through which community council decisions are formally announced to the community: "Once the association has been used in this formal way to sanction . . . community laws, any challenge or transgression becomes, however, automatically an association matter."[107] When Ngbe co-opts a community decision, this automatically becomes a 'law of Ngbe,' and Ngbe assumes overall sanctioning authority. The association then becomes, to paraphrase Ruel, the reified and incorporated community council. The transformation of the Ngbe into the community is made possible through an ingenious device which permits all the influential community leaders to become members of Ngbe. It is this fact of overlapping membership which enhances the political importance of the Ngbe secret cult.

If Ngbe is indeed a reconstituted community council, why the resort to this elaborate subterfuge? Why is there a need for the council to operate under cover of the Ngbe? The answer to this puzzle, Ruel suggests, lies in the nature of the Banyang corporate structure.[108] Two interrelated but seemingly contradictory principles define this corporate structure and also determine the role of associations in general and that of Ngbe in particular vis-a-vis Banyang society. The first of these principles requires that corporate political action be based upon the consensus of the members of the group involved; and the second principle emphasizes the need to accommodate within such collective action the diverse interests of the individual members who make up the whole. In short, group decisions imply broad-based political participation and input reflecting all shades of interest in the community--unity in diversity. The Ngbe association is an organization of people who share some common values and interests over and above those that are purely local and parochial in nature. Ngbe owes its sense of group solidarity to the shared common values of its membership and is able to maintain its solidarity character because it permits memberhsip to participate in the formulation of group policies and decisions. Ngbe therefore plays a central role in the process of defining Banyang corporate political structure.

Summary

What can be said about these traditional societies based on the brief ethnographic survey just attempted? In re-examining the data already assembled about the three ethnic groups and directing attention to the socio-political organizations, some striking similarities and differences emerge. The two segmentary systems do share many features, just as they register some significant differences in other areas. On the whole the data indicate that the segmentary groups are markedly different from the centralized chiefdoms.

To demonstrate the breadth of similarities and differences between the two segmentary groups and how far removed they are, in spite of their own internal differences, from the centralized kingdom, a review of the data along three dimensions will be attempted here: (1) within each of the societies, who are the people who have been vested with the right to exercise power? (2) what is the basis upon which the right to govern is anchored?[109] and (3) what are the criteria for appointment and succession to leadership roles? Later on, another variable--the role of associations within each of these societies--will be added to the analysis in an effort to demonstrate that its presence clearly affects the socio-political organizations of these traditonal systems. It will be seen that inspite of their many similarities significant differences still exist between the segmentary societies (Kpe and Banyang) which compel us to be very cautious against any crass lumping together of the two. A consideration of the role of associations also uncovers a strengthening in the already existing polarization between segmentary systems on the one hand and centralized kingdoms on the other.

In both the Kpe and Banyang societies, leaders are dependent for their role upon those whom they represent. As the Banyang describe it, leadership is a community property and a leader is essentially a representative and not an autocrat who imposes his will on the people. He in fact rules by the people's consent and any attempt on his part to overstep his authority runs the risk of provoking a withdrawal of the people's respect and obedience--the very basis of his legitimacy. This egalitarian feature of the two segmentary societies contrasts sharply with the authoritarianism of the centralized Bafut kingdom. Where in segmentary systems the leader's role is traditionally defined as non-authoritarian and non-coercive, in the centralized Bafut system, his role is vested with a wide range of decision-making authority and extensive command powers. In this system, authority derives from the Fon and is exercised on his behalf. The reverse is true of the segmentary Kpe and Banyang where authority derives from the people and is exercised on their behalf by leaders appointed by them.

Succession to leadership roles in the segmentary societies generally is determined by heredity and wealth, as well as by the personal qualities of the candidate. Among the Kpe, for instance, a village head earns his respect not on the basis of some fictive divine authority but by virtue of his position as "father of the village"; a position which he holds because he is, first, an elder; second, because he is a direct descendant of the founder of the village (heredity), and third, because of his personal attributes. The Banyang believe leadership is achieved through the demonstrated ability of an individual to penetrate and to wield influence within the inner chambers of the councilar bodies in his community. Any person who can succeed in doing this clearly has demonstrated his worth as a leader and hence merits the respect of his people.

Among the Bafut, birth plays a decisive role in matters of succession and only people with 'royal blood' are eligible for the Fonship. However, some very important offices are appointive, for instance, noblemen in the kweyifon, and the head of this society. Although not all leadership roles are ascribed, the dichotomy between nobles and commoners inevitably creates a highly stratified society with pronounced status distinctions kept alive by equally pronounced dominance-submission relationships. The hierarchy of statuses is sustained through a web of values that stresses obedience, loyalty, and deference to superiors. All these make for an authoritarian system in contrast to the egalitarianism of the segmentary system where heredity and superior-subordinate distinctions are played down. To be sure, status distinctions do exist but these are not as institutionalized nor as enmeshed in the socio-political fabric as is the case in Bafut. The Banyang, for instance, distinguish between small leaders from hamlets and big leaders from villages and orient their relationships toward them accordingly. As has been shown among the Kpe, elders and direct descendents of founding fathers are reserved a place of honor in the society. But in both cases personal qualities are crucial determinants of whether an individual gets appointed as a leader and whether he continues to receive respect and support from his people or not. Leaders whose powers have waned or been excelled by others quickly drop out of sight and are replaced by new ones. The presence of this 'safety valve' in the social system allows for flexibility in segmentary societies. There is mobility in both directions--upward and downward--as leaders rise and fall and are replaced, and the process is never ending.

Focus can now be shifted toward a comparison of the role of associations in these three ethnic groups. To put the analysis in proper perspective, however, it will be necessary to relate the discussion to the background of Paula Brown's conceptual framework of African authority systems.[110] In a highly engaging discussion on patterns of authority in Africa, Paula Brown takes issue with the Fortes and Evans-Pritchard typology of African political systems for two reasons: first, because the authors permitted a glaring omission by not considering "stateless" societies in which associations rather than a segmentary lineage system regulate political relations; and second, because they fail to distinguish different types of authority and political structure in states. She then suggests a classification of political systems based on (a) the structure of authority-wielding groups, and (b) the types of authority exercised by occupants of authority roles. Brown claims that a careful examination of the authority structures in African societies would reveal four basic types of society: first, societies in which authority is exercised only in and through kinship groups (elementary family, the extended family, lineage or corporate clan); second, societies where authoritative associations and kinship groups exercise authority; third, societies where authority is exercised jointly by kinship groups, associations, and state organization; and fourth, societies with state organization and subordinate kinship groups, with associations either absent or of minor political importance.

Defining authority as the ability of an authority-holder to obtain obedience from his subordinates through use of sanctions directly or indirectly applied, Brown proposes three types of sanctions, namely: moral sanctions, ritual sanctions, and legal sanctions or a combination of any of these. Moral sanction represents tradition and public opinion expressed in mass action or verbalized by a person holding moral authority. Moral sanctions are effective where the enforcer is held in high esteem by his subordinates or where the group shares a common set of values, the infringement of which automatically places one beyond the pale of his/her primary reference group. Ritual sanction derive from supernatural forces supported by traditions. A ritual sanction is effective only when the ritual leader is able to convince the offender of his authority to invoke supernatural sanctions against him. Legal sanctions are the application of threat of force, by a body so empowered, against those who have violated societal rules. The effectiveness of a legal sanction rests on the ability of the enforcer to apply the right amount of force to accomplish the desired punitive goal and also on the general willingness of the community to accept the directions of the authority.

Brown then classified holders of authority according to whether they control moral, ritual or legal sanctions, or some combination of these. In her first type of <u>society in which the kinship group exercises authority</u>, two tiers of authority roles are discernable: (a) an extended family head who is vested with moral authority (based on traditional respect towards elders, a value shared by the majority in the wider society) which he uses to maintain order within the extended family; and (b) the head of the larger kinship group, the maximal lineage or localized clan who often controls ritual and limited legal sanctions, combining the positions of chief priest and judge. In general, order and social cohesion in kinship groups is maintained through the application of moral-ritual, moral-legal, or rarely, legal sanctions. In <u>societies where associations and kinship groups exercise authority</u> (and here the focus is on those associations which exercise sanctions over groups extending <u>beyond</u> their own members) two kinds of associations may be distinguished: cult groups controlling ritual sanctions and secular associations controlling legal sanctions: all two exercising moral sanctions <u>within</u> their associations with some combining both ritual and legal sanctions. These associations exercise authority along with the lineage and clan heads that make up the kinship political community.

In those <u>societies in which authority is exercised by kinship groups, associations, and state organization</u> cooperation among these three component parts is achieved through the principles of centralization and division of labor. Usually a central executive council composed of lineage heads and leaders of the most important associations headed by the king is found. The king exercises ritual and legal authority aided by his council. Though his jurisdiction usually covers the entire state apparatus, for practical administrative reasons, local leaders are allowed some measure of ritual-legal sanctions in their various towns or villages except in serious offenses or disputes which require the attention of the king and his executive council. The fourth type of <u>authority system has a state organization and subordinate kinship groups with politically impotent associations.</u> The authority system is defined by a highly centralized organization, at the top of which is the king with wide legal powers at his disposal. The state usually covers a large territory and supports a heterogeneous population which makes it difficult for order to be effectively maintained through moral and ritual sanctions; the accent, therefore, is on legal sanctions. A highly organized state requires an elaborate legal system which defines and classifies all types of offenses and their appropriate punishments.

Having discussed Brown's taxonomy, I shall now try to apply it to the three ethnic groups being studied. The argument is that the introduction of the variable--authoritative associations--greatly affects the previous classification which regarded Kpe and Banyang as putatively similar on the basis of their being segmentary societies. Now it seems a much more refined distinction can be made between the Kpe and Banyang. The Kpe political system fits snugly into the first type of authority system, where authority is exercised only in and through the kinship groups. Among the Kpe the extended family is the basic political unit and its head is usually the eldest member descended from the founder of the village. Because of his limited coercive powers, the village leader relies heavily on moral sanctions whose effectiveness is generally guaranteed because of the traditional respect Kpe accord elderly people and those whom they elect to govern them. The Banyang also regard the lineage group as the basic political unit and follow almost the same procedure as the Kpe in selecting its head. Here the similarity ends, for the Banyang do have a number of politically powerful associations which in conjunction with the kinship groups jointly exercise authority. In the Banyang political community a clear cut division of labor exists between the lineage and village leaders. The former are primarily concerned with lineage matters and their authority is limited to moral sanctions. The more serious offenses and disputes are punished or arbitrated at the next higher level where there is a concentration on coercive sanctions. The village leader's jurisdiction begins where that of the lineage head's ends; beyond lineage group matters, the village leader enters the picture for it is he who presides over more serious matters like divorce and return of bride wealth, property inheritance, land disputes, etc. He, therefore, has access to both ritual and legal sanctions, especially when such important associations as the Ngbe are drafted into the law-and-order enforcement act. Whereas among the Kpe regulatory associations are few, primarily social and of little political importance, the Banyang count a multiplicity of associations that are politically potent. These associations actively participate in the political process and account for extensive ritual and command powers which they exercise over groups that are beyond their own members. The importance of associations is evidenced in the fact that all the important lineage and village leaders are de facto members of some of the all-powerful associations like the Ngbe, holding high offices in them. It is the combination between 'City Hall' and the 'Lodges' that defines Banyang political and authority systems, making them different from the Kpe's.

The Bafut political structure depicts the interaction of three important component parts: kinship groups, regulatory associations and the Fon. The various kinship levels of political organization (the compound and ward heads) in Bafut are vested with moral and (limited) legal authority. Each of the seven villages that make up the Bafut kingdom has its own chief who is autonomous to a certain extent but still regards the Fon as paramount. The various heads and village chieftains are all subordinate to the Fon who rules both as a secular monarch and a divinity aided by the all-important regulatory association--the Kweyifon. The kweyifon is also vested with secular and spiritual authority. Though Chilver and Kaberry see the Fon as "suzerain, distributor of rewards, as the dispenser of honours, as head of all associations of royals and commoners, as the centre of a web of political communications, and as the supreme judge,"[111] he still cannot maintain effective control over his entire domain without delegating some authority to subordinates, nor can he rule effectively without the active support of the Kweyifon. Unlike the Banyang who permit a system of overlapping membership which makes it possible for a village head to hold membership simultaneously in one or more councils--residential community council, village level council, its 'inner chamber,'--and also in the Ngbe society; a Bafut village chief does not automatically qualify for position in the Kweyifon since his elevation to that body depends on factors other than the fact that he is a village chief. The Banyang system of overlapping membership allows leaders to assume different authority powers and postures depending on which particular role is currently occupied. Thus, a lineage leader whose office entitles him only to the use of moral sanctions can by changing roles concomitantly expand his power horizons. As a village leader his powers are circumscribed by the functions he is allowed to perform, but in his capacity as a high Ngbe official this same individual assumes wider powers because his functions have expanded to correspond with the new status. Only the Fon in the Bafut context can behave in this chameleon-like manner and this is because it is he who delegates authority to subordinates. He can, if he so elects, confine all authority to himself. It is, however, the interplay in the authority domain, between kinship groups, secret associations and the Fon that distinguishes Bafut political community from the Banyang's.

On the basis of the preceding discussion, it is postulated that the variations observed in the social organizations and authority systems of these three ethnic groups will not vary with geographical location.

The Sample

Interviews were held with and questionnaires distributed to about 900 adult Cameroonians. The response rate was about fifty per cent. Four hundred and fifty-seven schedules and questionnaires were retrieved, of which 56 were discarded for incomplete information. The sampled n is 391, about

35 per cent of which were self-administered questionnaires. The sample obtained did not come from a normal distribution and as such it cannot in terms of probability theory be considered a true representation of the population. This non-probability sample was selected in order to facilitate subgroup comparisons in line with the major thrust of the study which was to investigate the impact of environment on ethnic group values and political orientations. Aside from the non-paremetric nature of the sample, the data obtained are grouped into either nominal or ordinal scales. These two factors impose severe limitations on the number and type of statistics and statistical tests that can be employed to test relationships. Consequently, the choice of statistical technique for hypotheses testing, as determined on the basis of scaling considerations and sampling assumptions, is the chi-square (x^2) test.

The level of significance was set in advance of .01. The region of rejection was defined in advance as consisting of all values of the given statistical tests and coefficients which are so large that the probability associated with their occurrence under the null hypothesis is equal to or less than 1 in 100. Hence, whenever a relationship or test was significant at the .01 level, the null hypothesis was rejected at that level.

Footnotes

1. J. A. Ngwa, *An Outline Geography of the Federal Republic of Cameroon*. London: Longman's Green & Company, 1967.
2. E. W. Ardener, *Coastal Bantu of the Cameroons*. London: International African Institute, 1956, p. 31.
3. Talcott Parsons, *Essays in Sociological Theory*. Glencoe: The Free Press, 1954 2nd ed.; and S. F. Nadel, "Witchcraft in Four African Societies: An Essay on Comparison," *American Anthropologist*, Vol. 54, No. 1 (January-March 1952).
4. Probably re-settlement is the more appropriate word here inasmuch as workers were imported from the hinterland areas and resettled in the coastal areas which supported plantation agriculture.
5. P. M. Kale, *A Brief History of Bakweri*. Lagos: Tika-Tore Press, 1939, p. 27; F. A. Wells and W. A. Warmington, *Studies in Industrialization: Nigeria and the Cameroons*. London: Oxford University Press, 1962.
6. Victor T. Le Vine, *The Cameroon Federal Republic*, op. cit., p. 49.
7. Bert F. Hoselitz, "Urbanization and Economic Growth in Asia," *Economic Development and Cultural Change*, Vol. 6 (1957), pp. 45-55; George M. Foster, *Traditional Cultures and the Impact of Technological Change*. New York: Harper & Row, 1962, p. 29.
8. Hoselitz, op. cit., p. 43.
9. Figures are based on the 1976 census. Ministry of Economic Affairs and Planning, *Main Results of the April 1976 General Population and Housing Census*. Yaounde: Central Bureau of the Census, 1978.
10. Rudin, p. 79.
11. Ardener, 1956, p. 24.
12. See Rudin, pp. 86, 193, and 365 for a more detailed account.
13. As the seat of government, it was populated by a large proportion of the territory's educated elite who were very politicized.

14. Another version of the folklore has it that Tiko was originally (and still is) referred by Kpe people as Keka; a renowned trading mart where fish was exchanged for farm produce brought in from the mountain slopes. On a trip to Keka to barter their cocoyams for fish, Kpe women returned to Buea with fish that was considered by their men folk to be less than what was expected. When it was suggested to these women that they had been cheated by the people of Keka, they wryly remarked that "E Keka ema tikoa"; which translated from Kpe means that "keka has changed!" Thereafter Keka was always referred to as the town that had changed (tikoa)--the word tikoa was later anglicized to Tiko.

15. For a detailed history of Victoria, the reader is referred to Victoria, Southern Cameroons: 1858-1958, ed. Victoria Centenary Committee, Victoria: Basel Mission Book Depot, 1958.

16. Robert Redfield, "The Folk Society," American Journal of Sociology, 52 (January, 1947), p. 293; for a critique of Redfield, see Horace Miner, "The Folk-Urban Continuum," Bobbs-Merrill Reprint, S-202, pp. 529-37.

17. Redfield, p. 294-5.

18. M. J. Ruel, 1960. The Asian experience is also a case in point where cities have always acted as catalysts of socioeconomic change through which Western influences filter down into the countryside. For a discussion of the Asian experience, see Robert I. Crane, "Urbanism in India," American Journal of Sociology, 60 (1955), pp. 463-70 and Norton Ginsburg, "The Great City in Southeast Asia," American Journal of Sociology, 60 (1955), pp. 455-62.

19. Ardener, et. al., 1960.

20. The Kpe and other coastal groups whose lands were sequestrated by the Germans never gave up the struggle to recover their lands. The Kpe, in particular, made representations at various times to the British Administration which had inherited the territory in 1916 on this subject. In 1946, the Bakweri Land Committee was formed by a group of leading Kpe nationals. This Committee in 1950 made representations to a U.N. Visiting

Mission challenging the Government's presumption of eminent domain over Kpe land and demanding an immediate return of all ex-enemy lands (which were now being held in trust by the Governors of Nigeria to be developed for the common good of all Cameroonians) to the Kpe people in whom ownership was traditionally and legally vested. The administration's response to the various Kpe land petitions were in the form of pious statements expressing indignation at the treatment this group received from the Germans. However, the British administration did purchase some land from various European owners which were declared 'native lands' and handed over to the Kpe. Between 1927 and 1932, the colonial authorities spent a total of ten thousand, five hundred pounds sterling to purchase 14,851 acres of land to be used by the Kpe and neighboring groups. Again in 1950, 25,000 more acres were made available to the Kpe from excisions of lands leased to the Cameroons Development Corporation. In all, 39,851 acres of land from the original 400-500 square miles alienated were returned to the Kpe. See C. K. Meek, <u>Land Tenure and Land Administration in Nigeria and the Cameroons</u>. London: Her Majesty's Stationery Office, 1957, pp. 404-8; <u>Report by His Majesty's Government to the League of Nations on the Administration of the Cameroons, 1924, 1932, and 1938</u> and <u>Report by His Majesty's Government to the United Nations on the Administration of the Cameroons, 1949 and 1950</u>.
    21. Ardener, et. al., 1960.
    22. Ibid.
    23. George M. Foster, <u>op</u>. <u>cit</u>., pp. 44-57.
    24. Frey, 1968, pp. 934-65.
    25. Almond and Verba, <u>The Civic Culture</u>; the Mexican sample was drawn exclusively from an urban population; with such a skewed sample caution has to be exercised in deriving broad and sweeping generalizations from their results. This methodological weakness has been criticized by Erwin K. Scheuch, "The Cross-Cultural Use of Sample Surveys: Problems of Comparability," in <u>Comparative Research Across Cultures and Nations</u>, ed. Stein Rokkan. Paris: Mouton, 1968, p. 194.

26. Banfield, 1958, pp. 77ff.

27. It was not possible to collect data from the hinterland as such only the Banyang and Kpe village groups are included in the subsequent analysis. This, of course, means that the village sample is biased in favor of the two segmentary traditional systems and excludes the centralized Grassfield systems. Although comparisons cannot be made between segmentary and centralized peoples living in villages, the data, however, can sustain comparisons between rural village political culture and that found in plantation camps and large towns.

28. E. W. Ardener in Social Change, pp. 89-90.

29. Rudin, Germans in the Cameroons, 1884-1914; Wells & Warmington, Studies in Industrialization: Nigeria and the Cameroons; also the following studies deal with the plantation system under the Cameroon Development Corporation: Sanford Bederman, The Cameroon Development Corporation: Partner in National Growth and Ardener, et. al., Village and Plantation in the Cameroons.

30. Bederman, op. cit., p. 16.
31. Wells & Warmington, op. cit., p. 133.
32. Meek, p. 406.
33. Johnson, pp. 97-8.
34. Wells & Warmington, p. 140.
35. Johnson, op. cit.
36. Bederman, op. cit.

37. See the typology developed by Meyer Fortes and E. E. Evans-Pritchard, eds., African Political Systems. London: Oxford University Press, 1940.

38. See Edwin W. Ardener, "The Nature of the Reunification of Cameroon," in Arthur Hazelwood, ed., African Integration and Disintegration. London: Oxford University Press, 1967 for a lucid discussion of this problem.

39. Ibid.

40. Adam Przeworski and Henry Teune, The Logic of Comparative Social Inquiry. New York: John Wiley Interscience, 1970.

41. E. M. Chilver and P. M. Kaberry, Traditional Bamenda: Precolonial History and Ethnography of the Bamenda Grassfields. Buea: Ministry of Primary Education and Social Welfare, 1967, p. 1. The authors use the term Western Grassfields to refer to all the ethnic groups that occupy the Bamenda highland. I am using the term Grassfield in a more restrictive sense to refer only to the Tikar, Chamba and Widekum ethnic groups.

42. Merran McCulloch, Margaret Littlewood and Idelette Dugast, Peoples of the Central Cameroons. London: International African Institute, 1954. Chilver and Kaberry, "The Kingdom of Kom in West Cameroon," in Forde and Kaberry, eds., West African Kingdoms in the Nineteenth Century. London: O.U.P., 1967, pp. 123-151.

43. For a discussion on situational ethnicity see, Immanuel Wallerstein, "Ethnicity and National Integration in West Africa," in Harry Eckstein and David Apter, eds., Comparative Politics. New York: The Free Press, 1963, pp. 665-668; A. L. Epstein, Politics in An Urban African Community. Manchester: Manchester University Press, 1958; and John Paden, "Urban Pluralism, Integration, and Adaptation of Communal Identity in Kano," in Ronald Cohen and John Middleton, eds., From Tribe to Nation in Africa. Scranton, Pa.: Chandler Publishing Company, 1970.

44. These Divisions were formerly called Bamenda, Wum and Nkambe. Bamenda was later subdivided into three divisions of Mezam, Bui and Momo while Wum took the new name of Menchum and Nkambe became known as Donga-Mantum.

45. The following account leans heavily on Chilvers' and Kaberry's excellent book Traditional Bamenda, all information given being from this source unless otherwise stated.

46. Chilvers and Kaberry, p. 13.

47. Ritzenthaler, et. al., 1962, p. 13; also McCulloch in Peoples of Central Cameroons, p. 11.

48. Much of this section is based on the Ritzenhalers' study of the Bafut, unless otherwise stated.

49. E. G. Hawkesworth, Assessment Report 1926. Unpublished Monograph, West Cameroon Archives, Buea, paragraphs 15-30; also McCulloch, 1952, p. 18.

50. The bukum are the nobles who advise the Fon. They are usually commoners who have been elevated to the rank of noble by virtue of their meritorious service to the Fon. They are not nobles by birth. There are about fifty bukum in Bafut, twelve of whom comprise the Fon's Council of Elders. The death of one of the twelve, necessitates the selection of a replacement from among the other thirty-eight bukum. Ritzenthaler, op. cit., p. 111.

51. Ibid., p. 13.
52. Ritzenthaler, et al., 1962, p. 116.
53. Ibid.
54. Ibid., . 117.
55. The coastal chiefdoms were carved out in order to destroy the trade monopoly of the coastal people. Those who cooperated with the traders and later colonial authorities were designated chiefs; it was the effete and the pliable ones who won this "coveted" title. Take the example of the Isuwu chief Bille who was given the title of "King William" in 1826 in recognition of the surrender of his sovereignty to England!

56. According to the Ritzenthalers, a rarity in Africa; see Radcliffe-Brown and F. Forde, eds., African Systems of Kinship and Marriage. Oxford: Oxford University Press, 1959, p. 25.

57. Ritzenthaler, et al., pp. 109-110.
58. Chilver and Kaberry, 1963, p.
59. Ardener, 1956, p. 82.
60. Ibid., p. 11.
61. Ibid., p. 17.
62. Allen, 1938; also Ardener, 1956, p. 24.
63. Ibid., p. 10. Allen also makes the ridiculous assertion that the Kpe-Mboko people are actually a conglomeration of groups of emigrants from all parts of Cameroon who united into one large group for reasons of self-defense and administrative convenience later cementing their union with a legend of common origin.

64. There is strong evidence to support this contention. For example, several Kpe villages have Mboko namesakes which causes Ardener to wonder if these villages did not directly spring from the original Mboko ones. Villages like, Wovea, Wokoso, Wonjia, etc. Ardener, 1956, p. 23.

65. Ibid., pp. 23-24. Another version of the origin of the name Buea says it is derived from Eye's name meaning the children of Eye. Kale, 1939, pp. 6-7.

66. Ardener, 1956, p. 24.

67. Bouchaud cites 1472 as the year Portuguese traders first established contact with the Cameroon coast: "Quoi qu'il soit, nous en savons assez pour fixer avec quelque certitude à l'année 1472 la date de la découverte du Cameroun et pour attribuer le mérite à la fois au Roi Alphonse V, a l'entreprenant Fernão Gomes et au hardi marin qui fut Fernão do Po," p. 43. La Côte du Cameroun dans l'histoire et cartographie dès à l'annexion allemande. Yaounde: IFAN, Centre Camerounaise, 1952.

68. Kale, 1939, dates this contact to around 1668, p. 16.

69. The London Baptist Missionaries established a station in Bimbia in 1844 from their base of operations in Fernando Po. This was subsequently transfered to the Victoria mainland in 1858. Victoria Centenary Committee, ed., Victoria: Southern Cameroons, 1858-1958. Victoria: Basel Mission Book Depot, 1958.

70. Harry Rudin, Germans in the Cameroons 1884-1914. New Haven: Yale University Press, 1938; also Kale, 1939, for an account of the German defeat from a Kpe point of view, pp. 19-25.

71. It has been estimated that of about 434 habitable square miles of land the plantations occupied over 300 square miles, Ardener, 1956, p. 14. Also C. K. Meek, Land Tenure and Land Administration in Nigeria and the Cameroons. London: Her Majesty's Stationery Office, 1957, pp. 404-408.

72. E. W. Ardener, "Social and Demographic Problems of the Southern Cameroons Plantation Area," in Social Change in Africa, ed., Aidan Southall, London: Oxford U. Press, 1961, p. 86ff.

73. Allen, 1938, p. 16.
74. Ibid.
75. Ibid., p. 15.
76. Allen, 1938, p. 17.
77. Ibid., p. 17.
78. Ibid., p. 18.
79. Ardener, 1956, p. 72.
80. Ibid., p. 72.
81. Ibid., p. 73.
82. Ibid., p. 75.
83. Ibid., p. 53.
84. Ibid., p. 54.
85. Other spellings of this group are Banyang, Bayangi, Banyangi, 'Nyangi, etc.
86. Figures taken from M. J. Ruel, "Migration in two Southern Cameroons Tribes: The Banyang of Mamfe Division," in Shirley Ardener, E. W. Ardener, and W. A. Warmington, Plantation and Village in the Cameroons. Oxford: Oxford University Press, 1969, pp. 230-47.
87. The thesis on Banyang origin was first advanced by a French colonial administrator, A. M. Ripert, who was at one time Chef de Circonscription in Dschang, French Cameroons. Memorandum by E. G. Hawkesworth, Secretary, Southern Provinces, Enugu to the Senior Resident, Cameroons Province, Buea, dated 15th July, 1929. West Cameroons Archives, Buea.
88. Ibid.
89. M. J. Ruel, Leopards and Leaders: Constitutional Politics among a Cross River People. London: Tavistock Publications, 1969, p. 280.
90. E. H. F. Gorges, Banyang Tribal Area Assessment Report, 1930. Unpublished Monograph. Buea: West Cameroon Archives.
91. A. C. Anderson, Assistant District Officer, A Preliminary Assessment Report of the Banyang Tribal Area, 1929. Unpublished Monograph. Buea: West Cameroon Archives.
92. Ruel, 1969, pp. 1-4.
93. Gorges, 1930, paragraphs 24-25.
94. I observed in the course of my research that Banyang did not as a rule make the distinction between Upper and Lower Clan groupings. It

was only when specifically asked that some bothered to refer to their Clan group.
    95. Rudin, 1938, op. cit.
    96. Ruel, 1969, p. 19.
    97. Ibid., p. 19.
    98. Banyang political community comprises the following: the village which is the major political unit; the village group which is a composite of a number of villages grouped together; and village sections--usually the largest villages are divided into a number of residentially distinct and partially autonomous hamlets.
    99. Ruel, 1969, p. 21.
   100. Ibid., p. 22.
   101. Ibid., p. 146.
   102. E. H. F. Gorges, 1930.
   103. Ruel, 1969, pp. 66-7.
   104. Ibid., p. 160.
   105. Ibid., p. 160.
   106. Ibid., p. 164.
   107. Beginning in the 1930's age groups began to wane and were gradually replaced by a plethora of modern young men's associations like the Ekan, Young Seven, Agency, etc. Ruel, 1969, Chapter 11.
   108. Ibid., Chapter 10.
   109. John Beattie, "Checks on the abuse of Political power in some African states: A preliminary framework for analysis," in Cohen and Middleton, eds., Comparative Political Systems: Studies in the Politics of Pre-Industrial Societies. N.Y.: Doubleday, Natural History Press, 1967, pp. 355-73. In this article Beattie tries to draw the line between power and authority.
   110. Paula Brown, "Patterns of Authority in West Africa," Africa, Vol. XXI (October, 1951), No. 4, pp. 261-78.

3
Contrasts and Similarities Among Three Ethnic Groups

This chapter will be devoted to a comparative analysis of the three ethnic groups along three dimensions: (1) demographic characteristics; (2) socio-political values; and (3) the nature of the processes through which the political beliefs and values of the respondents were molded.

Background/Demographic Variables

On the basis of means, medians and frequency distributions, we shall examine and in the process indicate the contrasts and similarities among the three ethnic groups along the following variables: age, education, occupation, religious affiliation, family status, and pattern of residence.

Age--The median age of the Banyang and Grassfield was twenty-eight years and thirty years for the Kpe sample. The Banyang and Kpe, however, registered a high within sample variance.

Education--The data indicate clearly that all three ethnic groups enjoy a high level of literacy. This is as it should be, since the country as a whole enjoys an equally high level of literacy with more than 65 per cent of school age children currently enrolled in schools.[1] Among the Banyang, 51.4 per cent had completed primary school compared to 41 per cent for the Kpe and 39.7 per cent among the Grassfield. While only 17 per cent Kpe respondents went on to secondary or post-secondary and technical educational institutions, the Banyang and Grassfields registered an impressive 24 per cent and 26 per cent respectively of their respondents with post primary education. The last two distributions are consistent (more or less) with the overall national average of 24 per cent (even though this figure applies only to post-primary technical education).[2] The low percentage of post-primary educated Kpe comes as a surprise, for the coastal ethnic groups--of whom the Kpe is one--have historically enjoyed a high level of literacy because of their advantageous coastal position which brought them into early contact with modernizing influences from the European world, in the form of schools especially. As a matter of record, the first school in Anglophone Cameroon was founded in the coastal Kpe town of Bimbia in 1844. It would appear that the Banyang (who like the Kpe are a minority ethnic group numbering no more than 40,000) have gained much ground in the area of literacy, in spite of their insular forest location. From the point of view of proportion, it may well be that the Banyang are becoming the most educated ethnic group in English-speaking Cameroon--a position once considered held by the minority coastal Kpe.[3]

Occupation--In 1970, 21 per cent of the active adults between twenty and fifty-five years of age were employed by the government and related agencies (such as mission schools which receive grants-in-aid from the government in order to stay in business).[4] The sampled frequencies of those who reported being employed overall do not vary considerably from the national mean. The Grassfield sample when compared to the other two ethnic groups has a relatively large proportion of its respondents working for the government. Thirty-one per cent of the Grassfield as opposed to 18 per cent among the Kpe and Banyang work for the Cameroon government. The largest proportion of respondents from all three ethnic groups (the figures are 52 per cent among the Banyang, 44 per cent and 41 per cent among the Grassfield and Kpe respectively) is involved in manual agricultural labor, either as small-scale, self-employed subsistence farmers or laborers for the plantation industry. When not engaged as government employees or working in the agricultural sector, a small porportion within each of the ethnic groups is engaged in semi- and skilled trades such as masonry, carpentry, sewing, motor mechanics, and the like.

Of the three ethnic groups, the Banyang report the highest unemployment, 26 per cent, in contrast to only 12 per cent for the Grassfield and 14 per cent for the Kpe. Incidentally, the Kpe and Grassfield unemployment figures are closer to the 11 per cent national median.[5] Two factors may have contributed toward the high unemployment rate among the Banyang--factors which can be traced to the sampling procedures. First, the Banyang sample was biased in favor of young persons who had just completed primary and post-primary schooling and were not yet employed. Secondly, the Banyang sample contained a large proportion of women, relative to the other two ethnic group samples, who were not actively engaged in any form of subsistence farming or small scale trading and were consequently coded as "unemployed." To test these suspicions, the Banyang data were submitted to a series of crosstabulations controlling for age and sex. It was found that close to 90 per cent of the Banyang unemployed were under thirty-five years old but less than one-third of these was in the seventeen to twenty-four years age bracket (the group most likely to include recent primary and post-primary school leavers). On the basis of these figures, the first explanation for the high unemployment rate among the Banyang sample was rejected. However, when I controlled for sex, the results confirmed my expectations. Women accounted for 64 per cent of the total unemployed and the majority of them were housewives. These were respondents who did not state that they were employed by the government or by the Cameroon Development Corporation, or were involved in some form of small scale private business enterprise. The high incidence of married unemployed housewives in the Banyang sample was thus responsible for inflating this group's unemployment figure.

The data analysis so far indicates that the sample for this study is by no means a deviant one. In terms of literacy level and occupational background, the sample of respondents interviewed here is very close to the universe from which it was drawn. One is thus confident that the sampling techniques, crude as they were, successfully captured a cross-section of the Anglophone Cameroon universe.

Religious Affiliation[6]--Roughly two out of three English-speaking Cameroonians are Christians. There are approximately 401,000 Christians--that is about 38 per cent of the population--in former West Cameroon. On the basis of membership figures, the Roman Catholic Church is far ahead of the other mission churches operating in this region. Its total membership of Christians and Catechuments is roughly 57 per cent of the proselytized population, as against 34 per cent for the Presbyterians and 9 percent for the Baptist mission. (See Tables 3.1, 3.2 and 3.3). The prodigious growth of the Roman Catholic Church has occurred in spite of the fact that it was the last of the major Western missions to engage in serious evangelical work in English-speaking Cameroon.

Missionary activities antedate the European colonization of Cameroon, going back to the 1844 visit the Reverend Alfred Saker of the London Baptist Missionary Society paid to the Cameroon mainland from his island headquarters in Fernando Po. With the founding of Victoria in 1858 by Saker and his followers, the missionary movement gained a significant beachhead from which to spread its proselytizing missions to other flanks of the Cameroon territory. One may correctly say then that the missionary scramble for Cameroon began in earnest with Saker's settlement at Victoria. In a very short time the field was cluttered with different missionary groups representing the major ideological strains of Western Christianity. Due to pressures brought to bear on them by a hostile German colonial administration, Saker's English Baptists were compelled to hand over in 1886 to the German Basler Evangelische Missionsgesellschaft (though headquartered in Switzerland, the Basler mission still maintained a branch in Stuttgart, Germany "partly to give itself a German character, partly to attract German money for its work").[7]

Differences in dogma, church organization and discipline compelled a faction of Saker's Baptists which had just been integrated into the German-Swiss Basler Mission to sever ties from this latter organization and to form an independent Native Baptist Church. After the first flush of euphoria over its independence, the Native Baptist Church sought external help and in 1891, the German branch of the American Baptist Society established ties with this group in Cameroon. The alliance, like the previous one, was stillborn and in 1898, the Native Baptists once more asserted their independence. However, at the close of the First World War, the North American Baptists had successfully co-opted the entire missionary operation in English-speaking Cameroon that had anything to do with the Baptists. The late-comer to the missionary scramble was the Roman Catholic Church, who came to Anglophone Cameroon in 1894 on the invitation of the Basler Mission.[8]

Partly as a result of German colonial administrative policy--which anticipated some degree of inter-denominational disputes unless firm ground rules of operation were clearly defined and agreed upon from the onset--and also partly on the basis of some sort of a "missionary pact" (perhaps the forerunner to the "colonial pact"), the different missionary groups agreed to stake their claims in different parts of the Kamerun territory. Over time they each came to control what one might call spheres of missionary influence. Beginning with Saker and up until the entry of the Roman Catholics, missionary activity in Cameroon of English-expression was confined exclusively to the coastal corridor. It was not until the turn of the century that missionaries started penetrating into the hinterland. In the initial years, only the North American Baptists "concentrated their best efforts in the Grassfields,"[9] while the other two missions kept themselves pretty much to the coast.

Table 3.1*
Distribution of Christians[1] in the Divisions of
the South-West Province of English-Speaking
Sector of the Cameroon Republic, According to
Denominations

Divisions	Catholics[2]	Baptists[3]	Presbyterians[4]
Fako	15.2% (n 35,052)	9.8% (n 3,294)	13.4% (n 18,266)
Meme	16.6% (n 38,393)	4.7% (n 1,586)	20.7% (n 28,414)
Manyu	9.5% (n 21,909)	.7% (n 245)	5.7% (n 7,906)
Ndian	1.2% (n 2,827)	nd	nd
Total for S.W.	42.5% (n 98,182)	15.2% (n 5,125)	40.0% (n 54,586)

[1]Figures also include catechuments.
[2]Figures are for the year ending 1970.
[3]Figures represent total Baptist membership as of March 1973.
[4]Figures are the for 1972 Presbyterian church census.

Table 3.2*
Distribution of Christians in the Divisions of the
North-West Province of English-Speaking Cameroon

Divisions	Catholics	Baptists	Presbyterians
Bui	7.5% (n 39,573)	14.9% (n 5,043)	*6
Momi	5.9% (n 13,584)	*5	
Donga & Mantung	4.0% (n 9,133)	34.5% (n 11,612)	15.4% (n 21,108)
Mentchoum	8.6% (n 19,958)	20.9% (n 7,043)	6.4% (n 8,809)
Mezam	21.7% (n 50,101)	14.3% (n 4,832)	4.2% (n 5,806)
			34.0% (n 46,461)
Total for N.W.	57.5% (n132,349)	84.8% (n 28,530)	60.0% (n 82,184)
Total for both Provinces	100.0% (n230,531)	100.0% (n 33,655)	100.0% (n136,770)

5Included under figures for Mezam Division.
6Included under Donga/Mantung.   n.d.-no data available

*Source for Tables 3.1 and 3.2: Annuaire de L'Eglise Catholique 1972-1973, Church Census 1972, Presbyterian Church in Cameroon, Buea, 16th May, 1973. Mimeo and personal communication from the Headquarters of the Cameroon Baptist Church, Buea, December, 1973. Note: Percentages were calculated by this author.

Table 3.3
Distribution of Christians in Areas Occupied by the
Ethnic Clusters Surveyed in this Study

Divisions	Catholics	Baptists	Presbyterians
Fako[1]	15.2% (n 35,053)	9.8% (n 3,294)	13.4% (n 18,266)
Manyu[2]	9.5% (n 21,909)	.7% (n 245)	5.7% (n 906)
Momo, Mentuchum[3] and Mezam	36.3% (n 83,643)	35.3% (n 11,875)	54.0% (n 73,375)

[1] Fako Division also includes ethnic groups like the Bafaw and Balong who are ethnologically related to the Kpe. See Ardener, Coastal Bantus, op. cit.
[2] The major ethnic group in this Division is the Banyang.
[3] People from these divisions--the Tikar, Chamba and Widekum-- have been classified in this study as Grassfield.

Looking at spheres of control from an historical perspective, the Basler Mission, as it were, heir to Saker's huge missionary legacy, remained firmly entrenched in the coastal and, to some extent, forest regions of English-speaking Cameroon. The North American Baptists focused their attention on the Grassland areas while the Catholics not only made impressive gains in the coastal areas but were also very active in the hinterland/Grassfield region. Table 3.4 shows the distribution of missionary activities in Kamerun around 1913.

Whereas the previous table maps out missionary activity in its early stages, Tables 3.1 and 3.2 attempt to present a more contemporary picture. We note with interest that there has been a dramatic shift in evangelizing work away from the coast to the Grassland areas. There are more church members in absolute and relative terms in the Grasslands than in the coast and forest regions. The commanding lead enjoyed by the Grassland region in terms of church membership is attested to by the fact that when we put together all the church members in Fako and Manyu divisions (divisions in which the Kpe and Banyang predominate), the total is just about equal to the number of Catholics in only three Grassfield divisions of Mentchum, Mezam and Momo! It would appear that in both absolute numbers and proportionately, there are more Christians among the northern Grassland people than among the Coastal southern population (see footnote 10). English-speaking Cameroon may be unique in this respect-- being one of the few post-colonial African countries with a southern coastal flank long exposed to western missionary influence yet still relatively less Christianized than the hinterland north.[10] The popular belief that the majority of African societies are usually polarized into a Christian south and a pagan (or Islamized) north does not hold in this particular society. If anything, the northern hinterland of English-speaking Cameroon is more Christanized than the coastal and forest south, in spite of the over half a century head start the latter had over the former in exposure to Christian missions.

I have gone into some detail in explaining missionary expansion and influence in the region being studied for two reasons: first, to give the reader an idea of the distribution of Christianity and the areas which have historically been under the influence of various missionary ideologies. And secondly, to underscore Professor Johnson's observation, that religious cleavages dramatically coincide with ethnic and geographical cleavages;[11] the Kpe and Banyang having been under the influence of the various Protestant missions (Basler and North American Baptists) while the Grassfield have had strong ties with the Catholic church. The information here updates and in part corrects the picture of missionary activities in Cameroon.[12]

The reader may wonder why throughout the discussion of religious affiliation the preoccupation has been primarily with Western Christian Missions. I have often 'wondered why only less than 10 per cent of the sampled universe considered themselves animists in contrast to Le Vine's astonishing claim that 65 per cent of English-speaking Cameroonians are animists.[13] An overwhelming 90 per cent of the sampled respondents from the three ethnic groups belong to the major ideologies of Western Christianity, although no attempt was made to distinguish between nominal and active (or practicing) Christians.

Looking at the distribution of denominational affiliation in the sampled universe reveals some interesting contrasts and similarities among the ethnic groups on the one hand and also some insights into the contemporary map of missionary activities in the country. About one half of both the Banyang and Kpe samples report that they belong to the Presbyterian Church. However, in contrast to Johnson's finding, there are more Presbyterians (41 per cent) than Catholics (38 per

Table 3.4*
Pre-World War I Missionary Activity in
German Colony of Kamerun

1913

Mission	# of Schools	# of Pupils Enrolled	# of Converts
American Presbyterian	97	6,545**	2,796
Basler Mission	319	17,833	13,176
Catholic	151	12,532	n.d.
London Baptist	57	3,151	3,128

Source: Rudin, Germans in the Cameroons, 1882-1939, pp. 360-382.

*In 1914 the number of converts had increased to 15,000.
**In another section, Rudin gives 9,313 as the number of pupils in Presbyterian schools in 1913, p. 376.

cent) and Baptists (12 per cent) among the Grassfield. The same holds for the Banyang who are divided as follows: 50 per cent Presbyterians, 30 per cent Catholics and 9 per cent Baptists. Overall, there are more Presbyterians than Catholics and Baptists among respondents in the three ethnic groups. I find that there have been major shifts in missionary spheres of influence: (1) the North American Baptists who have had a long record of contact with the coastal ethnic groups in general and the Kpe in particular claim only 14 per cent of this group's membership; (2) the Catholic Church seems to be fairly well established in Banyang country, with 30 per cent of the Banyang respondents as members of this church; (3) the struggle for the "heathen" Grassfield is between the Presbyterian and Catholic Churches, with the former having a slight edge; and (4) the contemporary map also indicates that all the missions now seem to be concentrating their best efforts in the Grassfield which was not the case at the beginning of the century. If membership figures are used as an indicator, we notice that 85 per cent of the Baptist Church membership, 60 per cent of the Presbyterian, and 57 per cent of the Catholic comes from this area.

Family Status--By family status, I mean the marital state of the respondent and his/her estimate of the size of the family in which he/she grew up. Table 3.5 shows that the highest proportion of married persons come from the Kpe sample, i.e., about 64 per cent, followed by the Grassfields with 50 per cent, and then the Banyang with 39 per cent. There are more individuals in each of the three ethnic groups who come from large families (families with over eight children) than small or medium sized ones. However, more Grassfields (31 per cent) and Banyang (28 per cent) than Kpe (25 per cent) come from medium sized families (families having between five and seven children).

Residential Patterns--One of the objectives of the research design was to control for the factor of exposure to the modernizing influences brought into Cameroon by the occidental winds of change. To hold this factor constant, at least for the urban areas and peri-urban plantation camps, it was decided that all interviewing would be carried out in the coastal multi-ethnic towns and plantation camps since these areas have had the longest record of contact with the Western world. Only those individuals who had spent at least ten years in the coast were sampled. Respondents were asked two questions:

> Where have you spent most of your life: a village, a town or some other place (please specify)?
>
> How long did you live in this place?

Table 3.6 shows that more Kpe respondents have spent the greater part of their lives in rural villages prior to coming to the coastal plantation camps and towns than have Grassfield and Banyang. Over 50 per cent of the Banyang and Grassfield respondents have lived in towns for over ten years.

Ethnic Group Values

The preceding pages were devoted to a comparative description of the differences and similarities among the ethnic subsystems along demographic variables. In this section, the comparative format will still be employed to describe the value patterns of the ethnic groups in question. It is necessary to admit at this juncture that the range of values which might be used to demarcate ethnic group boundaries is of course very broad. Here interest is on values that affect the ability of an ethnic group to maintain itself and persist over time. For the purpose of this study, therefore, ethnic group patterns of (a) authority and decision-making; (b) intergroup contact; and (c) orientation to innovation are the values which

Table 3.5
Marital Status and Family Size of
Respondents by Ethnic Groups

Ethnic Groups	Marital Status (percentage responses)			Family Size (percentage responses)			
	Married	Single	N	Small	Meidum	Large	N
Banyang	39.3	57.9	104	19.6	28.0	52.3	107
Grassfield	50.4	46.6	127	17.6	31.3	51.1	131
Kpe	64.1	34.0	150	19.6	24.8	53.6	150

Table 3.6
Number of Years Respondents Spent in Locality
By Ethnic Group

Years in Locality (percentage of ethnic group)

Ethnic Group	10-20 years		21-30 years		31-40 years		41-50 years		Over 51 years	
	Rural	Town	Rural	Town	Rural	Town	Rural	Town	Rural	Town
Banyang	24.1	47.3	9.3	8.3	4.6	0.0	4.6	.9	.9	.0
Grass-field	26.2	38.4	14.6	14.6	2.3	.8	1.5	1.5	.0	.0
Kpe	17.0	22.9	17.6	11.1	7.8	7.2	1.3	2.6	7.8	2.6

were judged to be of crucial importance for the maintenance and persistence of any social organization.

(a) <u>Patterns of authority and decision-making</u>--The study was interested in four aspects of the process by which socio-political values are authoritatively allocated in an ethnic society. The first aspect relates to the type of authority figures children perceive their parents to be; whether parents are considered to be authoritarian or permissive and how this perception of parental authority influences the informal relations between parent and child. Each respondent was asked four unstructured questions pertaining to their perception of parents as authority figures. The questions read as follows:

> Can you tell me something about your father? What was he like as a person? Was he strict and domineering, for example?
>
> What about your mother? What was she like as a person? Was she strict and domineering, for example?
>
> If you had some problem when you were young and living with your parents, to whom did you talk it over?
>
> Could you do this freely?

Secondly, I was interested in the decision-making process within the family. Respondents were presented with four questions, one of which was judgmental in intent, that is, the respondent was asked to evaluate the process of decision-making in the family. The four questions read:

> When some problem came up in the family when you were a child such as moving to another village or deciding on the future of your brothers or sisters, how was the problem solved? Did the whole

> family discuss the problem before arriving at a decision?
>
> Who had the main voice in the decision? That is, whose opinion had the most weight? Was it both your parents, only your father's, your mother's or some other person's?
>
> Looking back on your childhood, how would you characterize the way in which decisions were made in your family? Everybody took part or father made most of the decisions or mother made most of the decisions or both parents made most of the decisions or some other persons?
>
> As a child, were you satisfied with the way in which decisions were made in your family?

Third, I sought to establish the place of children in the entire framework. Three questions were posed:

> What about the children--did they have any voice in family decision-making?
>
> (If the children had some voice): Which problems could they discuss?
>
> (If they had some voice): Was it all the children or only the older children who could take part in family discussions?

Finally, an attempt was made to reconstruct the decision-making process within the ethnic group by presenting the respondent with a hypothetical problem that called for some sort of solution. Several alternative solutions were then offered and the respondent was only required to select one that was consistent with his/her ideal method for making decisions in a large group. In order to find out whether the individual's preferred method for making decisions was shared by other members of the ethnic group, each individual was also requested to select one decision-making method from those presented him which he thought most other persons in his ethnic group would probably choose. This question was stated in the following language:

> When a community has to make arrangements to build a road, there are three possible ways they can arrange things like location and who is going to do the work.
>
> 1. They can leave the decision to be made by the older or recognized leaders in the community;
>
> 2. Instead of only a few important families deciding, everybody in the community will be involved in the decision-making process until a decision agreeable to <u>almost</u> everyone is arrived at;
>
> 3. The whole community can be summoned to a meeting and everybody asked to vote. A decision will be arrived at based on what the majority of the people in the community agree upon.
>
> Which way of deciding do you think is usually best in such cases? Which of the ways do you think most other persons in your ethnic group would usually think is best?[14]

Each of the four dimensions of authority patterns will be discussed in turn.

(i) Parents as authority figures. About one half of the Banyang and Grassfield respondents described their father as very strict and domineering while only 40 per cent of the Kpe shared this characterization. Roughly one quarter of the respondents across the three ethnic samples were unable to give valid descriptions of their father (or mother for that matter). In such cases, the respondents were too young when they lost contact with either or both of their parents--through death, divorce, growing up with grandparents or other relatives, etc.--to grow up knowing their parents very intimately. Among those who had vivid recollections of their mother, a substantial majority across the three ethnic groups described her as permissive and not too overbearing. It is interesting to note that children who came from families with an overbering father usually had a permissive mother. One may posit an inverse relationship in parental authority where the more one parent displays a certain attribute, e.g., permissiveness, the less the other parent manifests this attribute and the more he/she demonstrates the reverse. The data also indicate that the parent who was considered permissive invariably ended up being the one in whom the children confided. More Banyang and Kpe children, as Table 3.7 indicates, were freer with their mothers than with their fathers. The reverse is true for the Grassfield sample which was evenly split between 37 per cent who confided in their father and 36 per cent who preferred to take their juvenile problems to their mother. Although some respondents expressed difficulty in communicating their problems to either or both parents, the overwhelming majority experienced no such communication gap. On the whole only one out of every five respondents raised this issue.

(ii) <u>Decision-making within the family</u>.
When asked whether the whole family participated in discussions on problems that affected the entire family, 72 per cent of the Grassfield, 69 per cent of the Kpe, and 58 per cent of the Banyang respondents replied in the affirmative. When respondents were further asked to indicate which member of the family had the major voice in the decision-making, most of the respondents were of the opinion that it was father's voice that carried the most weight (the figures were 55 per cent

Table 3.7

Childhood Confidants

Persons	Ethnic Groups (percentage making each choice)		
	Banyang	Grassfield	Kpe
Father	26.2	37.4	34.6
Mother	48.6	35.9	41.8
Both Parents	11.2	15.3	9.2
Close Friends	1.9	.8	.7
Others	6.5	6.9	9.2
N.A.	5.6	3.8	4.6

for Banyang and Grassfield to 48 per cent for the Kpe--See Table 3.8). A distinction seems to have been established between participation in the decision-making process on the one hand and the final determination and allocation of decisions that are binding on the whole family on the other hand. The distinction also reveals the interplay among family members in the process of arriving at group decisions. By participation, one is simply referring to a situation where all (or most) of the family is allowed to join in on discussions of problems that affect the family as a whole. However, this procedure does not mean that family decisions reflect the consensus of polled opinion of family members. The real locus of power within the family out of which final and binding decisions originate is quite different. To give this point greater clarity, let us briefly analyze the pattern of responses of one ethnic group, the Grassfield. In the first question, I am interested in finding out if family decisions receive prior discussions in which everybody is involved; 72 per cent of the Grassfield respondents held that such was the case. When asked who had the main voice in molding family decisions, 55 per cent (almost a 20 per cent difference) of the Grassfield wrote that it was their father. Furthermore, when this same group was asked to characterize the way in which decisions were made in the family only 9 per cent mentioned that everybody took part in making them. This pattern of responses is shared by the other two ethnic groups. What is the significance?

The data reveal that although some participation is allowed every member of the family in the discussion of family problems, the domain for the actual <u>determination</u> of authoritative family decisions remains the prerogative of parents. And the father appears to have preempted this privelege for himself.

A second generalization that can be drawn from the data suggests that though <u>organically</u> different, ethnic groups may share common features with regard to how decisions are made within the family. Note the convergence of opinion between the structurally hierarchical Grassfield and the segmentary Banyang and Kpe on the question of decision-making at the family level. For instance, as Table 3.10 reveals, the Kpe are closer to the Grassfield in their near unanimous rejection of the notion that everybody contributes equally to the final determination of family decisions. Whereas 16 per cent Kpe and 9 per cent Grassfield do not feel that every family member has an equal vote, close to 21 per cent of the segmentary Banyang feel the same way. The point to be made here is that those who share this view are in the minority in all three ethnic groups.

Finally, respondents were asked to express satisfaction or dissatisfaction with the way decisions were made in their family. Few had anything negative to say about the situation. The difference between those who were satisfied and those who were not was in the ratio of 4:1.

(iii) <u>Children in the decision-making process</u>. When asked whether the whole family took part in domestic discussions, it was mentioned

Table 3.8
Whose Voice Had the Most Weight in Family Decision-Making

Persons	Ethnic Group (percentages)		
	Banyang	Grassfield	Kpe
Both Parents	29.0	38.2	39.2
Father	55.1	55.0	48.4
Mother	9.3	3.8	9.2
Other	4.7	3.1	2.6

Table 3.9
How Decisions Were Made in Respondents' Family

Who Participated	Ethnic Group (percentages)		
	Banyang	Grassfield	Kpe
Whole Family	57.9	71.0	68.6
Only Some Members	36.4	26.7	27.5
N.A.	5.6	2.3	3.9

Table 3.10
Responsibility for Day-To-Day Decisions Taken in Respondents' Family

Decision-Making Units	Ethnic Group (percentages)		
	Banyang	Grassfield	Kpe
Everybody	20.6	9.2	15.7
Father alone	33.6	36.6	42.5
Mother alone	7.5	5.3	7.8
Both parents	37.4	46.6	32.0
Other	.9	1.5	1.3

Table 3.11
Children in Family Decision-Making Process

Did Children Participate?	Ethnic Group (percentages)		
	Banyang	Grassfield	Kpe
Yes	43.9	45.4	43.1
No	54.2	53.1	53.6
N.A.	1.9	1.5	3.3

that a clear majority in the three ethnic samples mentioned that everybody in the family was allowed to participate in family "fireside chats." To clarify this claim let us analyze the data on children's role in domestic decision-making. Since by definition children represent the most junior members of the family, their participation or non-participation would serve as the acid test of the proposition that everybody was an equal partner. The definitional problem aside, it was also felt that an understanding of the role played by children in this aspect of decision-making might prove helpful in the analysis of the dynamics of national political orientations. One of the major objectives is to establish relationships between political orientations and certain other independent variables, of which childhood socialization into patterns of authority and decisionmaking was considered to be an important one.

Three questions were posed to respondents about the role of children in the formulation of family decisions. Roughly 54 per cent of all the respondents admitted that children were not usually permitted to take part in family decision-making and were limited to the marginal role of discussing purely children's problems, such as school fees, choice of marriage partners, and the like. Age was a pivotal determinant: older children were more likely than the younger siblings to be invited to take part in family consultations. This generalization holds true for all the three ethnic groups (after discounting the 50 or so per cent that gave no answer, the figures for each ethnic group indicating that older children were permitted into family privy councils read as follows: Kpe 42 per cent, Banyang 37 per cent and Grassfield 36 per cent).

(iv) <u>The ideal method in group decision-making</u>. Turning now to the last of the four levels of decision-making, respondents were presented with a hypothetical problem together with three decision-making alternatives from which to select one method that the individual thought was personally the best, and then to select an alternative which the individual believed most members of his/her ethnic group would consider most acceptable. The alternative methods for arriving at group decisions that were suggested were: (1) all decisions that affect the ethnic group should be made by the older or recognized leaders of the community, (2) everybody in the community should be involved in the decision-making process such that group decisions reflect the consensus of group opinion, and (3) group decisions should be based on what the majority of people in the community are agreed on. Results are given in Tables 3.12 and 3.13.

The second method was resoundingly rejected by respondents in the three ethnic groups--only 15 per cent of the Kpe, 9 per cent of the Banyang, and 8 per cent of the Grassfield respondents thought it was a wise thing to let everybody in the community take part in making binding decisions for the group. The larger proportion of respondents from the two segmentary subsystems, the Banyang and Kpe, preferred the third method where decisions invariably reflected the views of the majority in the community. Whereas 55 per cent of the respondents from these two groups took the majoritarian position, only 36 per cent of the hierarchical Grassfield subsystem respondents subscribe to the same view-point. Consistent with their ethnographic profile, more Grassfield respondents--53 per cent--are committed to the belief that decisions affecting a community should be legislated by the elders of that community. This alternative represented the authoritarian or elitist decisional pattern in the typology, as opposed to the other two more egalitarian approaches. The data suggest that the structural differences of these ethnic groups are reflected in group values toward decision-making.

Table 3.13 shows the distribution of scores not on individual preferences but individual projection of how other ethnic group members would react to the situation. We are interested here in the degree of consistency between individual preference and their projective statements. The majority of Banyang and Kpe as individuals preferred the egalitarian-majority position but in their projections of the preferences of fellow ethnics only 36 per cent of the Banyang (as opposed to 54 per cent of the Kpe) thought that their fellow members would opt for the majoritarian position. More Banyang--49 per cent--this time selected the first alternative, i.e. decisions should be made by community elders and leaders. The Grassfield and the Kpe, unlike the

Table 3.12
Respondents' Choice of the Ideal Method of Arriving at Group Decisions

	Ethnic Group (percentages)		
Method	Banyang	Grassfield	Kpe
Elitist	32.7	52.7	24.8
Consensual	9.3	8.4	15.0
Majoritarian	55.1	35.9	54.9
D.K.	2.8	3.1	5.2

Table 3.13
Respondents' Projections of What Fellow Ethnic Group Members Would Consider Ideal Method of Arriving at Group Decisions

Method	Ethnic Group (percentages)		
	Banyang	Grassfield	Kpe
Elitist	48.6	45.8	24.2
Consensual	10.3	11.5	15.0
Majoritarian	36.4	35.9	53.6
D.K.	4.7	6.9	7.2

Banyang, maintained their relative positions between individual preferences on the one hand and projections of group preferences on the other.

(b) Patterns of Intra-group Contact--The concept of ethnic group implies a collective of people who are bound together through common cultural ties and who consider themselves different from other ethnic groups. The assumption is that for an ethnic social system to persist over time, its members must share in a broad range of values. My intention was to investigate the patterns of intra-group contact with emphasis on two dimensions, one dealing with cultural symbols or artifacts (language) and the other involving attitudes (identity and loyalty).

(i) Language as a cultural artifact. Two questions to tap this dimension read as follows:

> Do you speak any indigenous Cameroonian language(s)?

> (If 'yes') Which ones do you speak?

The proposition that language controls the thought process and is the cornerstone of any cultural edifice is not original to us.[15] Language can also be viewed as the link in an unbroken chain holding together the old and new generations, the past and present. It is the medium through which an older generation is able to communicate with the new order, in the process transferring spiritual and material elements of their shared cultural heritage. To speak a language, therefore, is to support and perpetuate a culture. A dead language is a dead culture and conversely, a dead culture implies a moribund language.

The sampled universe unanimously and unequivocally rejected any implications (from the interview schedules) that their cultures were dead. Close to 99 per cent of the coastal Kpe respondents indicated that they were fluent in their mother-tongue, a revelation which is significant indeed in the light of the fears and apprehensions expressed by many Kpe elders that their culture is dying since the younger generation of Kpe has shown no interest in learning that language or upholding ethnic customs and traditions. With more than 50 per cent of the Kpe sample being made up of respondents between the ages of seventeen and thirty-five years and the near unanimity in the overall response, it would appear that the younger generation as well as the older one does take pride in its language and does in fact speak it rather fluently. In sum, the apocalyptic sentiments frequently expressed by elderly Kpe parents that survival of their language is in serious doubt because of the lack of use by the younger members is unjustified or at least highly exaggerated. Of course if this generation of Kpe youth neglects to teach its offspring the rudiments of their language, then one may have cause for worry.

In reviewing the data for the other two ethnic groups I find that here too the overwhelming majority of the sampled respondents admitted being fluent in their mother tongue; 95 per cent of the Grassfield respondents were fluent in their native language, while 94 per cent Banyang spoke

Kenyang (the language of their ethnic group). It is worth pointing out that about 90 per cent of the Banyang sample and the entire Grassfield sample is made up of immigrants who have been living in the coastal area of Cameroon for many years. Some of them can be legitimately considered "native coastals," in the sense that their family trees have been deeply rooted in the coast for several generations. An obvious conclusion to draw from this is that the process of inducting children into their ethnic group--part of which is the transmission of language from parent to offspring--does not cease as a result of people leaving their ethniclly homogeneous areas for the multiethnic coastal towns and plantation camps. (This subject will be taken up in chapter four.)

One of the phenomena of ingroupness is the compulsion to speak in one's native tongue when among people from one's own particular ethnic group. Our respondents were asked which language was most frequently used in conversations with fellow ethnic group members. Across the three ethnic samples, a staggering nine out of ten respondents said conversations were usually carried on in the respective mother tongues.

(ii) Group identity and loyalty. I mean by loyalty and identity (and no attempt will be made here to distinguish one from the other--rather they will be used interchangeably) the subjective or behavioral identification between a culture-bearer and his/her ethnic group whose culture involves the mutual identification of individuals because they come from the same ethnic group. A prerequisite for group cohesion is that members not only identify with each other but also maintain a high sense of pride in and loyalty toward the group. A major assumption of the study was that a sense of ethnic group identity would manifest itself in the friendship network (and marriage patterns) of the ethnic group members in question. That is to say, a member who is proud of his/her ethnic group will not only speak laudably of it but will also have a friendship network which includes many members from his/her ethnic group. To test this assumption, respondents were asked the following questions:

> Would you say that most of your friends are from your ethnic group or different ethnic groups?
>
> Suppose a son or daughter of yours was planning to marry someone from a different tribe and he/she came to ask for your permission, how would you react? You would be happy to hear that your child has finally decided to get married; disappointed that your child chose a spouse from another tribe but still give them your permission; be very angry to hear that your in-law to be is from another tribe and so oppose the marriage or it would make no difference whom your child chose for his/her spouse since it is entirely his/her business.
>
> If you had to choose a husband for your daughter from an ethnic group other than yours, which ethnic group would you want your future in-law to come from?

Sifting the data I find that roughly two out of every three Banyang and Grassfield respondents select their close friends from people in different ethnic groups. With the Kpe there was an even split between those who elected their friends from within the Kpe culture group--45 per cent--and those whose friendship network encroached into other ethnic groups (50 per cent). It would seem, therefore, that the Kpe ethnic group displays more cohesiveness than the other two groups. Is this really the case?

The data for cross-ethnic marriage preferences compound this confusion. The Banyang and Grassfield in contrast to the Kpe appear more loyal to their ethnic groups. Table 3.14 shows that the Kpe are less likely to be angry and more likely to be happy over the idea of their children marrying into different ethnic groups, while the Banyang and Grassfield are more inclined to be indifferent or angry. When parents were asked to choose spouses for their children more Banyang and Kpe (59 per cent and 58 per cent respectively) than Grassfield (47 per cent) respondents said they would select someone from an ethnic group that was different from theirs. But 40 per cent of the Grassfield respondents as opposed to 32 per cent Kpe and 30 per cent Banyang would insist that the new in-law come from an ethnic group whose customs were similar, or from the same ethnic group.

When sex was examined separately, the data showed that among the Kpe and Grassfield men are more open to cross-ethnic marriages than women. The Banyang, however, are evenly split on this issue and there are as many women in favor of cross-ethnic marriages as there are men (see Table 3.16).

Table 3.14
Respondents' (as a parent) Feelings Should an Offspring Choose to Marry Outside the Ethnic Group

Feelings	Ethnic Group (percentages)		
	Banyang	Grassfield	Kpe
Happiness	40.2	33.6	46.4
Disappointment	7.5	15.3	15.0
Anger	9.3	6.1	3.3
Indifference	41.1	41.2	33.3
O.K.	1.9	3.8	2.0

To summarize the findings, (a) the degree of participation in ethnically homogeneous friendship networks in relatively higher among the Kpe than the Banyang and Grassfield; and (b) the propensity for corss-ethnic marriages is shared by

Table 3.15
Respondents' Preference for Ethnic Group of
Children's Spouses

Type of Ethnic Group	Ethnic Group (percentages)		
	Banyang	Grassfield	Kpe
Whose customs are different from respondent	58.9	46.5	57.5
Whose customs are similar	16.8	22.1	11.1
Definitely my own group	12.1	17.6	20.9
O.K.	19.6	13.7	10.6

Table 3.16
Relationship Between Sex and Non-Ethnic Marriage Partner

Type of Ethinc Group	Ethnic Group (percentages)					
	Banyang		Grassfield		Kpe	
	Male	Female	Male	Female	Male	Female
Customs are different	28.8	26.8	26.2	20.8	30.7	24.2
Customs are similar	4.6	7.4	14.6	7.7	6.5	4.6
Definitely my own group	9.3	3.7	10.8	6.9	8.5	11.8
O.K.	14.8	4.6	10.8	2.2	7.8	3.3
Sub total	57.5	42.5	62.4	37.6	53.5	43.9

all three groups though more so among the Kpe.
However, this is not consistent with the pattern
of social network participation observed in the
course of this investigation. My prior knowledge

of the Kpe and the other groups, further buttressed by extensive participant observations, led me to expect a low level of group identification and cohesion among them, with the reverse situation holding for the Banyang and Grassfield.

In a series of indirect questions that dealt peripherally with the issue of group solidarity, I discovered that the Kpe readily admitted that as a group they lacked a strong sense of "togetherness" in contrast to other ethnic groups, including the Grassfield and Banyang. Perhaps a sample of some of the comments made will underscore the point.

> We Kpe don't trust each other; a Kpe big man would rather have a Graffi [meaning Grassfield] driver than ask one of us to drive his car. [Kpe mechanic-driver in his late teens.]

> When Graffi and Nyangi [meaning Banyang] people get posts ['cos pidgin for high office], they make sure that their tribes' people are given jobs. When it comes to Kpe--well, we are so selfish and greedy that we only care for our own bellies. [Kpe civil servant in his mid-thirties.]

> Our women would rather be deceived into befriending Graffi men because these blokes have a lot of money to spend on them. But look at the way they mess up our girls--get them banged up [meaning pregnant] then refuse to marry 'em! Yes these stupid girls never learn a lesson--they still prefer the short term enjoyment with a rich foreigner than long term union with their fellow Kpe men. [Kpe youth in his early twenties].

> [This sentiment was shared by a cross-section of the Kpe male respondents

and was subsequently rendered in various ways but the central meaning was clear--that Kpe girls have broken bounds by fraternizing with non-Kpe.]

I can never understand you Kpe boys. What do you see in these Graffi and Nyangi women that your own women don't have? I suppose you find them attractive because they are willing to play the submissive role. [Kpe female stenographer in her mid-twenties, expressing a sentiment we found to be commonly held by a broad distribution of Kpe women, who feel they have been betrayed by their men.]

Because I believe that the high acceptance of the Banyang and Grassfield respondents of friends from other ethnic groups could be explained in terms of their immigrant status in the coast rather than as an expression of low group identification, I shall not spend time trying to explain the figures. On the other hand, the attitude of Kpe towards each other merits some attention in these pages because this question has been raised rather frequently. An assessment report of the Kpe prepared for the incoming British colonial administrators in the immediate, postwar years found this group displaying very low positive identification with their traditions and customs. The low level of group cohesion was attributed to the imposition of an alien German system of government and the resultant destruction of indigenous socio-political systems.[16] Added to this was the introduction of Christianity and the invidious distinction missionaries made between so-called primitive African idol-worshipping and the civilized approach to religion as represented by the White Churches-- a distinction which led to the systematic destruction of indigenous religion.[17] Another attempt to explain the sense of defeatism and fatalism displayed by the Kpe traces it to their defeat and conquest by the Germans, which was followed by the appropriation of their land without compensation. The Kpe, by this explanation, never succeeded in making a satisfactory adjustment to the shock of conquest.[18]

In seeking to explain why so many Kpe make the sort of statements (of which the selection above is only representative) that suggest low group cohesion, due allowance should be made for these factors. However, the position taken here is that the low sense of group solidarity stems primarily from the loss of political hegemony by this ethnic group. The Kpe as an ethnic collective now find themselves no longer the politically potent force in the country they once were, having been reduced to a secondary position as a result of the emergence of a new power class which upset the old hegemony. Historical and geographic factors conspired in favor of the Kpe: their strategic coastal position exposed them very early to modernizing Western influences from traders, missionaries, and later colonizers. The net effect of this exposure is that the Kpe took off with a head start over the other ethnic groups in English-speaking Cameroon. Writing in the early 1950's, the British anthropologist Ardener considered this group to be the most "westernized" of all ethnic groups in the then British Cameroons. He was of course referring to the high educational and occupational levels enjoyed at that time by the Kpe.

Accounting for a disproportionate share of the educated manpower in the British administered trust territory of Cameroon, the Kpe intelligentsia quickly rose to the forefront of the nationalist struggle for independence. The Bakweri Land Committee which was organized in the late 1940's to press for the return of Kpe land alienated during the period of German colonial occupation could be considered a quasi-political organization. It was part of an umbrella movement--the Cameroon National Federation--under which budding Kpe nationalists tested their skills in negotiations, political bargaining, and petitioning the United Nations Trusteeship Committee.

Another nationalist movement, also spearheaded by leading Kpe intelligentsia, had earlier surfaced in Lagos, Nigeria, in 1939. This was the Cameroon Youth League whose founder and president, P. M. Kale, was a Kpe. Although the Cameroon Youth League leadership was predominantly Kpe, it nevertheless had a membership roster that included most of the political luminaries in English-speaking Cameroon.[19] Thus, in the initial stages Kpe intelligentsia contributed enormously to the crystallization of political consciousness in Cameroon. This is not to imply that educated people from the other ethnic groups did not participate in the struggle against colonial domination in Cameroon; one simply wishes to underscore the fact that the elite of Kpe society were the premier political leaders and the vanguard of the nationalist struggle in English-speaking Cameroon.

The first Leader of Government Business and subsequently first Premier of the Southern Cameroons Region was Kpe. This Kpe-led administration under Dr. E. M. L. Endeley was in power for five years between 1954-1959 until it lost a general election to Dr. John Ngu Foncha, a Grassfield. The rise of Foncha ushered in a new order, in which the Grassfield and not the Kpe were to become the dominant political force in English-speaking Cameroon.

A careful reading of the political history of the country leads one to the conclusion that the change of government from Endeley to Foncha was a political act with heavy symbolic content and repercussions in terms of the psychological outlook of Kpe and other Cameroonian ethnic groups. For this marked the transfer of power and authority from the so-called "sophisticated" and "civilized" southern Kpe gentlemen to the so-called "bush" Grassfield people from the North. It signaled the supreme reversal of political roles and statuses that had been taken for granted for the last two decades where a minority coastal people by virtue of their educational attainment led the rest of the population. The loss of political power and authority to, of all people, the Grassfield group must have been a deep blow to the pride and even arrogance of the southern Kpe aristocrats.

As the majority Grassfield (accounting for over 50 per cent of the population of Anglophone Cameroon) began asserting themselves, they became ubiquitous in the higher echelons of government and in the private sector. They pre-empted for themselves the choice jobs in the country and the choice coastal lands; and a powerless Kpe people were in no position to stem the tide of Grassfield domination. The antecedent factors for this shift in power focus are traceable to the alleged "selfishness" and "greed" of Kpe leadership, as one of them bitterly stated:

> When the government was in our hands we filled all the top executive positions with Nigerians then gave more scholarships to Grassfield people. These Grassfield people were the ones who took over after the Nigerians left. The irony of it is that the very Grassfield chaps Endeley trained are the ones who kicked him out of office and are today the fellows making all the important policy decisions in this region. And you talk of the Kpe solidarity! Hell, I only hear it when some politician needs my vote.

(c) <u>Orientation to Change</u>--The last of the ethnic group values to be examined deals with individual and group orientations toward change. In his monumental study, <u>The Decline of the West</u>, Oswald Spengler made the following statement with regard to time: "It is by the meaning that it intuitively attaches to time that one culture is differentiated from another."[20] For him time can be broken down into a timeless historical Present, and the ultra-historical projection into the Future.

Florence Kluckhohn, on the other hand, identifies three ideal types of orientations to change: (1)

a relatively timeless, traditionless, future-ignoring Present; (2) a realizable Future; and (3) the maintenance and restoration of the Past.[21]

Defining change as the receptivity of a society to innovative propensity to change demonstrated by many societies.[22] Apter's central problem is to explain why some traditional systems can innovate more easily than others. His conceptual framework recognizes two value models of receptivity to change: an instrumental and a consummatory value type. Each type corresponds to a particular kind of socio-political organization. Traditional systems with instrumental value orientations toward change are usually hierarchical with all authority concentrated in one single authority (usually the King). Where the predominant value orientation toward change is consummatory, the traditional system is pyramidally organized with its chief or political leader responsible to his social group rather than to a paramount chief. According to Apter, instrumental-hierarchical systems innovate with ease until the kingship principle is challenged, and then the entire system joins together to resist change. Consummatory-pyramidal systems, on the other hand, are highly resistant to change in all its forms and where change is forcefully imposed, external political groupings that form as new solidary associations emerge to oppose the older traditional ones.

In this study three types of perspectives toward change were identified: (1) traditionalist, (2) neo-traditionalist, and (3) progressive or modernist. The traditionalist perspective is defined as one which holds that there is nothing intrinsically good about change and new ways. This view is ultimately predicated on a fear of the unknown and is prompted by a basic insecurity about the future precisely because it represents uncharted territory; a path that has never before been trodden upon. Because of the uncertainty of the future, the traditionalist insists that old customs and beliefs must not only prevail but where they have been forcibly uprooted, should be brought back with haste.

Where the traditionalist sees no compromise between the old ways and the new, the neo-traditionalist can be considered as the transition zone or the confluence of traditionalism and modernity. The neotraditionalist is defined as one who does not embrace change for the sake of change nor does he/she a priori eschew the past for its putative primeval values and customs. Rather he/she looks into the past for explanations and solutions to contemporary problems. There is no hesitation on the part of the neotraditionalist to enlist traditional values in the service of innovation. The neotraditionalist, to borrow Apter's definition (even though he uses it in a slightly different context) is one who explains the contemporary world by appealing to antecedent traditional values. He is a syncretist in the sense in which Thomas Hodgkin applies the term.[23]

Unlike the other two perspectives toward innovation which are timebound, the modernizing or progressive posture is timeless. In this respect, the modernist is one who treats the past as a matter of history which has very remote impact for the present or future. The modernist is an innovator par excellence.

The concept of change was measured, in this study both as an abstract concept and as a concrete phenomenon. The idea of change as an abstraction was employed to elicit the consensus of group beliefs as to the importance of time in human relations. The second formulation placed the concept of change within a concrete situation such that the individual could easily identify with it. The different conceptual formulations also necessitated different methodological approaches; in the first instance change was phrased within a forced-choice context, whereas in the second, it was presented in an unstructured format. The question of change as an abstract concept reads as follows:

People have very different ideas about what has gone before and what we can expect from life. Here are three ways of thinking about these things: (1) Some people believe that it is best to give most attention to what is happening now in the present; to keep those aspects of the old ways that one can-- or that one likes--but to be ready to accept the new ways as we confront them [this was labelled the Neo-traditionalist]; (2) Others think that the ways of the past were the most right and best, and as changes come things get worse; therefore we should work hard to maintain the old ways and try to bring them back when they are lost [labelled Traditionalist Orientation]; (3) Some believe in the future, that the best way to live is to look a long time ahead, work hard and give up many things now so that the future will be better [Modernist Orientation].[24]

Respondents were then asked two questions: (a) "Which of these ways of looking at life do you think is best?" (b) "Which of these ways of looking at life do you think most other persons in your ethnic group would think is best?"

Table 3.17 shows that across samples more Grassfield than Banyang and Kpe respondents, in that order, selecting the Neo-traditionalist view of life. Within the sample again the largest number of Grassfield (47 per cent) and Kpe (35 per cent) opting for the Neo-traditional orientation. Forty-six per cent of the Banyang respondents prefer the modernist orientation, compared with 40 per cent preferring the neotraditionalist. Across sample more Banyang than Grassfield (40 per cent) and Kpe (34 per cent) interpret life from the perspective of a futuristic orientation. It is worth noting that the Kpe who have enjoyed a long history of contact with Western influences come out no more "modern" in their orientations toward change than the other two ethnic groups. Although the traditionalist orientation is the third choice for all three groups, it is a strong third for the Kpe (24 per cent) and a poor third for the remaining two groups (10 per cent for the Grassfield and 8 per cent for the Banyang).

In projecting into the minds of their fellow ethnic members, the Banyang and Grassfield maintain their relative positions (as indicated in Table 3.18). The major shift is within the Kpe sample, 36 per cent of whom predict that more of their fellow Kpe would prefer the future orientation. The question was asked of all respondents:

> If it were possible for you to be alive in the year 2023 A.D. how would you like Cameroon to be like?

Table 3.19 shows the coded responses. The distribution of responses generally was in favor of the country becoming more industrialized and highly developed. However, it is most intriguing to glance at the distribution of responses for the item: "No change--still under present regime." Thirty per cent Grassfield, 18 per cent Banyang and only 11 per cent Kpe elected this item. Why are almost three out of ten Grassfield respondents and only one in ten of the Kpe favorably disposed toward the present regime to the extent that they are willing to see it remain in office for another half century? Can this wide margin reflect the level of identification these groups have with the national political system? This would suggest that the Kpe and Banyang more than the Grassfield are alienated from the political system. And one explanation would be that the former groups do not feel that the government represents their interests. The most frequent complaint voiced was: "gov'men dey na for Graffi dem hand" (Government is controlled by the Grassfield).

Table 3.17
Orientations to Change

Orientation	Ethnic Group (percentages)		
	Banyang	Grassfield	Kpe
Traditionalist	8.4	9.9	23.5
Neo-traditionalist	39.3	46.6	35.3
Modernist	45.8	39.7	34.0
D.K.	6.5	3.8	7.2

Table 3.18
Projections of Fellow Ethnic Group
Members' Orientations to Change

Orientation	Ethnic Group (percentages)		
	Banyang	Grassfield	Kpe
Traditionalist	26.2	23.7	26.1
Neo-traditionalist	30.8	38.2	24.8
Modernist	32.7	33.6	35.9
D.K.	10.3	4.6	13.1

The Socialization Process

It is generally agreed that the processes of socialization constitute the crucible within which adult attitudes are formed. A study of adult political attitudes cannot, therefore, be divorced from the context that gives them shape and form. This should not only hold true for societies where one single institution stands out as the pre-eminent socializing force but also in these social contexts where several significant agencies contribute (either in collusion or collision) to equip the individual with the right set of political orientations. Having hypothesized that the interactive experiences within the ethnic group assist the individual in shaping his political

Table 3.19
Ideas of What Cameroon Should Be Like in the Year 2023 A.D.

Desired Characterictics	Ethnic Group (percentages)			
	Banyang	Grassfield	Kpe
Modern, industrialized & highly developed	58.9	55.7	68.6
No change, still be under Ahidjo's government			
Modern but very Africanized	17.8	29.8	11.1
United and well integrated	1.9	.8	0.0
A welfare state	0.0	.8	1.3
More democratic	0.0	0.0	1.3
Less neo-colonial	0.0	0.0	2.0
As it was during German times	.9	0.0	1.3
Like Paradise	0.0	.8	.7
A.K./N.A.	0.0	1.5	1.3
	20.6	9.8	12.4

outlook, the study set out to investigate (a) who the people are with whom the individual associated in his/her formative years (b) how and when the individual first became exposed to discussions of political issues and (c) what people were responsible for preparing the adolescent individual for possible participation in the new and broader context of the national society.

(a) <u>Socializing into specifically ethnic traditions and values, i.e., ethnicization</u>--To test the assumption of the centrality of the ethnic group in the socializing process, respondents were asked four questions:

> I would like to find out something about your childhood. As you were growing up how much time did you spend around people from your ethnic group? All of the time; most of the time; some time or no time at all?

> Whom did you associate with in your growing up years? Elderly people from your ethnic group, members of your family; your father; your mother or your age mates? [Multiple responses were permitted.]

> As you were growing up, where would you say you learnt the most about the traditions of your ethnic group; for example proper behavior toward elders, folk stories, etc. From your parents; the elders in the village; your grandparents; the school; your age-mates or some other people? [Multiple answers swers were permitted.]

> [Based on your answer to the above question] How much time was spent learning about these traditions? Quite a lot of time; some time but not much; very little time or no time at all? [Multiple answers were permitted.]

On the question of time spent with ethnic group members, over two-thirds of the respondents from the three ethnic groups reported having spent varying lengths of time with fellow ethnics. There was some variance within and across samples as to the actual amount of time respondents spent with ethnic group members. On the whole more people across the three ethnic samples spent very little time with ethnic group members (the figures are 39 per cent for both Banyang and Kpe and 38 per cent for the Grassfield). Also, more Kpe and Grassfield respondents were with their fellow ethnic group members for considerable periods of time than were the Banyang. (See Table 3.20)

In comparing the preceding results with those on time spent learning ethnic group lore, the same pattern of responses is discernible; only a minority of the respondents selected the "No time at all" item--as a matter of fact less than 3 per cent, as revealed in Table 3.21. Over 70 per cent of the respondents in the three samples spent some or a lot of time learning about ethnic group values and traditions. On the whole the most evident conclusion to be drawn from these two tables is that the overwhelming majority of the respondents in each of the ethnic groups grew up for the most part surrounded by fellow ethnic group members from whom they received first-hand information about ethnic group traditions and customs. This finding coincides with a major assumption of this study that for the majority of Cameroonians the ethnic group remains the single most important socializing agency.

With whom do youngsters in the three ethnic groups associate? Mostly their parents and elders, as Table 3.22 shows. Of the two parents, the father appears to be more popular than the mother in two of the ethnic samples--the Kpe and Grassfield.

It is interesting to note that fewer Banyang than Grassfield and Kpe mentioned the category of elders as persons with whom they associated as

Table 3.20
Amount of Time Spent With Co-Ethnics During Adolescence

Ethnic Groups (percentages)

Amount of Time	Banyang	Grassfield	Kpe
A lot of time	15.0	23.7	30.1
Some time	32.7	29.8	22.2
Very little time	39.3	38.2	38.6
No time at all	13.0	7.6	7.8
N.A.	0.0	.7	1.3

Table 3.21
Amount of Time Spent by Respondent Learning About Ethnic Group Values and Traditions

Ethnic Groups (percentages)

Amount of Time	Banyang	Grassfield	Kpe
A lot of time	45.8	48.9	35.9
Some time	33.6	36.6	37.3
Very little time	16.8	12.2	22.9
No time at all	1.9	2.3	2.6
N.A.	.9	0.0	1.3

youngsters. It is expected that persons from a segmentary social system where the principle of egalitarianism is a major cornerstone would be permitted easy access across generational groups. That is to say, the distinction between elders and young ones, while present, would not be so rigidly maintained that relations between these two groups would be strained. Thus, my expectations were that more Banyang and Kpe respondents would mention having spent a great deal of time with their ethnic elders. This assumption has been seriously challenged by the low score given this category by the segmentary Banyang respondents. Only forty per cent of the Banyang associated with their ethnic group elders during their formative years while 46 per cent (compared to 69 per cent for the Grassfield and 76 per cent for the Kpe) attribute their knowledge of ethnic lore to grandparents. Does this indicate a generational gap built into the Banyang social system which sustains a social distance between young and elderly and restricts informal contact between the two groups?

Table 3.22
Persons with Whom Respondent Associated During Adolescence

Associates of Respondent	Ethnic Groups (percentages; multiple responses permitted)		
	Banyang	Grassfield	Kpe
Elders	40.1	90.8	90.1
Family Members	63.5	60.0	67.6
Father	62.5	76.7	76.0
Mother	89.3	48.7	48.7
Age Mates	66.3	67.0	67.8

(b) The transmission of political values, i.e. politicization--How, when and with whom do individuals first begin discussing politics? What advantages do individuals derive from these early political talks? To answer these questions, respondents were exposed to a battery of unstructured questions:

> Did anything happen in your family or when you were growing up that made you think a lot about the way your country was governed?

Table 3.23
Persons from Whom Respondent Learnt the Most
About the Values and Traditions of Ethnic
Group

Ethnicization Agents	Ethnic Groups (percentages; multiple responses permitted)		
	Banyang	Grassfield	Kpe
Parents	80.3	90.8	90.1
Elders	59.7	60.0	67.6
Grand Parents	45.6	76.7	76.0
School Teachers	53.7	48.7	48.7
Age Mates	44.4	67.0	67.8

(If yes to above question): What was it that made you start thinking seriously about government and politics in this country?

The majority of respondents in all three ethnic samples responded negatively to the first item. Roughly two-thirds of the Kpe and one-half of the Grassfield and Banyang respondents reported having no recollections of anything that took place in the family during their formative years that might have had any impact on their political outlook. Of the minority who still held on to some vivid recollections of past activities of a political nature, the second question was relevant. Since this was an unstructured question, their responses on the factors that triggered interest in politics were coded and are here reported in Table 3.24. Looking at this table, one finds that of those who responded, a plurality of the Banyang and Grassfield attribute the crystallization of their political consciousness to an early exposure to the sordid aspects of party politics in the country. When translated into specific language, it meant frequent disagreements, polarization, dissension, fear and distrust over political issues and parties not only within the family but spilling over into the broader context of the ethnic group. Some of the comments will highlight the point:

> My parents were always arguing over which party or candidate to support during election time. My father supported the K.N.C. [Kamerun National Congress] and its leader, Dr. Endeley while some of my relatives supported Mr. Kale's K.P.P. (Kamerun People's Party). [40 year old Banyang male.]

> Grown-ups behaving like little children--abusing each other, engaging in fights, burning up houses, etc. just to convince each other that their respective parties stood for the ultimate in - democratic government. I could not have been more disgusted. [Banyang civil servant in his mid-thirties.]

> Tam for multi parti days be be tam way any man de helep 'iself. No man no talk true talk--de leader dem sep sep be b'in lie people. Dem be jus de fight for dem garri and we small small people de fight we self. [Plantation worker from Grassfield in his late forties.]

> My first recollection of politics goes back to the late '40's and early '50's with the formation of the K.N.C. and K.N.D.P. [Kamerun National Democratic Party.] I remember clearly an intra-tribal disturbance around 1950 in the kingdom of Nso in which the Fon himself was involved. I believe this had to do with party preference or something. [Grassfield male in his mid-forties.]

> What made me start thinking seriously about politics in this country? Well this was during the campaigns leading

to the U.N. plebiscite on the question of reunification with former French Cameroons or integration with the Federation of Nigeria. The atmosphere in Bamenda then (where I was living and going to primary school) was very tense. There were frequent fights between K.N.D.P. [pro-unification] and C.P.N.C. [anti-unification] militants. In my school, children whose parents supported the C.P.N.C. were severely beaten by an overwhelming crowd of pro-unificationists. [Grassfield youth in his early twenties.]

Yes, I remember just how badly affected my parents and other tribal elders were when our tribe's most prominent politician, the Reverend J. C, Kangsen lost his ministerial post. [Rev. Kangsen--now moderator for the Presbyterian Church of Cameroon--was a K.N.C. legislator representing Wum Division and also a member of the Endeley led Executive Council in the then Southern Cameroons House of Assembly. His party later lost to Foncha's K.N.D.P. in a 1959 general election.]

Of the 25 per cent Kpe respondents who have recollections of things happening in the family that got them interested in politics, three items seem to have been involved: (a) the evils of colonialism; (b) poverty and the squalor in which they grew up; and (c) discrimination against them because they were an ethnic minority. On a comparative basis, we may note that no Grassfield respondent and only 7 per cent of the Banyang, as opposed to 31 per cent of the Kpe who answered the question, mentioned the evils of colonial rule as a factor that ignited political awareness. Ironically, the Kpe, who of the three ethnic groups have had the longest contact with Europe, and whose members have been dubbed (either in admiration or derision) the most "Europeanized" group in English speaking Cameroon, turn out to be the one group that found this history of contact painful and pernicious. A sense of prolonged suffering under the brutal white domination emerges from the comments of the Kpe:

> Many, many years ago there was an airplane crash on Fako [Mount Cameroon, the slopes of which the Kpe inhabit] and the Whitemen came into Ewonda, Bova and other villages, conscripted all able-bodied men they could find and marched us up the mountain to the site of the plane crash. At gun point we were ordered to carry down to Buea, the corpses of the victims of that crash. We had no choice but to comply with the Whiteman's orders. Anyway, a few men who were smarter than us fled the villages when they heard the crash so as to avoid being called to act as pall-bearers--as if they knew! Some even got to the site before the colonial authorities and made away with some very valuable things [laugh]. [Kpe man in his late fifties.]

> Boy, those Germans were tough as they come. During German times any infraction of the law was punishable by thrashing. If you did not go to school, the policeman came after you, dragged you back to school, and in front of your school mates, your teacher administered 12 strokes of the cane on your bare buttocks. Of course, we grew to be well disciplined but I am convinced there are better ways of instilling discipline in youngsters. [Former headmaster trained under the Germans now in his mid-sixties.]

> The Germans came, stole our lands then forced us to live on the most unproductive part of the mountain where the rocks

> make it so difficult to cultivate crops
> and the hills are so steep that a Kpe
> woman who climbs them every day sooner
> or later begins to look sixty when she
> is only thirty years old. We joined the
> English in driving away the Germans in
> two world wars; one would have thought
> that they would at least correct the
> wrongs of the Germans and give us back
> our lands. Instead, they handed it over
> to the C.D.C. and soon the whole area was
> infested with people from other parts
> of the country who now talk and act as
> if they have more claims on these lands
> than a Mokpe. Talk about injustice!
> [Kpe technician in his mid-thirties.]

In reconstructing their individual political histories, some Kpe inveigh against alleged ethnic group discrimination. Of those who hold on to some early recollections about 22 per cent of the Kpe respondents describe their early introduction to politics as a consequence of first-hand experience with ethnic group discrimination. Feelings such as the following are common:

> After passing my First School Leaving
> Certificate Examination with credits in
> all the three subjects, I was admitted
> to Sasse College. I ended up not at-
> tending Sasse because of lack of fi-
> nancial assistance. Yet, I know of many
> Graffi boys who did not have as many
> subjects as I had in the F.S.L.C. but
> won government scholarships to study
> either at Bali or Sasse. [Kpe youth in
> his early twenties.]

> It is strange that I cannot be allowed
> to own land in the Grasslands yet some
> of the largest landowners in the coast
> are people from that area. When we were
> much younger, it was taboo for a non-
> Kpe to cross the village fence into
> our enclave but today they not only

Table 3.24
Events that Started Respondents Thinking Seriously about Government and Politics

Responses	Ethnic Groups (percentages)		
	Banyang	Grassfield	Kpe
Was struck by the depth of poverty in the country	5.6	6.9	5.9
Ethnic group discrimination (tribalism)	2.8	2.3	5.2
Saw how corrupt and divisive party politics were	10.3	14.5	3.3
Through family involvement in party politics	3.7	0.0	1.3
Struck by high degree of corruption among government officials	1.9	2.3	0.0
Witnessed the birth of a quasi-autonomous Southern Cameroons region	.9	1.5	-
Struck by the evils of colonial rule	1.9	0.0	7.2
Other	0.0	0.8	0.0
Don't recall/nothing happened, etc.	72.9	71.8	76.5

cross with impunity but have literally bought up our lands. I feel very sorry for you young boys who are growing up. After you complete your studies, where is there going to be land in your country to build a bungalow? There isn't much we can do; after all, the government is in their hands. [Kpe elder, about 55 years old.]

Look here, I finished Ombe [formerly a Trade School now a Technical Institute] at the top of my class. Before I knew it, all the vagili [Kpe for Grassfield] fellows in my class had landed top jobs with the P.W.D. But for the sympathetic and timely intervention of a British civil servant, I would have ended up in my village tending pigs and planting cocoyams. He gave me a job and saw to it that I received my just and fair rewards for services rendered. After we got our so-called independence, the man left and I was back where I began. The government now firmly in the hands of the vagili saw to it that their boys got all the promotions. Hell, I got so disgusted that I left to become a chomeur [French for unemployed now part of the 'cos pidgin lexicon.] [Kpe technician in his early thirties.]

The recollections of these Kpe about their experiences with ethnic discrimination when viewed against the background of their collective history adds up to the following: the Kpe realize that they are a minority ethnic group in the ethnic pantheon of Cameroon; they find that even on their native turf they are outnumbered by immigrants from the Forest and Grassfields; and finally, they have in the last two decades lost their political hegemony over English-speaking Cameroon. The fact that fewer Banyang and Grassfield respondents selected this item suggests the low relevance it has for these groups. Without denying the validity and legitimacy of some of the complaints raised by these Kpe respondents, it is this writer's impression that the Kpe preoccupation with ethnic discrimination could be regarded as grasping at straws.

As displayed in Table 3.24, the factors that had an early impact on respondents' political outlook were (1) their first-hand experience of poverty which, translated into dialectical language, means an early exposure to the economic stratification of the country into "haves" and "have-nots"; (2) witnessing ethnic group cleavages expressed in the form of inter-group conflicts or the subjugation of minority ethnic groups by the more policitally and economically powerful groups; and (3) an early exposure to party politics and its legacy of hatred, bitterness and general distrust. These three factors seem to reflect the general attitude of the respondents who answered this question with respect to their "coming of age" in the political arena. Combined, they account for over 60 per cent of the total responses volunteered (the actual percentages were: 61 per cent for the Kpe, 69 per cent for the Banyang and 70 per cent for the Grassfield).

The respondents were next asked to indicate the types of topics and issues discussed by parents and other ethnic group elders. The primary objective here was to determine the amount of politicization that one is likely to receive from an average Cameroonian home and what part, if any, ethnic group elders and other people besides the individual's nuclear family play in the political education of youth. The following questions were asked:

> Do you remember any discussions of politics in your family when you were a youngster, let's say when you were around sixteen years old? Did your parents talk about political things?

(If yes to above question): What were the discussions about?

As a youngster growing up in the town/plantation camp/village, can you remember whether your ethnic group leaders and elders ever discussed politics or government in the presence of children your age?

(If yes to above question): Can you remember what the discussions were usually about?

In interpreting the data, it should be borne in mind that the questions sought to establish whether politics were ever discussed by parents and elders in the presence of children. The assumption here is that much can be learned about politics from listening into discussions without the individual actually taking part in the debates. On the question of whether families discussed politics while children were present, the Grassfield are evenly split, a plurality of the Banyang are affirmative, while the reverse is true for the Kpe. When the locus is shifted to village elders, the Kpe continue to deny being present while politics was discussed, the Banyang are evenly split, and this time it is the Grassfield plurality that rejects this position. (See Tables 3.25 and 3.26).

If political values are transmitted by allowing youngsters to participate (either as silent observers or active participants) with their parents and elders in political discussions, this did not happen with the sampled universe. Close to three-fifths of the sampled respondents in the three ethnic groups either reject the proposition or have no recollections of witnessing political discussions. How then do the youth of Anglophone Cameroon become informed about the political system--its leadership and institutions? Who are the primary agents in the process of imparting political knowledge and information? Respondents were asked two direct questions whose responses

Table 3.25
Parents' Discussion of Politics

Responses	Ethnic Group (percentages)		
	Banyang	Grassfield	Kpe
Yes	32.7	32.1	28.8
No	29.9	32.8	39.8
Don't Recall	37.1	35.1	31.4

Table 3.26
Elders' Discussion of Politics

Responses	Banyang	Grassfield	Kpe
Yes	32.7	31.3	26.1
No	32.7	37.4	56.2
Don't Recall	34.6	31.1	17.7

we hoped would shed some light on all the issues of political socialization among our sample:

> Who, in your opinion, taught you how to be a good citizen?
>
> How was this done? I mean, how did these persons go about teaching you to become a good citizen?

The data suggest that parents are, along with school teachers, the prime sources of political attitude formation among Cameroonian youth. Seenty-five per cent of the Banyang, 74 per cent Kpe and 70 per cent Grassfield reported that their parents (either separately or together) were primarily responsible for teaching them the precepts of good citizenship. (The figures for school teachers were 14 per cent among the Grassfield, 13 per cent among the Banyang and 9 per cent for the Kpe.) When asked what methods and values were stressed,

80 per cent of the Grassfield respondents, 73 per cent of the Kpe and 69 per cent of the Banyang indicated that much was learned about good citizenship through informal conversations with their parents and teachers. It was during these conversations that political values such as obedience to and respect for authority, proper behavior toward other members of society, respect for the rights of others, and so on, were stressed. When these values were not passed on in informal situations, the youngsters learnt them through formal classroom instructions (through such subjects as civics and history), and through participation in such activities as Sunday School, Boy Scouts, and Girl Guides. It is also important to note that political lessons were draws from folk tales, by observing the behavior of older people, and in the administration of punishment or reward for acts of omission or commission (lying, stealing, cheating, fighting, and so on).

Summary

In the chapter on ethnographic descriptions, it was shown that in many respects the orthodox distinction between hierarchical and segmentary societies did have strong theoretical validity. It was the intention of this chapter, among other things, to demonstrate to what extent these theoretical descriptions were isomorphic with reality. In our introductory chapter it was hypothesized that the theoretical differences observed between the two types of traditional societies should be supported by the empirical data gathered for this study. To test this assumption, several questions were put to members of three ethnic groups to examine the differences and similarities with respect to the following patterns: authority and decision-making; intra-group contact and loyalty; orientation to change; and processes of socialization and politicization.

It was found that in all three ethnic groups, patterns of authority and decision-making were generally similar at the sub-societal level--i.e.

within the family. For both segmentary and hierarchical societies, family decision-making was found to be unrepresentative and limited in participation to only a few members. Respondents in the three ethnic groups shared the view that though most members in the family were theoretically allowed some participation in family discussions, this did not necessarily include children, the majority of whom were disqualified outright by virtue of age, with only the older ones experiencing some limited degree of participation. Nor did the theoretical fiction of equal participation in family discussions necessarily translate to mean that major family decisions reflected family consensus, since in the majority of cases all the crucial decisions were made unilaterally by the father as head of household or by both parents.

The data also indicate that ideally the majority of respondents in the two segmentary societies prefer the majoritarian model of group decision-making, at the societal level; and the Kpe, moreover, in selecting this for the other members of their group further lent validity to the assumption that this, indeed, is the prevailing mode of decision-making in segmentary societies. In contrast, the consensus of members from the hierarchical society showed a strong preference (either as individuals or when speaking on behalf of the collective) for the unrepresentative, elitist decision-making model. In this one instance, the data strongly confirmed ethnographic distinctions between segmentary and hierarchical traditional societies that differentiate these two systems on the basis of their decision-making structures.

On the matter of intra-group contact and identification, the first measure was degree of fluency in the mother-tongue. It was found that the overwhelming majority of respondents in all three groups were strongly attached to their indigenous languages and used them with some degree of frequency in conversations with fellow ethnic members. The fact that one of the groups (the

Kpe) studied is indigenous to the coast and has had a long history of contact with the West has not led to a corresponding decline in its members' mastery of the native language. The finding also strongly suggests that groups migrating from the hinterland to the costal areas do not find it necessary to cast off their own languages in favor of creole or languages original to their hosts. Because language identifies a culture, it can be said that these ethnic groups are not sociological fictions but empirical realities whose survival is guaranteed to the extent that these languages are not lost amidst the confusion brought about through rapid social change.

Looking at the other dimension of group loyalty and identification, it was found that slight differences could be observed in the manner in which members from the different societies reacted to their groups. These differences were more in degree than in kind. Although the majority of respondents from the three groups showed a fairly high level of group identity and loyalty, subsequent analysis tried to point out certain discrepancies between reported postures and reality. A major surprise was in the pattern of responses by the segmentary Kpe. Contrary to popular belief and the author's own extended observations, this group emerged with a significantly high level of group loyalty and identity. (It is our belief, for reasons already discussed, that this state of affairs is more apparent than real.)

Another area in which the three groups registered some differences was in their pattern of orientations toward change. The studies by Le Vine and Apter led to the expectation that the two segmentary societies would be most resistant to change, while the reverse would be true for the hierarchical society. Based on the typology of change suggested, the segmentary systems should have come out more in favor of the traditionalist orientation toward change or at least the neo-traditionalist. As it turned out, the results make any neat categorizations rather hazardous. One of the segmentary groups (Banyang) interpreted change within a modernist framework. In contrast, for the other segmentary group (Kpe) and the lone centralized society (Grassfield), change was defined in essentially neo-traditionalist terms. Only the Kpe group's orientation to change came close to confirming my theoretical expectations. Clearly, group perceptions of change are not necessarily associated with particular types of ethnic systems. In other words, the theoretical assumption that hierarchical systems would be least resistant to change has not been borne out in this study. Nor does the length of time an ethnic group has been involved in modernizing processes (reference here is to the Kpe who have enjoyed a long exposure to Western contact) necessarily result in that group subscribing to modernist values associated with change.

Finally, an examination of the processes of ethnic group socialization revealed little variations among the three groups studied. The data showed that within these two types of traditional societies, a reasonable amount of time and effort was contributed by older members toward the instruction of their younger ones about the values, customs, and traditions of their group. In an apparent paradox, it was also found that in one of these groups, inter-generational contact (i.e., frequent interaction between old and young members) was very limited. While for the segmentary Kpe and centralized Grassfield a larger percentage of the respondents reported a high level of contact between young and old members, this was not the case for the segmentary Banyang. Here again, as with the pattern of responses recorded with respect to group orientation toward change, the two acephalous societies occupy opposite extremes of the continuum.

Another aspect of the socialization process examined was the transmission of political values from parents to children. For the majority of respondents in the three groups, introduction to politics occurred late in life. Very few of those interviewed reported any sense of political awareness during the first sixteen years. This could largely be explained by the low percentage of respondents who reported that politics was discussed by elders and parents in the presence of children. However, many felt that their views on politics were derived from instructions given to them by their parents and school teachers.

   A major conclusion of this chapter is that despite differences in history, traditions and socio-political organizations, when members of ethnic groups describe their own societies (in terms of functions and processes), their responses reveal no significant differences between types of systems. The one exception to this observation was in the decision-making arena at the higher societal level. Here the data carefully distinguishes between segmentary societies on the one hand and hierarchical on the other. The former are characterized by a representative and egalitarian mode (either majoritarian or consensual) of decision-making in contrast to the latter's unrepresentative elitist decisional process. This distinction was only made clear at the group level; it was not the case at the subsocietal family level, where the mode of decision-making was essentially hierarchical and unrepresentative for both segmentary and centralized societies. What this seems to suggest is that a more precise method of differentiating between traditional societies would be an analysis of their patterns of authority and decision-making _especially_ at the societal level.

Footnotes

1. This statistic however masks the uneven distribution of educational facilities in the Cameroon. As Clignet has pointed out, the 1970 school enrollments included no less than 64 per cent of the population aged between six and thirteen years in Francophone Cameroon as opposed to 46 per cent in the Anglophone sector. Even within the Francophone sector there is a noticeable variation in the number of children exposed to educational institutions based on regional variation; for instance, only 22 per cent of school-age children are enrolled in school in the Islamized North against 94 per cent in the Center South. R. Clignet, The Africanization of the Labor Market. Berkeley and Los Angeles: University of California Press, 1976, p. 31.
2. Clignet, p. 31. As of 1968, there were 4,531 Anglophone Cameroonians enrolled in post-primary educational institutions with fewer than 7 per cent attending the national university in Yaounde. When compared to its population of one million, the level of post-primary school enrollment for English-speaking Cameroon is pitifully low. See Rubin, pp. 166-167.
3. Ardener, the ethnographer for this group, did in fact claim that the Kpe are in his words the "most Europeanized tribe in the British Cameroons." I would like to believe that Ardener's choice of the term "Europeanized" simply meant exposure to western education. Op. cit.
4. Clignet and Foster, p. 21.
5. Rubin, p. 175.
6. This section relies heavily on field notes compiled by Ms. Cherry Dyer, who kindly made them available to me.
7. Rubin, op. cit., p. 363.
8. The Baslers were the favorite mission group of the German colonial administration and as such exerted enormous influence on the question of which missionaries could come to The Kamerun colony.
9. Victoria Centenary Committee, Victoria, Southern Cameroons: 1858-1958, p. 40.

10. There are proportionately more Christians among the Grassfield people than among the peoples of the southern forest and coastal regions. About 40.5 per cent of the Grassfield population (drawn from the five administrative divisions that make up the North-West Province) is Christianized as opposed to 34 per cent for the rest of English-speaking Cameroon.

11. Johnson, op. cit., p. 87.

12. Basing my calculations on the 1957 census estimates for Southern Cameroons and using church membership figures for the same year, I found that 31 per cent--or roughly one out of every three persons--of the population of Victoria Division (now referred to as Fako) is Christianized. By 1970, the proportion had jumped up to 44 per cent.

13. Le Vine, 1970, p. 71.

14. With some minor modifications to make it culture-specific, this question comes from the Kluckhohn and Strodtbeck comparative study of value orientations among several American sub-cultures. The study was both excellent from a theoretical and methodological standpoint. Kluckhohn and Strodtbeck, op. cit.

15. See citations in Ndiva Kofele-Kale, "Our Colonial Mentality: Europe's Legacy to Africa," The Pan-Africanist, No. 3 (December 1971), pp. 11-17.

16. J. G. E. Allen, op. cit., p. 5.

17. Ibid., p. 5.

18. Ardener, 1956, p. 82.

19. The Bakweri Land Committee is discussed in some length in Ardener et. al., 1960, esp. chapter 16. A first hand account of the rise of the C.Y.L. is contained in P. M. Kale, A Political Evolution of the Cameroons. Buea: Government Press, 1967.

20. Oswald Spengler, The Decline of the West cited in Florence Kluckhohn and Fred Strodtbeck, Variations in Value Orientations. Evanston: Row, Peterson and Company, 1961.

21. Kluckhohn and Stodtbeck, op. cit.

22. David Apter, "The Role of Traditionalism in the Political Modernization of Ghana and Uganda," <u>World Politics,</u> 13 (October 1960), pp. 45-68.

23. Thomas Hodgkin, <u>Nationalism in Colonial Africa</u>. London: Muller, 1956.

24. Question also borrowed from the Kluckhohn and Strodtbeck study.

4
Environment and Ethnicity: Contrasts in Rural-Urban Attachment to Ethnic Group Values

The impact of urban life on traditional values and the extent to which townspeople sever links with their ethnic group as a result of geographical mobility from village to city is a subject that has occupied much of classical and contemporary anthropological writing on Africa. Coming out of this preoccupation is the belief that Africans who leave their traditional rural villages for the new towns and industrial/labor camps become increasingly estranged from their traditional culture. This view has its roots in colonial anthropology which split the African universe into two halves, one tribal and the other non-tribal.[1] Out of this misconceived and artificial dichotomy emerged the concept of "detribalization" and its derivative, the detribalized African; a rootless town-dweller whose moorings in traditional culture have been badly shaken as a result of culture contact in the towns. Detribalization came to mean different things to different people. Godfrey Wilson used it primarily in the demographic sense, to describe the movement of people out of rural into urban areas.[2] Hellman gave the term a distinctly sociological interpretation as characterizing the social relationships marked by a complete severance of ties with the kinship group living in the rural village.[3] Like Beals,[4] she equated detribalization with "the rejection of tribal modes of behavior, and the lapse of social relationships with people living in tribal areas."[5]

The tribal/detribalized dichotomy is false because, as Max Gluckman argues, it was predicated on the premise that:

> . . '. . the tribe was the 'zero point,' the start from which people changed as they came under urban and other Western influences: hence the starting point

of analyses was the original tribe and the original tribesman. Correspondingly, when some anthropologists began to study Africans in the towns, they saw the problems to be studied as those arising from the adaptation of tribesmen to urban conditions, and formulated these in terms of a process of 'detribalization,' which had to be analysed and measured as the tribesman slowly changed.[6]

It is not that Gluckman disagrees with the concept of "detribalization," for he goes on to say that "... in a sense every African is detribalized as soon as he leaves his tribal area, <u>even though he continues to be acted on by tribal influences. He lives in different kinds of groupings, earns his livelihood in a different way, comes under different authorities.</u>"[7] (my emphasis). Gluckman gives an entirely different meaning to the notion of "detribalization"; he uses the term detribalization to denote a situation in which an African who (having crossed the tribal boundary to live in the town) becomes cut off from tribal government and authority but <u>not</u> from tribal influences and values as such. As he saw it "detribalization" was not a continuous process of change but an action that describes or distinguishes two types of African peoples: one living in the rural villages and the other in towns.

Gluckman believes that different social systems exert different kinds of pressures which affect and condition the values and outlook of those who live within these structures. To understand the behavior of a townsman, one must analyze him within the context of the town, bearing in mind that residence in the city for a period of time will have some concomitant effects on his underlying value system and overt behavior.

In trying to move beyond the oversimplified view of change embedded in the concept of detribalization, Gluckman proposes a perspective which allows for both the traditional (rural) and modern (urban) African to be understood on their own terms. But this redefinition of detribalization as the process of individual adaptation to a nontraditional milieu, useful and important as it is, has been rightly criticized by Cohen and Middleton.[8] They point out that Gluckman's framework envisages the actor as "two different persons," but in actual fact, Cohen and Middleton argue, it is one actor caught in the vortex of social change playing the roles of two different "persons." That is, in the rural community this actor "acts out" his "ruralness" while in the urban context this role changes as the same person now plays the part of an urban resident.

It is for this reason that we consider rural village, plantation camp and town to be morphologically different environmental types containing relatively stabilized and permanent populations.[9] Though the residents, individually and collectively, belong to different ethnic groups and make periodic trips across these localities, at no one given time are they objectively located as residents in more than one locality. A plantation camp resident is a plantation camp resident as distinct from a villager. He cannot be placed within the two localities at the same time; for this reason, any attempt to examine and understand his values and behavior must be carried out within the particular environmental context.

Although the town dweller in many respects is the product of a town "culture," this does not render him "detribalized." On the contrary, the villager who leaves his rural village for one reason or another--to live in a plantation camp or town--brings into these localities the cultural values of his ethnic group. For the duration of his stay in this new setting a continuous interplay goes on between his antecedent ethnic values and the prevailing influences of the current locality. Thus where significant differences exist between a rural person and a town dweller, these differences are occasioned more by pragmatic adjustments to a new experience and less by quantum shifts in the underlying ethnocultural value system.

The environment <u>per se</u> does not destroy the underlying ethnocultural fabric; rather, it superimposes itself on it. What distinguishes a rural person from an urban resident is not the assumed belief that one is a "tribal" man where the other is "detribalized." What distinguishes them is their respective locations in space, i.e., <u>locality</u>. One type of locality may make it possible for ethnic values to express themselves unrestrainedly, while a different locality may impose certain restrictions on self-expression. In principle, therefore, an ethnic man is an ethnic man irrespective of his objective location in space. To the extent that X and Y have internalized the values of their ethnic group, they will remain ethnically similar regardless of the fact that X has lived all his life and will probably die in the village while Y seeks his fortune in the urban context. X, by living in the village, may have greater opportunities to "act out" his ethnic values while Y in the city is forced by circumstances arising out of the urban experience to appeal less and less to his ethnicity and perhaps more and more to his "urbanity." In any case, between these two persons, the difference in ethnic loyalty and attachment is one of degree, <u>not</u> kind.

The analysis of the effects of environmental location upon individual and group attachment to ethnic values raises several important questions: Do populations with different traditional sociopolitical structures respond differently to environmental changes? What aspects of ethnic values are more susceptible to environmental influence and hence change? Or put differently, which ethnic values resist change as a result of contact with urban and so-called modern ways of life? Are the effects of environmental change on individual and group ethnic values linear or curvilinear? Or are these ethnic value discontinuities occasioned by the rural-urban shift stabilized at a threshold level?[10] This chapter will examine these questions. It will do so by testing the ethnic system value consistency hypothesis which holds that variations in environmental location do not produce concomitant changes in the values subscribed to by populations from dissimilar traditional systems. Formulated in its null form, the hypothesis reads:

> THERE WILL BE SIGNIFICANT DIFFERENCES BETWEEN RURAL AND URBAN RESIDENTS FROM DISSIMILAR TRADITIONAL SYSTEMS WITH RESPECT TO THEIR ATTACHMENT TO ETHNIC GROUP VALUES.

Operationally, three types of values have been singled out as constituting the most crucial elements in any ethnic society insofar as it <u>must</u> perform those functions that Parsons refers to as pattern maintenance and adaptation. Under pattern maintenance, I have selected for testing (1) authority and decision-making patterns and (2) patterns of intragroup contact and solidarity. Under pattern adaptation, I shall examine ethnic group orientations toward change. It is hypothesized that those populations which share <u>similar</u> ethnic background will demonstrate very <u>little</u> intragroup differences with respect to these three basic values even across different geographical localities. To take one example, it is expected that populations from the centralized ethnic systems will, regardless of locational variation, show a marked preference for an authoritarian form of decision-making structure. Correspondingly, segmentary group members will be more disposed toward an egalitarian decision-making system.

Findings

Patterns of Authority and Decision-Making

Traditional African societies are characterized by a high degree of variability with regard to who enjoys power and how this is exercised. This pattern of authority varies with the structural properties of ethnic groups, as Fortes and Evans-Pritchards have shown. Previous discussion of the structural differences of the three ethnic groups under consideration has already established that in the centralized Grassfield chiefdoms interpersonal relations are conducted within a context of superordinacy-subordinacy which stands in marked contrast to the egalitarian and almost laissez-faire character of the segmentary Kpe and Banyang groups. This segment of the discussion will delineate the continuities and discontinuities in traditional patterns of authority and decision-making as these come under the influence of environmental change, i.e., urbanism and modernism.

(1) Childhood Images of Parental Authority--Relatively few persons--less than 20 per cent--had vague images of parental authority. The overwhelming majority of respondents had vivid recollections of what the authority of their parents was like. Of those who did recall, the majority sketched out their fathers as very authoritarian figures in contrast to mothers who were relatively permissive. This pattern of authoritarian father versus permissive mother permeates the entire social fabric and cuts across geographical locations.

The majority of respondents from the centralized traditional system regardless of locality described their fathers as disciplinarians, a description shared by a preponderance of the segmentary population groups. However, significant variations appear when locational differences are taken into consideration. More camp and town respondents from the segmentary system in contrast to village respondents assigned to their fathers an authoritarian personality. When the systems are compared, centralized people show more of a tendency toward strict and authoritarian fathers than those from segmentary groups.

Finally, the data also show that permissiveness is a characteristic the majority of the respondents from both systems attribute to their mothers. The view appears consistently in all three localities. The structural properties of these ethnic groups are not reflected in children's images of parental authority.

(2) Allocation of Domestic Authority--As Tables 4.1 and 4.2 indicate, the structural properties of the three ethnic groups compared here fail to carry over into the structure of domestic decision-making. Large majorities in all groups describe decision-making within the family as elitist, with ony a few persons actually involved in prescribing decisions for all. Interestingly enough, in all groups there is wide agreement that more family members are allowed to participate in decision-making even though few actually make the decisions. Thus, the proportion of Grassfield families where decision-making involves everybody increased from 68 per cent among camp families to 77 per cent among urban residents. Correspondingly, the proportion of Kpe and Banyang families with a similar pattern of decision-making remains about the same across environmental locations. The data suggest that environmental changes have a minor effect on the character of decision-making among the three groups; there are no marked differences between rural families and those living in the peri-urban camps and urban areas.

As to which member among the significant few who make family decisions is the dominant voice, Table 4.2 indicates that in all three groups, fathers enjoy a preeminent role in decision-making. This is true for both rural and urban families. However, among families in the peri-urban labor camps, fathers share domestic authority with their spouses; this is true for 49 per cent of the segmentary groups, while the corresponding proportion among Grassfield camp families is 33 per cent. This greater propensity for camp parents to share in family decision-making reflects the presence of women in the plantation labor force and their increasing role as bread-winners in their families. The plantation economy has assited in liberating the female from her traditional subordinate status.[11] As Ruth Simms observed years ago: "Women, by their personal achievements and their potential status as equal partners in the domestic family, are coming to expect a parity in status with the men."[12] This observation finds support in my own and several other studies.[13] In peri-urban and urban areas where women are active in the labor force and thus are financially secure, if not independent, they now insist on being included in family decision-making as equal partners with their husbands.

(3) Structure of Intra-Group Decision-Making--This research tried to ascertain the preferences individuals expressed with respect to patterns of decision-making above the level of the nuclear/extended family. Three prototypes of decision-making were proposed: an elitist type in which all decisions were made by a few; a consensual mode where decisions reflected the consensus of the members; and a majoritarian form which emphasized decisions arrived at by the majority in the group. It was predicted that individuals from the centralized Grassfield group would express a preference for the elitist model in marked contrast to the consensual or majoritarian model preferred by the segmentary groups. As anticipated, the political structure of the three ethnic groups is reflected in members' preference for decision-making styles. Among the centralized Grassfield the elitist mode is preferred; the Kpe and Banyang indicate a preference for the majoritarian model.

When the effects of environmental change are taken into consideration, the analysis of preferred modes of decision-making becomes quite complicated. Among the segmentary rural and urban population and the centralized urban residents the majoritarian model is preferred (the proportions are 60, 46, and 39 per cent respectively). Correspondingly, among the segmentary camp population the preferred decision-making method is the elitist. This is also the choice among centralized camp residents. The preference for the elitist model is most striking among the segmentary groups because it departs from their predicted ethnographic profile. It can be hypothesized that this departure reflects the hierarchical structure of authority patterns in the plantation camps. Plantations, as a rule, are characterized by their large force, small supervisory staff, and a decision-making structure that is highly centralized. Like a business enterprise, the plantation system is hierarchically organized such that decision-making powers rest at the apex, though some are delegated to subordinate officers. Each plantation employs an elaborate chain of command, at the head of which is the plantation manager, followed by divisional managers, field assistants, overseers, and then the mass of the people--laborers.

Within camp society itself, the overseer is the representative of and the direct link to the plantation command system. As a representative of the plantation hierarchy, the overseer has an impressive array of command powers. At first glance he does appear to be wearing two caps--one identifying him as an agent of the plantation system and the other as the workers' mouthpiece. This appearance, however, is misleading. The overseer has direct access to the plantation manager (or his delegate) from whom he receives instructions with respect to plantation work to be done. These instructions are then communicated to the laborers. This then puts the overseer in direct and close contact with the labor force. But it does not make him the people's representative because the overseer is a taskmaster. He is in a position to assign workers to specific jobs and to impose his supervisory presence on them. Because

Table 4.1
Participation in Family Decision-Making

WHO PARTICIPATES	FOR SEGMENTARY KPE & BANYANG RESIDING IN			FOR CENTRALIZED GRASS-FIELD RESIDING IN		
	VILLAGES	CAMPS	TOWNS	VILLAGES*	CAMPS	TOWNS
Every Family Member	66.7	64.0	62.7		67.5	76.5
Only a Few	28.0	33.0	31.8		28.7	23.5
NA	5.3	3.0	5.5		3.7	
Total	100.0	100.0	100.0		100.0	100.0
N	75	77	109		80	51

*Data not available

Table 4.2
Allocation of Domestic Authority

MAJOR DECISION-MAKER	AMONG SEGMENTARY KPE & BANYANG RESIDING IN			AMONG CENTRALIZED GRASS-FIELD RESIDING IN		
	VILLAGES	CAMPS	TOWNS	VILLAGES*	CAMPS	TOWNS
Father	56.0	44.0	52.7		57.5	49.0
Mother	10.7	27.0	12.7		5.0	2.0
Both Parents	28.0	49.0	30.0		32.5	47.1
Other	5.3	4.0	4.6		5.0	1.9
Total	100.0	100.0	100.0		100.0	100.0
N	75	77	109		80	51

*Data not available

Table 4.3
Group Preference for Decision-Making Models

Preference	AMONG SEGMENTARY KPE & BANYANG RESIDING IN			AMONG CENTRALIZED GRASS-FIELD RESIDING IN	
	VILLAGES	CAMPS	TOWNS	VILLAGES*	CAMPS	TOWNS
Elitist	18.7	54.5	31.2		55.8	29.4
Majoritarian	60.0	33.8	45.9		33.8	39.2
Consensual	13.3	7.8	16.5		6.5	19.6
No Answer	8.0	3.9	6.4		3.9	11.8
Total	100.0	100.0	100.0		100.0	100.0
N	75	77	109		77	51

*Data not available

he can reward and punish, he is usually a feared man. It is within his power to reward diligent workers by assigning them to less demanding jobs, to recommend them for promotions and pay increases, and similarly to punish recalcitrant workers by making them perform the most difficult jobs and not recommending them for pay raises. Whether we call this an incipient patronage system or something else, the fact remains that overseers in plantation camps enjoy and exercise considerable clout. It is this clout which reinforces their authority image in the minds of workers; an image which evokes obedience and deference. The relationship between overseer and workers has institutionalized the roles of superordinacy and subordinacy.

Theoretically, the overseer's formal authority role is confined only to those hours of the day during which he is directly involved with the supervision of plantation workers. In practice, however, he continues to wear the cloak of his office even after work hours. Thus, whether in the formal settings of plantation work or in the informal atmosphere of camp life, the aura surrounding the overseer as an authority figure persists. One might liken him to a sergeant-major who as the highest ranking NCO represents military authority within the barracks. The overseer is not exactly like a union steward whose loyalties are primarily to the workers he represents, nor should he be confused with an orginization-backed alderman whose loyalties are split between his constituents and the political machine. And he is certainly not even a remote equivalent of the tribal elders or respresentatives that Epstein found in the towns of the Copperbelt. The overseer is essentially an extension of the plantation hierarchy and in every way part and parcel of that command structure. It is to this system that he owes his status and directs his primary allegiance.

Indeed, the plantation system breeds a certain kind of hierarchical relationship between workers and managers (broadly conceived) in which status distinctions are unequivocal. From this lop-sided system comes an elitist decision-making structure. The relationship between the overseer and his manager is one of submission and deference; the one gives commands while the other must comply. The relationship between overseer and laborers parallels that between overseer and manager again it is one of commands and obedience. It is not important here that the overseer is merely one end of a chain of command. What is important is that from the workers' perspective the instructions that emanate from the overseer appear to originate with him. The overseer becomes a sort of lawgiver. This view will persist because it is consistent with the workers' entire camp experience. Workers are therefore more likely to associate decision-making with the orders and instructions frequently received from their overseers; they generalize from their experience. As a result, camp residents are more likely to define decision-making within the framework of the elitist principle. This is precisely what the segmentary camp residents were describing. However, the preference for the majoritarian model among the centralized urban residents is influenced by the long period of contact this immigrant population has had with the acaphalous indigenous coastal groups. It is hypothesized that this long exposure to the egalitarian authority structure of the Kpe among this Grassfield subsample seem to have had an effect on their preference for the majoritarian form of decision-making.

In summary, it has been shown that the influence of environmental location on the structure of authority and decision-making does not follow any uniform pattern. In terms of the allocation of domestic authority and environmental change, the fact that ⋅in families from all three ethnic groups resident in the plantation camps domestic authority is shared by both parents suggests a curvilinear relationship. This model of change holds that modernization fosters new patterns of behavior, followed by a partial restoration of traditional patterns; i.e., processes of change and stabilization alternate through time. In this case, the traditional role of the African wife as a passive follower in domestic decision-making changes in the plantation camp where women have entered the labor force and become wage earners like their spouses, enjoying a certain degree of financial security, and sometimes complete independence from their husbands. They have thus earned the right to participate jointly with their male partners in domestic decision-making. But this behavioral and role change is confined only to the peri-urban plantation camps. In the urban centers, the traditional status of the female prevails, which suggests that traditional practices are not completely abandoned.

The noticeable shift in the distribution of preferred modes of decision-making as segmentary camp and centralized urban residents make pragmatic adjustments to new forces and experiences suggests a linear relationship between environmental change and group decision-making preferences. These individuals, as a rsult of their participation in novel structures, tend increasingly to abandon traditional patterns of behavior and to adopt new behavioral dispositions.

Patterns of Intra-Group Contact and Solidarity

(1) <u>Language Fluency</u>--Proficiency in one's mother tongue and the ability to communicate in it when among fellow ethnic group members will be used here as indicators of the level of intra-ethnic group contact and solidarity. We want to discover what impact environmental change has on people's ability to express themselves fluently in their indigenous languages and how this in turn affects the cohesiveness and solidarity of the ethnic group. The importance of language as a cognitive symbol and as a medium of communication in any society is well-recognized.[14] In selecting it as an indicator of ethnic group contact and cohesiveness, it was argued that the survival of an

ethnic group is highly related to the persistence of its medium of communication. Language cannot exist divorced from the human community which it serves as a functional and symbolic tool; neither can a society endure for long denied of a means of communicating among its members. In this sense then, a peoples' cultural genius does not rest exclusively on its achievements and past glories but also rests on the symbols and artifacts employed in distinguishing the insiders from the outsiders. Language serves as a vital link and a crucial determinant of ethnic group persistence and solidarity.

Language seems to be a unifying symbol for both centralized and segmentary people. Of those respondents questioned the overwhelming majority in both systems report fluency in their mother tongue. Ninety-six per cent of the segmentary subsample and 95 per cent for the centralized group have some command of at least one indigenous Cameroonian language. A higher proportion of centralized people (94 per cent) than segmentary individuals (87 per cent) report being fluent in their mother tongue (see Table 4.4).

When community location is controlled, the data show that the segmentary Kpe and Banyang camp residents have a weaker command of the mother tongue than their fellow ethnics living in villages and towns. For both groups the data also show that the highest level of language proficiency is found among town residents. Thus 40 per cent of town residents compared to 26 per cent for the village and 23 per cent camp, within the two segmentary system groups, speak their mother tongue. When this same system's data were examined by locality (within-locality analysis), we find that the proportion of respondents who express themselves in an ethnic language is high for all three localities. The figures were 96 per cent of the town respondents, 85 per cent village and 77 per cent camp. In short, locational variation does not compromise the ability of segmentary peoples to be proficient in their mother tongue.

A test of independence yielded a chi-square of 24.534 with 10 degrees of freedom at the .0063 level of significance. Since this was significantly greater than the expected chi-square value, the null hypothesis was rejected. The expectation that locational difference would have no significant impact on respondents' ability to express themselves proficiently in the ethnic language was borne out by the data on the two segmentary groups.

A within-system analysis of the centralized group responses shows that the majority proportion of camp residents (56 per cent) in contrast to town residents (37 per cent) speak with some degree of fluency a language indigenous to that system. Unlike the segmentary group, where the lowest proportion of ethnic members fluent in a mother tongue was concentrated in camps and the highest in towns, the reverse clearly is the case for the centralized system. But like the segmentary groups, locational variation does significantly affect the language skill of Grassfield peoples.

Since my interest in language centered on its role as a symbol around which group pride and solidarity converged, it was reasoned that where the latter attributes are highly manifested, the language "traffic" between peoples of the same group will be equally high. That is, people who express high ethnic group pride will tend to communicate with their fellow members exclusively or a great deal more in their ethnic group language. Since a language is preserved through its continued use, people who take pride in their language will make efforts to preserve it. When members who share the same culture select their language over other existing languages as the medium through which feelings and ideas will be communicated, then such members are concerned about the preservation not only of their language but the cultural individuality of that group.

The traffic in ideas among members from the same ethnic system using their ethnic language as such a vehicle of transmission could serve as the measure for intra-group cohesiveness, contact, solidarity, and pride. It would logically follow that where the traffic is heavy there will be a correspondingly high level of group contact and solidarity. I have hypothesized that whatever the level of group solidarity among persons from the same ethnic system, it will not be affected by environmental variations. Thus, if a given group manifests a high level of intra-group cohesion and pride, then regardless of where the members are collectively located, this high level of group pride will persist.

The preceding analysis of respondents' ability to express themselves in the mother tongue has clearly demonstrated that the preponderance of individuals interviewed are fluent in a native language. This finding led me to expect that the use of ethnic languages as vehicles of communication among co-ethnics will be equally high. This expectation is borne out by the data, which reveal that in both centralized and segmentary systems, intragroup communication is made possible through the frequent, though not exclusive, use of an ethnic language. As Tables 4.4 and 4.5 show, large majorities in both traditional systems and across all three localities use an ethnic language when in the company of fellow ethnics. The widespread use of <u>cos' pidgin</u> (a language which, though indigenous to Cameroon, is not bound to any particular ethnic group) by an equally large proportion of respondents for the universe sampled is also noted. Equally noteworthy is the very limited use of English--one of Cameroon's two official languages--among the mass of Cameroonians.

In examining the <u>total</u> proportion of respondents from both systems who mention use of an ethnic language in conversations with co-ethnics, and comparing them across localities, differences in the structural properties between segmentary and centralized systems become quite apparent. Of the 78 per cent segmentary respondents who speak an ethnic language in the company of fellow ethnics, town and village account for over one half (29 per cent and 26 per cent respectively) with the remaining 21 per cent coming from camp respondents. This division parallels that discerned earlier on the item dealing with individual proficiency in a mother tongue. There it was noted that the largest proportion of respondents who were weak in the mother tongue came from the camp population group. It comes as no surprise, therefore, that fewer camp respondents than residents from the other localities do communicate in their indigenous language when among fellow ethnic group members.

Looking at the data on centralized system members, of the 91 per cent respondents who usually carry out conversations with other group members in an ethnic language, a higher proportion (55 per cent) come from the camp in contrast to 36 per cent from the town. Here too, the cleavage parallels that found in the examination of population group fluency in an ethnic language.

The expectation that locational difference will not significantly affect individual and group language skills and the ability to communicate in an ethnic language when in the company of fellow ethnics has not been entirely sustained by the data. Locational variation does exert some pull away from ethnic system solidarity and cohesion (understood as a function of language proficiency and communication). Furthermore, the evidence suggests that locational differences do not affect the two traditional systems in a uniform pattern. Thus, tests of independence show no association between location and ethnic language as a medium of communication for the segmentary system population (chi-square was 171.352 with 34 degrees of freedom); while a relationship was discerned for the centralized system (chi-square = 16.244 with 22 degrees of freedom). For the latter system, the finding is that environmental variation does affect the ability of its members to express themselves in the ethnic language. The finding then is that for the centralized system, unlike the segmentary one, the level of intra-systemic contact varies with locality.

Table 4.4
Ability to Speak Ethnic Language by
Traditional System

Respondents who Speak	Centralized System	Segmentary System
Own Ethnic Language	93.8%	87.4%
Other	.8	8.0
None	5.4	3.5
Total	100.0%	100.0%
N	129	261

Table 4.5
Languages used in Communicating with Fellow
Ethnics Among Segmentary Peoples

Respondents who Speak	Village	Camp	Town
Own Ethnic Language	95.5%	89.5%	88.9%
'Cos Pidgin	62.7	79.2%	75.1
English	30.7	51.9	38.0
Total	188.9%	230.7%	202.0%
N	75	77	109

*Multiple responses permitted

Table 4.6
Languages used in Communicating with Fellow
Ethnics Among Centrtalized Peoples

Respondents Who Speak	Village*	Camp	Town
Own Ethnic Language		92.3%	90.4%
'Cos Pidgin		71.2	68.7
English		39.0	39.3
Total		202.5%**	198.4%
N		77	

*Data not available
**Multiple responses permitted

(2) <u>Structure of the extended family</u>--It has been observed that as Africans migrate from the rural to urban areas, there is a tendency for the nuclear family to become isolated from the extended family kin group. This contraction of the extended family is usually evidenced in the small size of the nuclear family. The implications of this tendency for patterns of intra-group cohesiveness and solidarity are grave, given that the extended family is the epicenter of the vast network of kinship ties which bind together members in traditional African society. My data show that the extent of contact between nuclear family and extended family kin group varies little with environmental location. Among Grassfield urban residents, 88 per cent live within an extended family structure; the corresponding proportion is 72 per cent for the two segmentary groups. Regardless of ethnic origin, the shift from a rural environment to an urban context is uniformly associated with an increase in the importance placed on the extended family. In short, urban conditions do not weaken extended family ties; parents still send their children to relatives in the rural areas for holidays or even for upbringing. Urban households, like those in the rural areas, take in relatives from the rural villages, and far from shrinking, the urban family remains large,

with an average size of 8 members (see Table 4.8). This aside, the data also reveal a pattern of rural-urban continuity maintained through frequent trips between town and village and vice versa. The majority among segmentary and centralized urban residents maintain strong ties with their villages. Roughly 4 out of every 10 segmentary urban residents return to their village for visits at least once every month if not more. Only 16 per cent of respondents from the centralized group report not ever returning to their villages for visits. These strong ties with the rural area are not unique to Cameroon, as Gugler observed among urban residents in Eastern Nigeria;[15] Pfefferman among urban industrial workers in Senegal;[16] Hans Dieter Seibel among migrated industrial workers in Ibadan and Lagos;[17] Adepoju among immigrant household heads residing in Ife and Oshogbo;[18] and Caldwell among Ghanaian urban residents.[19] These studies all conclude that the African townsman considers himself an absentee villager and continues to conceive of himself as a member of a rural community. The Ghanaian sociologist, Kofi A. Busia, has described this seemingly permanent bond between urban migrant and villager in these words:

> A person's membership of his lineage binds him forever to the village where the lineage is located. Wherever he may go, however long he may be away, he belongs to his lineage town or village. The economic and social obligations of kinship such as those connected with funerals, marriages and divorce, as well as political allegiance and jural rights and status which are also tied up with kinship, keep alive his attachment to his native town or village.[20]

It is this enduring attachment which helps explain the strong rural-urban continuity observed in this study.

Table 4.7
Family Size Among Segmentary and Centralized Group Members

SIZE OF FAMILY	FOR SEGMENTARY KPE & BANYANG RESIDING IN			FOR CENTRALIZED GRASSFIELD RESIDING IN		
	VILLAGES	CAMPS	TOWNS	VILLAGES*	CAMPS	TOWNS
Large (over 8)	56	46.7	55.5		53.7	47.1
Medium (5-7)	24	33.3	22.7		25	39.2
Small (under 5)	20	20	19.1		20	13.7
No Answer			2.7		1.3	
Total	100.0	100.0	100.0		100.0	100.0
N	75	77	109		80	51

*No data available

Table 4.8
Family Composition Among Segmentary and Centralized Group Members

	FOR SEGMENTARY KPE & BANYANG RESIDING IN			FOR CENTRALIZED GRASSFIELD RESIDING IN		
	VILLAGES	CAMPS	TOWNS	VILLAGES*	CAMPS	TOWNS
Extended	54.7	72.0	71.8		48.7	88.2
Nuclear	40.0	24.0	26.4		48.7	11.8
No Answer	5.3	4.0	1.8		2.6	
Total	100.0	100.0	100.0		100.0	100.0
N	75	77	109		80	51

*No data available

Orientation to Change

To find out the extent to which environmental differences affect ethnic group values with respect to change, respondents from both segmentary and centralized systems were offered three choices of innovative postures. These were: (1) a traditionalist posture which rejects change and advocates the preservation of the past; (2) a neo-traditionalist perspective which represents a symbiosis of the past and the present; and (3) the progressive or modernist viewpoint, future-oriented and disdainful of the past.

When ethnic system distinctions are ignored and the data examined for the sampled universe, we find that more respondents either chose the neo-traditional (40.2 per cent) or modernist (39.1 per cent) view of change. There was, therefore, a clear rejection of the militantly traditionalist posture toward social change. Only a small fraction (15 per cent) of respondents selected this category. However, when across-locality comparisons are made, this high rejection of the traditionalist attitude toward change is confined to the multi-ethnic camps and towns. The data reveal that: (a) in the village subsample, comparatively more respondents are either traditionalists (35%) or neo-traditionalists (35%); (b) the largest number of camp respondents (45 per cent) cluster around the neo-traditionalist position; and (c) the orientation of town respondents is the progressive-modernist one. Tests of independence showed no clear relationship between locality and orientation toward change. The chi-square value of 38.571 with 6 degrees of freedom at the .0001 level of significance was greater than the expected value, compelling a rejection of the hypothesis that locational difference affects people's orientations to change.

Looking at the two traditional systems, the results of the test of independence showed that environmental difference has a greater impact on persons from centralized systems than on segmentary population groups. A within-system analysis of the centralized subsample across the board revealed two perspectives that enjoy widespread support and account for over 80 per cent of the frequency score: the neo-traditionalist (46.6 per cent) and modernist (40 per cent). When localities are compared, more camp respondents lean toward the traditionalist position while the majority of town respondents favor the modernist posture. In neither of these localities did the neo-traditional orientation to change receive a substantial proportion of the frequency score; it was selected by 18 per cent of the town respondents and only 5 per cent in the camp group. Table 4.10 presents the results for the centralized system. The obtained chi-square of 7.126 was less than the expected value--evidence that environment does significantly affect the dispositions of centralized peoples toward innovation.

Table 4.9
Respondents' Own View of Change by Location: Segmentary

Orientation	Rural Village	Plantation Camp	Town
Traditional	34.7%	41.6%	35.8%
Neo-Traditional	34.7	5.2	13.8
Modernising	24.0	42.9	45.9
N.A.	6.7	10.4	4.6
Total	100.0%	100.0%	100.0%
N	75	77	109

$\chi^2 = 29.22876 \quad P = .0001$

Table 4.10
Predictions of How Ethnic Group Members see
Change by Location: Centralized

Respondents Who Predicted	Rural Village*	Plantation Camp	Town
Traditional		50.6%	37.3%
Neo-Traditional		5.2	17.6
Modernising		40.3	41.2
N.A.		3.9	3.9
Total		100.0%	100.0%
N			

$$X^2 = 7.12619 \quad P = .3093$$

*No data

The comparison of segmentary system scores across the three localities shows that orientations to change differ somewhat among the community groups but no clear cleavage emerges as did with the centralized system. Segmentary persons are more inclined toward the modernist orientation in sharp contrast to the centralized group's strong identification with the neo-traditionalist position.

In examining the general pattern of frequency distribution for the segmentary subsample, two tendencies are noted. First, there is a tendency for town and camp respondents to cluster in fairly large numbers on both extremes of the innovation value continuum; they tend to be either traditionalists or modernists. The figures are displayed in Table 4.9. The rural village population is evenly split between traditionalists and neo-traditionalists. However, a cross-tabulation of locality with orientations to change for this system yielded a chi-square value which was larger than the expected value, thus a rejection of the null hypothesis. The conclusion then is that locational differences do not affect orientations toward change for persons who belong to a segmentary traditional system.

Having found out how respondents as individuals felt about change, we next asked them to venture "educated" guesses on the position of other system members on this value. The results displayed in Table 4.11 reveal that for the centralized group <u>individual</u> orientation preferences are consistent with expectations of <u>collective</u> preferences. As many respondents from the centralized system, as individuals, who selected the neo-traditionalist position over the other two, also selected the neo-traditionalist orientation as that which would prove most appealing to their fellow ethnic members.

The data on individual preferences and projections of group-members' preferences for the segmentary system contradict the conclusions already made with reference to the centralized system. Although the proportion of individuals from this subsample who expressed a preference for the modernist orientation and projected the same preference for the rest of the system members was about the same (39 per cent individual preference to 35 per cent predicted preference for modernism), there were some noticeable discrepancies between individual preferences and predictions of group preferences with respect to the other two innovative dispositions. Individual preferences were comparatively high for the traditionalist perspective (37 per cent) and low for the neo-traditionalist (17 per cent). The two positions, however, were about equally selected (26 per cent and 28 per cent respectively) on behalf of fellow ethnic system members.

When tests of independence were performed for both systems (obtained chi-squares were 19.626 for the segmentary subsample and 9.645 for the centralized subsample, both with 6 degrees of freedom) the results were consistent with the conclusions formulated earlier based on data for individual preferences. I, therefore, find that environmental difference only affects centralized people.

In conclusion, the data provides partial confirmation for the theoretical assumption that individual and collective group orientations toward change will remain consistent regardless of habitational variation. This was more true for segmentary system people than for the other system, suggesting a reformulation of the hypothesis which takes into consideration variations in traditional systems.

Summary

On the whole, the data presented in this chapter strongly support the hypothesis that degree of attachment of ethnic system values is not subject to indiscriminate shifts in response to environmental variations. In testing this hypothesis I have considered a number of important variables. Special attention has been paid to the pattern of images children have of parental authority, rules governing family decision-making, participatory role of children in the decisional process, models of decision-making in ethnic systems, patterns of intra-group contact, and finally, orientations toward change. Throughout the analysis the comparative method was adopted; first, systemic distinctions were dropped so that analysis was carried out for the entire sample assuming it was drawn from a homogeneous universe; then comparisons were made between the two traditional systems; and finally, within-systems analysis was done for both systems examining environmental differences.

The data revealed few inter-systemic differences and substantial similarities between the two systems on a number of variables. It has been found that recollections of parental authority, patterns of family decision-making, and intra-group contact were essentially the same for both systems. It turned out that the majority of segmentary and centralized respondents had authoritarian fathers and mothers who were relatively permissive and came from households in which the method of decision-making was hierarchical with the father playing a very dominant role, and in which children, as a general rule, were non-participants in the decisional process. Members from both groups also shared a high sense of pride and solidarity, as manifested in their ability to speak their ethnic language and the propensity to use it in communications with fellow members. These in broad terms are the similarities shared by a substantial proportion of members from both segmentary and centralized systems.

Differences were also observed. Although a consensus emerged at the lower levels of society with respect to the decisional process, when this process was examined at the broader societal perspective differences appeared. Segmentary persons defined the decision-making process at the group level as one in which decisions arrived at by the majority are binding on all members. On the other hand, most centralized people believed that decision-making in their group was elitist. Besides decision-making, significant inter-system difference was also observed in group dispositions toward change. Segmentary people were generally in favor of a progressive orientation while the majority of centralized peoples showed an inclination toward the neo-traditionalist posture.

Testing for the effects of environment on these values we found most of them held regardless of where respondents were located. There was a high degree of consistency in individual and group attachments to ethnic system values across localities. The one exception was with respect to language proficiency where the impact of environmental influences was selective, in that it produced variations only for centralized population groups and not for segmentary persons.

Table 4.11
Predictions of Group Members' Predispositions
Toward Change

Orientations	Centralized System	Segmentary System
Traditionalist	24.0%	26.1%
Neo-Traditionalist	37.2	27.6
Modernist	34.1	34.5
N.A.	4.7	11.9
Total	100.0%	100.0%
N	129	261

That locational differences do not _significantly_ affect the basic structure of ethnic group values is a major conclusion of this chapter. The implications of this finding are clear: (1) rural ethnic man and urban ethnic man are essentially the same with regards to exposure and attachments to some critical ethnic group values; and (2) subsequent explanations of social behavior, especially in the case we are studying, political orientations toward the national system, should not call on this attribute to explain group differences. If attachment to ethnic group values is a systemic characteristic held in common by the majority of members, then it cannot be employed to explain within-system variations. Since it is held as a constant for all system members, its explanatory power is non-existent. Its predictive usefulness would come into play if, and only if, as an attribute it were shared by some but not all the members of a society. Under such circumstances, it can logically be assumed that it is the differential possession of the attribute that probably explains variations in some other area.

Having shown that attachment to group values varies little with environmental differences, I propose to investigate variations in national political orientations as a function of geographical location in space. I shall, therefore, argue and attempt to demonstrate with empirical evidence in the next two chapters that it is the locality in which an individual lives that conditions his perceptions and shapes orientations toward the national political system.

Footnotes

1. Max Gluckman, "Tribalism in Modern British Central Africa," in Irving L. Markovitz, ed., *African Politics and Society*, New York: The Free Press, 1970, pp. 81-95.
2. Godfrey Wilson, *An Essay on the Economics of Detribalization in Northern Rhodesia*, Rhodes-Livingstone Institute (Livingstone, 1941-42), papers 5 and 6.
3. E. Hellman, *Rooiyard: A Sociological Study of an Urban Native Slum Yard*. Capetown: Oxford University Press, 1948, Rhodes-Livingstone Institute Paper, No. 13, p. 110.
4. R. C. Beals, "Urbanism, Urbanization and Acculturation," *American Anthropologist*, iii, 1 (January-March, 1951), pp. 5-6.
5. J. C. Mitchell, "Urbanization, Detribalization and Stabilization in Southern Africa: A Problem of Definition and Measurement," in UNESCO, *Social Implications of Industrialization and Urbanization in Africa South of the Sahara*, Paris: UNESCO, 1956, pp. 693-711.
6. Gluckman, op. cit., pp. 82-83; also "Anthropological Problems Arising from the African Industrial Revolution," in Aidan Southall, ed., *Social Change in Modern Africa*. London: Oxford University Press, 1961, pp. 67-68.
7. Gluckman, "Tribalism in Modern Africa," p. 83.
8. Ronald Cohen and John Middleton, eds., *From Tribe to Nation in Africa: Studies in Incorporation Process*. Scranton, Pa.: Chandler Publishing Co., 1970 "Introduction" p. 3.
9. J. C. Mitchell, op. cit.
10. For a discussion of these various models of social change, see Remi Clignet, "Environmental Change, Types of Descent, and Child Rearing Practices," in Horace Miner, ed., *The City in Modern Africa*, New York: Praeger, 1967, pp. 257-296; and W. Moore, *Social Change*, Englewood Cliffs, N.J.: Prentice-Hall, 1974, chapters 2 and 5.
11. The camp sample was drawn from three camps one of which, Tole Tea Estate, was selected because of its unique work force. It is probably

alone among all the Corporation's plantations with a labor force that is predominantly made up of women. In 1966, out of a total work force of 790, women accounted for over two-thirds (435) and plans were afoot to hire an additional 800 or more over the next ten years. When you include figures for contractual labor, i.e., those hired during the peak harvesting season, the labor force in 1973 stood at 1,061--814 females and 287 males. Here was a very unique laboratory to observe the effects of the changing role of the female on the structure of domestic decision-making. See Bederman, op. cit., p. 52 and "Analysis of Employees by Tribes, Tole Tea Plantation, 1973," Plantation Manager's Office, Tole Tea Estate.

12. Ruth Simms, Urbanization in West Africa: A Review of the Current Literature. Evanston, Illinois: Northwestern University Press, 1965.

13. See, for instance, Tanya Baker and Mary Bird, "Urbanisation and the Position of Women," The Sociological Review, VII, 1 (July 1959), pp. 99-121; S. Leith-Ross, "The Rise of a New Elite Amongst the Women of Nigeria," International Social Science Bulletin, VII, 3 (1956), pp. 481-488.

14. See S. I. Hayakawa, Symbol, Status, and Personality. N. Y.: Harcourt, Brace and World, 1953; Frank Ford Nesbit, Language, Meaning and Reality. New York: Exposition Press, 1955; and Leslie A. White, The Science of Culture. N. Y.: Farras, Straus and Cudahy, 1949.

15. Josef Gugler, "Life in a Dual System: Eastern Nigerians in Town, 1961," Cahiers d'Etudes Africaines Vol. 11 (1971), pp. 400-21.

16. Guy Pfefferman, Industrial Labor in the Republic of Senegal. New York: Praeger, 1968.

17. Hans Dieter Seibel, Industriearbeit and Kulturwandel in Nigeria: Kulturelle Implikationen des Wandels von einer traditionellen Stammesgesellschaft zu einer modernen Industriegesellschaft Ordo Politicus 9. Koln/Opladen: Westdeutscher Verlag, 1968.

18. Aderanti Adepoju, "Migration and Socioeconomic links between urban migrants and their home communities in Nigeria," Africa Vol. 44 (1974), pp. 383-95.

19. John C. Caldwell, <u>African rural-urban migration: The Movement to Ghana's Towns</u> New York: Columbia University Press, 1969.

20. Kofi A. Busia, <u>Report on a Social Survey of Sekondi-Takoradi.</u> London: Crown Agents, 1960, p. 73 cited in Josef Gugler and William G. Flanagan, Urbanization and Social Change in West Africa. London: Cambridge U. Press, 1978, p. 69.

5
Environment and National Identity: Contrasts in Rural-Urban Orientations Toward the Nation

One of the most influential conceptualizations of political culture defines it as "the particular distribution of patterns of orientation toward political objects among the members of the nation and the political system as internalized in cognition, feelings, and evaluations of its population."[1] The objects toward which people orient their political behavior have been operationally organized for empirical testing into four broad systems: identity, symbol, rule, and belief systems.[2] The identity system, following Devine's formulation, is the community which

> ... provides the structure for attachment to the political system as a whole and to members of the same political system considered as co-nationals. The rule system is the repository of support for the fundamental political agreements governing a particular society; the political constitutions, the norms of the regime, the 'rules of the game.' The symbol system is the structure for support of the basic political artifacts deemed valuable in the culture. The belief system is the repository of the fundamental principles and goals supported by the members of the political system.[3]

This chapter will examine rural-urban differences in members' orientations to the identity and symbol systems of political culture. Together the two represent the psychological proximity between Cameroonians and their political system as well as among Cameroonians themselves. Within the identity system a distinction will be made between (1) national identity, meaning the vertical relationship between members and their political system; and (2) community identity, which refers to the horizontal identification among members of the same nation.

Identity System

Sense of National Identity

Three levels of national identity were measured in this study: (1) political awareness, a term which refers to the degree of involvement in the political process by members of a political system. This level of political culture has been bifurcated by Almond and Verba (1963) into input cognition (the frequency with which people follow or pay attention to political and governmental affairs), and output cognition (the extent to which people perceive the political process as having an effect on themselves); (2) Political Knowledge; i.e., the ability of people to identify their national and local leaders; and (3) System Affect; i.e., the emotional attachment an individual has to his/her country.

Political Awareness/Input Cognition. In trying to assess the extent to which citizens are involved in governmental affairs and with what degree of infrequency, the data show, as expected, that more camp (80 per cent) and town (78 per cent) respondents stayed close to governmental and political affairs than did villagers, only 53 per cent of whom shared this position (as shown in Table 5.1).

However, when respondents were asked whether they thought politics was beyond the comprehension of the average citizen, a noticeable shift occurs with 69 per cent of the village and 68 per cent for the town respondents compared to only 40 per cent of the camp subsample subscribing to the view that the average citizen is incapable of this comprehension.

Since the item did not ask how the respondent himself felt about politics but called upon him to

Table 5.1
Relation Between Community and Political Awareness: Input Cognition Aspect

Community (percentages)

Exposure to Political Affairs	Rural Village	Plantation Camp	Town
Regularly	27.6	28.4	30.6
From time to time	25.0	52.9	48.1
Never	47.4	13.5	17.5
N.A.	0.0	5.2	3.7
Total	100.0%	100.0%	100.0%
N	76		

$$x^2 = 42.22 \quad p = <.001$$

give an opinion about the average citizen's reaction, the responses cannot be interpreted as indicative of the <u>actual</u> level of political comprehension among respondents. To reveal the citizen's own opinion of <u>his</u> level of political comprehension and awareness, the following item was put to the respondents: "Do you think you can understand some of the policies and programs that the national government has been undertaking? For example, the construction of the Tiko-Victoria highway?" The results indicate that the majority of respondents in all three communities understood (or thought they did) the significance of this particular governmental program. However, more town and camp respondents (68 per cent and 67 per cent respectively) than village respondents (52 per cent) report a higher level of political awareness with respect to the input process.

This finding is of interest since it is consistent with findings drawn from the data on media exposure. That is, village folk lag somewhat behind camp and town residents with respect to their exposure to the news media and the level of involvement with day-to-day happenings in the political arena. Since camp and town folk, as the data reveal, tend to listen more to political broadcasts than village residents, they are also more aware of important policy announcements and programs than people from the village.

Political Awareness/Output Cognition. Does the citizen perceive that the government has an impact on his day-to-day life? How does he assess this impact? Is it favorable or not, and why? Large majorities of village, camp, and town respondents see their national government as having some impact on their daily lives. On one extreme are the camp respondents, 92 per cent of whom attribute an impact (either great or moderate) to their national government. The other extreme is occupied by 86 per cent of town respondents, and the middle with 83 per cent respondents attributing some or great impact to their national government in the village subsample. Less than 4 per cent of the camp respondents and under 15 per cent of the village and town respondents attribute no effect to their national government. When the results of the question to determine whether citizens considered the impact favorable or not are examined, the pattern that emerges is similar to the one just discussed (though of course there were some substantial drops in the frequency score). A higher proportion of respondents in all three communities consider the impact of government beneficial to their lives.

The broad picture presented so far seems to suggest that Cameroonians, no matter where they live, feel the impact of governmental activities and policies. Although the majority of the respondents evaluate this impact as favorable, camp (77 per cent) and town folk (65 per cent) subscribe more highly to the view than village residents (47 per cent). As Table 5.2 shows, of those village respondents who found the impact of government far from beneficial, an overwhelming majority gave as their reason the unequal distribution of economic resources in the country, which not only expanded an already wide developmental chasm between the towns and rural areas but also reinforced the stratification between "haves" and "have-nots."

A few illustrations taken from the village responses are given below in thematic sequence:

(1) Unequal distribution of amenities and services; especially the fact that political rewards were still being dictated by regional and ethnic considerations.

Advantages enjoyed by government employees have not yet been extended to workers in the private sector. For instance, a whole lot of fringe benefits, like child allowance, house rents, generous leave allowances, etc. enjoyed by civil servants have been denied those of us working in the private sector. [Male plantation camp worker in his mid-forties.]

A worker in East Cameroon [meaning francophone Cameroon] who does the same job I do earns more money than I. Yet they tell us we are one and united! [Female school teacher in her mid-twenties.]

Tribalism still plays a very crucial role in the distribution of wealth and allocation of important positions in this country. You will notice that only some tribes (especially those from the coast whose men are no longer in power) have a disproportionate number of persons in the ranks of the unemployed. [Male Post-Secondary School graduate, early twenties.]

Most of the basic services, like pipe born water, electricity, good roads, etc. are all concentrated in the towns while those of us in the rural areas are left to languish. And yet we all pay our taxes like decent citizens. How come the government doesn't care about us, the common people? [Male villager in his late thirties.]

(2) The second most frequently mentioned reason given to support the position that governmental activities were far from favorable for some people was the gap between the rich and poor in Cameroon; which many felt was increasing rather than closing up.

The common man is suffering. People without jobs are asked to pay taxes and those who can barely make a living out of their meagre salaries are being assessed taxes that should logically be paid by the rich people. [Male villager in his early thirties.]

There are some people working in the government whose monthly allowances alone double my monthly salary. I am talking about their <u>allowances</u> not even their basic salary; not to talk of the bribes they take. With my few francs, I have to buy food in the same market with these people; pay for hospital drugs; send my children to school and be assessed the same amount for school fees. This is not fair! [Male junior civil servant, early thirties.]

If you look around you will notice that there are two tribes in this country. One tribe is the Mercedes-Benz tribe made up of wealthy businessmen, landlords, senior civil servants, Ministers, etc.; and the other is composed of the mass of Cameroonians--the common people. We are poor, jobless, underpaid and overcharged. The gap between us and them is never going to close up at the rate things are going. [A minister of the Church.]

(3) Many complained about the exclusion of most citizens from political participation and that there was no way consumers of government policies and programs can make significant input into the policy making process. A twenty year old village woman summarized this position in this very succinct statement:

> I hear only what I have to do for the government but the government never listens to me.

(4) Many people were visibly concerned with the unemployment problem and some of the ridiculous steps one had to go through in order to get a job.

> To get a job, I have to distribute bottles of whiskey to my prospective employers under cover of darkness. Where in the world am I supposed to get the money to buy them these expensive 'mimbo' [Creole for liquor] when I hardly even have a job? [Recent secondary school graduate.]

> I was expected to attend a job interview in a hotel room. To sleep with every man who interviews me for a job? Shit! I am not the 'horizontal' type. [Female been-to Secretary-Typist.]

> I completed school and stayed home for what amounted to donkey years without a job. Finally, I agreed to get married. [Woman in her mid-twenties.]

(5) A few people were disturbed by what they perceived as the denial of basic human rights in Cameroon and the fear that the country was gradually becoming a police state.

> I know of only two countries in Africa where so much restriction is imposed on

free movement of persons within the country's borders--South Africa and Cameroon. The parallel is not far-fetched for in Cameroon people are still required to carry Identity-Cards; while a Laissez-passer issued from the Provincial Security Service is a necessity if one wants to travel between provinces [this was abolished in 1975--author]. Twenty years ago, to travel from British Cameroons to French Cameroons one needed a passport. We attributed that to a colonial conspiracy. Ten years ago we voted to remove this artificial boundaries that separated brothers and so the Federal Republic of Cameroon was born. Today, a trip to Douala from Tiko, still requires a travel document. I tell you son, we have gone full cycle! [An old man in his late fifties.]

The highly critical stance taken by rural people reflects their genuine concern over the fact that their relative isolation from the centers of power has denied them their fair share of national goods and services. Their concern for social and economic justice in the distribution of national resources has long been recognized by the government. Beginning with the Second Five Year Economic and Social Development Plan (July 1966-June 1971) and continuing with the Third Five Year Plan (July 1971-June 1976) and the Fourth Five Year Plan (June 1976-July 1980), the Cameroon government has given prominence to the regional approach to economic development in the hopes that this strategy of decentralization will accelerate a balanced distribution of investment resources and the fruits of economic progress to all parts of the country. The Third Five Year Plan saw as its goals the maintaining of: (1) "equilibrium between ethnic groups and regions, none of which can be treated with special favour or disfavour but which must certainly improve their knowledge of each other to promote friendship; (2) equilibrium between town and country, agriculture and industry, manual workers and civil servants; so that economic development can be realised in a climate of national solidarity; and (3) equilibrium between cultures which must attain their full development and give birth to authentic Cameroonian civilization." In this plan, rural development was designated as one of the priority sectors receiving 9.2 per cent of the total investment program, double what it received under the Second Five Year Plan. This commitment to close the rural-urban gap through the revitalization of the rural environment was well articulated in the President's address to the National Assembly when the Third Year Plan was inaugurated.[5] It would appear from the above responses that few people in the rural villages have been impressed by the government's rhetoric. The last decade has witnessed a large scale rural exodus to the towns and cities such as Baffoussam, Douala, Edea, Kumba, Yaounde, and the Buea-Tiko-Victoria complex, as villagers escape from the relative poverty and deprivation of their rural environment in order to take advantage of the economic benefits which abound in the urban centers. In 1963 the rural population stood at 84 per cent, by 1970 it had dropped to 78 per cent and in 1976 to 71.5 per cent. In the space of thirteen years 12.5 per cent of the rural population, roughly three-quarters of a million persons have been added to the urban areas. These included a large percentage of the working age population and in particular young school leavers.[6]

Thus, in spite of government's efforts through resource allocations, villages continue to lag behind towns and cities on all the major indices of development: electrification, employment, income, education, housing, and so on, as the 1976 general population and housing census dramatically reveals, and as these rural respondents have long felt. One of the reasons for the persistence of these gross economic disparities among Cameroonians and among the regions of the country is the government's failure to translate policies to action. In his critical analysis of the provisions of the Cameroon Investment Code as well as the investment policies of public financial institutions--all of which were legislated into existence to strengthen the government's regional approach to development--a leading Cameroonian economist, Dr. Ndongko, concludes that these legislations have failed to reflect and give support to the government's objective of balanced regional development. Almost fifteen years after this strattegy for development was first articulated, the backward regions still remain relatively underdeveloped.[7]

Although the picture is slightly blurred in Table 5.3, we still find that many town respondents who found government impact to be beneficial mentioned the rapid pace of social and economic development; while a higher proportion of camp respondents cited the stable political situation. Clearly political stability and steady economic growth are positive aspects of governmental policies, although the responses of the camp community emphasize one while those of the town emphasize the other. Table 5.3 also indicates that village respondents who found government to be favorable saw this in the light of the stable political climate and the strides in the area of socio-economic development.

In summary, village, camp, and town respondents are agreed on the general impact of government on their lives though they differ on the diirection of this impact. Majorities in camp and town tend to see its effects as salutary. In contrast, village respondents assess the impact of government on their lives in a very negative way.

Political Knowledge. The pattern of responses illustrated in Table 3.4 which deals with the ability to identify government Ministers indicates that sharp differences exist between camp/town, on the one hand, and village on the other. The table reveals that only 32 per cent of the village respondents can correctly identify three cabinet

Table 5.2
Reasons Given by Respondents Who Found
Government Impact Unfavorable

	Community (percentages)		
	Village	Camp	Town
Poor Economic Policies Widened Gap Between Haves and Have-Nots	59.46	14.28	30.95
Unemployment	8.11	8.57	9.52
Civil and Political Liberties Denied	8.11	8.57	28.57
Other	0.0	5.71	2.38
No Reason	0.0	2.86	19.05
MD/MA	24.32	65.71	7.14
Total	100.00%	100.00%	100.00%
N	(37)	(35)	(42)

$x^2 = 52.2922 \quad p = < .001$

Table 5.3
Reasons Given by Respondents Who Considered
the Impact of Government to be Favorable

	Community (percentages)		
	Village	Camp	Town
Peace and Political Stability in the Country	26.31%	43.33%	16.34%
Big strides in economic development	34.21	26.67	40.38
No Reason	39.47	30.00	43.26
Total	100.00%	100.00%	100.00%
N	(38)	(120)	(104)

Ministers compared to 60 per cent for the camp and 62 per cent for the town. This low frequency of informed village respondents is consistent with the low percentage of the village subsample not exposed to the news media. The village group emerges as the least exposed to the communications media and the most poorly informed of all three communities.

Table 5.4
Ability to Identify Cabinet Ministers

Community (percentages)

Can Identify	Rural Village	Plantation Camp	Town
3 Ministers	32.9%	60.0%	61.9%
2 Ministers	15.8	9.0	9.4
1 Minister	21.1	3.9	5.6
0 Minister	30.0	26.5	22.5
N.A.	0.0	0.0	0.6
Total	100.0%	100.0%	100.0%
N	(76)	(155)	(160)

$x^2 = 34.9699 \quad p = < .001$

Tables 5.5 and 5.6 which report respondents' knowledge of the National and Local Party leaders reveal no variation in levels of information along community lines. These tables strongly suggest that large majorities of respondents in the three communities cannot identify their local party leaders or even name one national party official. This phenomenon is evenly spread through all three communities. However, the town does enjoy a slight edge over the other two communities with a fairly high proportion of well-informed residents.

The data also indicate that locality is significantly related to respondent's knowledge of national and local political party leaders but

Table 5.5
Ability to Identify National Party Leaders

Community (percentages)

Can Identify	Rural Village	Plantation Camp	Town
4 Bureau Members	14.5%	7.7%	18.1%
3 Bureau Members	2.6	8.4	8.1
2 Bureau Members	5.3	6.5	8.7
1 Bureau Member	21.1	11.6	7.5
0 Bureau Member	56.6	65.8	56.9
N.A.	0.0	0.0	0.6
Total	100.0%	100.0%	100.0%
N	(76)	(155)	(160)

$x^2 = 10.8553 \quad p = < .01$

Table 5.6
Ability to Identify Party Leaders

Community (percentages)

	Rural Village	Plantation Camp	Town
Identify Section President	17.1	18.7	32.5
Not Identify	81.6	80.6	66.2
N.A.	1.3	0.6	1.2
Total	100.0%	100.0%	100.0%
N	(76)	(155)	(160)

$x^2 = 10.8553 \quad p = < .01$

not related to knowledge of national Cabinet Ministers. (The latter when cross-tabulated with location where respondent lives yielded a Chi-square of 33.848 with 8 degrees of freedom which was not significant at the .01 level; failing to confirm the null hypothesis that locality affects respondents' civic knowledge.) Cross-tabulations of community with respondents' knowledge of party leaders at both the local and national levels resulted in Chi-squares that were significant at the .01 level of significance, thus confirming the first relationship between the two sets of variables.

Certainly, after reviewing the body of data for this section, the most evident conclusion is that Cameroonians have very low knowledge of who holds public office, and this is more so for their party leaders than cabinet ministers. Two questions then arise. How does one explain the apparent imbalance in the pattern of political knowledge revealed by the data? Why is it that respondents have less difficulty identifying cabinet ministers (given their high turnover rate in Cameroon) than they have the relatively stable party leaders? This discrepancy becomes even more significant when we realize that in practice, the Cameroon political system allows for an overlap between cabinet position and national party office. Thus, many cabinet ministers also combine active duties within the only party in the country--the Cameroon National Union. This is consistent with official doctrine, in which party and government collaborate. Most surprising is the apparent inability of a large majority of the respondents even to identify local party leaders--those with whom they are most likely, presumably, to come into contact.

Several explanations can be advanced for this low level of political knowledge in general and the coincidental high information level on cabinet ministers. The high success in recognizing ministers is in my view idiosyncratic; it is a by-product of sampling biases of either a reactive or interactive nature occurring in the course of the testing.[8] These biases were probably prompted by the fact that interviewing took place during a period of intense political activity after a momentous constitutional change. The shift from a federal system to a unitary state took place in May, 1972, and the move resulted in the appointment of a new cabinet and the reorganization of provincial administrative services.

The reorganization of the reconstituted provincial administrative services necessarily involved new appointments and movement of personnel. The investiture ceremonies for these new appointees, especially in the upper echelons, were well attended by the public and usually presided over by the minister in whose ministry the officer was a functionary. It may well be that the presence of ministers during these ceremonies afforded the public unparalleled opportunities to get acquainted with their national leaders. For the ministers too, these occasions heightened their visibility. As a result, when in the course of interviewing, respondents were asked to identify their cabinet ministers, only relatively few had difficulty recalling their names. Thus the high visibility of ministers occasioned by their frequent (if brief) exposure to the populace during this period of constitutional change increased the memory of respondents.

Without this intervening factor (timing of the testing), respondents' ability to recognize cabinet ministers would have been just as low as their ability to name their party leaders. This, of course, leads one to wonder whether there is a high level of mass alienation from the Cameroon political system, especially the national leadership.[9] To test if this was the case and whether it was not limited to the party hierarchy, an item was included in the questionnaire which sought to tap people's affective images of their cabinet officials. Respondents were asked, "If you had to choose a career for your child, what would you not want him/her to become? A lawyer, businessman, government minister or nurse?" On the whole, more people rejected a cabinet post for their children. Discounting the 38 per cent who elected not to express an opinion, only 4 per cent of the respondents did not want their children to become nurses; 11 per cent were against their becoming business entrepreneurs; 14 per cent were opposed to a career in law; while the plurality of respondents--32 per cent were against their children becoming government ministers. The most frequent reason given for this negative attitude toward cabinet ministers is the public's belief that ministers are very corrupt and generally more involved in the pursuit of self-interest than the public good. The evidence leads me to conclude that the Cameroon public, regardless of locality, is highly critical, cynical, and distrustful of its national leaders. This undifferentiated public also experiences great difficulty in correctly identifying its national leaders. The one apparent difference--a greater ability to recognize cabinet ministers--appears to be a clear example of coincidental reaction to external stimulus (i.e., the setting and timing of the research act).

The inability of Cameroonians to recognize their party leaders can be attributed to either or both of the following reasons: the fact that (1) party leaders are not highly visible to their constituents; and (2) an imperfect integration exists between the Cameroon National Union and the public. The evidence reveiwed so far suggests that ministers were easily recognized because of this high visibility. The fact of exposure does not go far in explaining respondents' failure in correctly identifying other leaders for, as I indicated earlier, many ministers also serve as party officials (either in the national bureau or section executive). Nor does it help to explain why the overwhelming majority of respondents failed even to identify by name any of their local party leaders--those with whom the public presumably has greater access. The low information level uncovered by the data strongly suggests the existence of a gap between the C.N.U. and the Cameroonian masses.[10]

To begin to understand this gap between party and people, a brief word must be said about the organizational structure and general orientation of the Cameroon National Union.[11] The Cameroon

National Union is what Johnson and Rubin have described as an elitist/patron party as opposed to a mass political party of the Leninist type. It began as (and has remained) a party which united the leadership of the nation rather than the membership of the various constituents.[12] Although the party's original intention was to transform itself into a mass movement to mobilize the Cameroon people toward the goals of national unity and socio-economic development, the CNU has not succeeded in casting off its elite/patron image. Nor is this problem of passing off an elite party for a mass movement uniquely Cameroonian. It is a problem shared by some of the more prominent one-party states in Africa.[13]

It is this writer's impression--and it must remain nothing more than an impression--that the orientation of the Party is toward rewarding those political leaders and their clients who have given up leadership positions in their respective parties in order to join Ahidjo's Union Camerounaise. The composition of the 1973-78 Parliament is a case in point. The elections of May, 1973, far from slating a completely new cast of political leaders merely returned to power carry-overs from the dissolved assemblies of the former federated states (i.e. former C.U.C., C.P.N.C., K.N.D.P., and U.C. politicians.)[14] The continuity at the leadership level is remarkable since it has succeeded in giving Cameroon one of the more stable African governments.[15] Yet the fact that it represents an unbroken chain of command of patron/leaders who have dominated the Cameroon political stage for two decades further suggests that the elitist profile of the CNU has not changed. A party organized as an elite/patron club runs into serious credibility problems when it seeks to present itself as a mass movement.

Another dimension of this imperfect integration between party and masses may be more a function of the historical recency of the CNU and less of its organizational edifice. The CNU did not come into existence until late 1966. (It existed prior to this date as the Union Camerounaise and confined all its activities to the francophone sector of the country.) Consequently, the party (1) is still in its early stages and is therefore not yet in a strong enough position to evoke widespread grass-roots partisan attachments; and (2) the C.N.U.'s historical recency, especially in English-speaking Cameroon, only serves to demonstrate that this sector of the country quite literally never had a single party political culture until the arrival of the CNU (West Cameroon enjoyed a measure of parliamentary democracy between 1954-1968). This factor in itself is capable of generating sufficient and powerful centrifugal forces to challenge, if not repeal, efforts at the national center to popularize the party at the mass level.

In summary, the data on political information suggest that a gap exists between the Cameroonian people and their national party. The gap, in this writer's opinion, reflects in part the structural and orientational deficiencies inherent in the CNU, and in part historical factors of which the party may have become an unwitting victim. Without reading too much into the data, it would appear that the impact of the CNU on the population has been limited, leaving open for debate the party's claims of having mobilized mass support for its goals and programs.

System Affect--

Attitudes Toward National Independence. In examining the first two dimensions of the identity subsystem of political culture, we were able to discern gaps between town/camp on the one hand and village on the other with respect to exposure to the communications media, level of political awareness, and content of political information on their national leaders. The system affect dimension is concerned with the feelings people have for their nation, its institutions, leaders, etc.

One of the items respondents were confronted with required them to select between a movie on how Cameroonians celebrated their tenth anniversary of independence from colonial rule and another depicting America's space explorations.[16] Although large majorities in the three localities chose to watch the movie on Cameroon, the distinction between town and countryside revealed in earlier analyses still lingers. Comparatively more town and camp respondents (81 per cent and 73 per cent respectively) than village respondents (65 per cent) opted for the movie of their country's independence celebration.

Table 5.7
Pride in Country: As a Cameroonian, What Things About This Country are you Most Proud of?*

	Community (percentages)		
	Village	Camp	Town
Political institutions & politics	3.9%	12.2%	16.8%
Political leadership	36.8	49.7	43.1
Economic development	13.2	29.7	18.8
People, heritage, culture	16.0	1.9	4.9
Nothing in particular	29.0	1.3	8.7
MD	1.3	5.2	7.5
Total	100.0%	100.0%	100.0%
N	(76)	(155)	(160)

$x^2 = 77.5989 \quad p = < .001$

*This was an open-ended item

National Attributes Which Evoke Pride--

Enlightened Leadership of President Ahidjo. Respondents were then asked an item aimed at discovering those attributes of the nation in which they took pride. The responses are displayed in Table 5.7. Two attributes, enlightened presidential leadership and the rapid pace of socio-economic development, need mention since they received the highest proportion of frequency scores for the entire sample. We find that all three localities rate their President very highly. Two points are germane here. The first is that the distribution of responses is somewhat influenced by locational difference. When we examine the proportion of respondents who perceive their pride in the Cameroon nation as influenced by the enlightened leadership of President Ahidjo, faint lines of cleavage appear separating localities. There are more camp respondents (50 per cent) than town (44 per cent) and village (36 per cent) who mentioned presidential leadership as a source of national pride. Secondly, the high regard respondents have for their president contrasts sharply with the low regard they have for his lieutenants (cabinet ministers especially). Apparently, Cameroonians do make a distinction between their president and the ministers who serve under him. They not only have little difficulty identifying him (as clearly expressed in the high proportion of respondents who mentioned his leadership as a factor generating high system pride) but are warmly and affectively oriented toward the person of Ahidjo.

Ahmadou Ahidjo: A Profile: The following are some of the adjectives that have been used to describe Cameroon's leader and de facto president-for-life: "wise," "ruthless," "pragmatic," "nondoctrinaire," "indispensable," "domineering," "fatherly," "shrewd," "modest," "simple," "francophile," "progressive," and so on. Whether he is any or all of these things, one fact emerges clearly, and it is that Ahidjo has, through a prudent mixture of moderate tactics and heavy-handed measures, succeeded in keeping his office and remaining in undisputed control of the country for over two decades; longer than any other African head of state. Born in 1924 at Garoua of Muslim parents

Ahmadou Ahidjo entered the colonial administration as a <u>commis</u> in the Posts and Telecommunications department in 1942 a year after finishing his secondary schooling. There he remained until his election to the Assembly of the French Union in June 1951 and to the Cameroun Territorial Assembly in March 1952.

As leader of the northern Young Muslim movement and the head of the Union Camerounaise group (which controlled 30 of the 67 seats in the French Cameroun Legislative Assembly) Ahidjo had no trouble getting appointed to the dual posts of Vice-Premier and Minister of Interior in the Mbida government. Following the collapse of this government, he became Premier in February 1958. With the support of the conservative northern-based Union Camerounaise, Ahidjo quickly acquired control over the state and in time succeeded in "reducing the other parties and their leaders to participation in minor roles either within the structure thus created or in opposition to it."[17] Ahidjo and his closest associates of this period, notably Moussa Yaya and Sadou Daoudu, the so-called "Northern Mafia," have remained in control of Cameroon politics ever since. Through the judicious combination of the carrot-and-stick approach, Ahidjo quickly neutralized political leaders in Francophone Cameroon and then moved in on their colleagues across the Mungo shortly after reunification. The techniques he employed are quite sophisticated and can be reduced in number to four. The first is cooptation of all political leaders of note. In the specific case of English-speaking Cameroon, this was formally achieved in 1966 when all political parties in the country were dissolved--not as voluntarily as party <u>griots</u> would have us believe--and replaced by a national party, the Cameroon National Union.[18] With the country as one huge patronage system at the disposal of the President, he spared no efforts in buying the silence of those co-opted Anglophone political leaders such as Endeley and Jua who initially opposed him or S.T. Muna and Egbe Tabi who were irresistably drawn towards him. As their reward, these politicians were appointed to the CNU national political bureau and/or to the ineffective, largely decorative National Assembly or given ministerial positions. But the use of co-optation as a technique for buying silence has not been restricted to politicians; even intellectuals have fallen victims to its seductive charms. Perhaps the most celebrated case is that of Professor Anomah Ngu, a surgeon of international repute who has now traded his scapel for the largely ceremonial vice-chancellorship of the University of Yaounde and with it a seat in the political bureau.

A second strategy adopted in aggrandizing power is that of forcing the retirement of erstwhile political allies like Foncha, Effiom and Elangwe who it is felt have outlived their usefulness to Ahidjo. These gentlemen are usually sent back to their villages on pensions generally considered one of the most generous in all of Africa. A good example is former Vice-President John Ngu Foncha, who with Ahidjo consummated the reunification struggle in 1961 but found himself unceremoniously and involuntarily dumped from the cabinet in 1970, coincidentally when the federation which he fought so hard to establish was being replaced by a unitary system. He retired to his palatial home in the village of Bafreng built with taxpayers' money where he lived in seclusion until his recent appointment as a Grand Chancellor of the Republic.[19] In the classic Stalinist policy of frequent purges of top leadership, especially those who are becoming too powerful, Ahidjo has managed to indulge in a game of musical chairs with his ministers and other top civil servants. These officials are rusticated from office--the phrase in Cameroon is "appélé à d'autres fonctions"--and sent into hibernation for a period of time and then without any warning rehabilitated and reinstated in government service. The most recent example is that of Mr. Nzo Ekangaki, once an <u>eminence grise</u> in Ahidjo's cabinet, later elected to the illustrious position of Administrative Secretary-General of the O.A.U., a position he was forced to resign from in disgrace in 1974.[20]

Upon his return to Cameroon, the expectation was that he would be given a top government position but this was not to be; so he tried his hand, with notable lack of success, in business. Banished from the corridors of power where he once strode like a Roman senator, Ekangaki retreated to his village in Nguti until 1979 when he was summoned back to Yaounde as a "<u>conseilleur</u> <u>technique</u>" (a position which in Cameroon means one gets paid for doing nothing) in the ministry of Territorial Administration. He was placed, ironically, under minister Ayissi Mbodo who was lured back to Cameroon from his job with the International Labor Organization by Ekangaki himself when he was Cameroon's Minister of Labor and Social Welfare. A final solution to recalcitrant politicians and dissidents is simply elimination. Many of the regime's critics have disappeared without any trace, others are in exile and still others are in the many jails that serve this purpose (there are an estimated 300 political prisoners in Cameroon today and many believe this is a very conservative figure).[21]

    The combination of these methods of control has helped in giving Cameroon one of the most stable and continuous regimes in post-colonial Africa. This stability has also led to the deification of Ahidjo and the enthronement of the myth of an indispensable leader, a kind of <u>deus ex machina</u> to whom all segments of the Cameroonian population, plebians and patricians alike, are beholden. The public view of Ahidjo as an omnipotent, omniscient, and all-loving President who is above the weaknesses that afflict ordinary mortals is widespread. Yet the public recognizes that he presides over an imperfect society where nepotism, injustice, economic inequality, official corruption and various socio-economic infirmities prevail. In trying to reconcile this apparent contradiction of a near-perfect secular pontiff reigning over an imperfect society, the public simply turns on his lieutenants. These officers become the target of their wrath and the scapegoat for the failure of policies and programs worked out by a collective leadership. That President Ahidjo, as the pre-eminent force behind this collective leadership, is ultimately responsible for the publis behavior of his ministers and must perforce share in the blame is a view that remains quite muted in Cameroon.

Socio-Economic Development. The second response category that received relatively high frequency scores was socio-economic development. What is interesting here is that the proportion of respondents who selected this attribute fairly corresponds to those who mentioned national accomplishments in the areas of socio-economic development as one of the salutary effects of governmental policies and programs.

Strength of Attachment to Fatherland. Finally, respondents were asked whether they would like to swap their Cameroonian nationality for that of another country. On the whole, large proportions of respondents in all three community groups indicate a willingness physically to desert the fatherland (46 per cent village, 47.1 per cent camp, and 55 per cent town). Lest the overall results be hastily interpreted as a sign of low system effect, let it be emphasized that responses

Table 5.8
System Affect as Evidenced by Willingness to Change Nationality

Choice Expressed	Community (percentages)		
	Rural Village	Plantation Camp	Town
Change Nationality	46.0%	47.1%	54.5%
Not Change	32.9	18.7	28.1
N.A.	17.1	34.2	17.5
Total	100.0%	100.0%	100.0%
N	76	155	160

$x^2 = 36.715 \quad p = < .001$

to a follow-up item which asked why respondents wanted to change nationalities seem to indicate an urge for adventurism and not an expression of dissatisfaction with the Cameroon nation. A fairly high proportion of respondents who expressed the desire to switch nationalities indicated a preference for those countries that were considered: "as peaceful as Cameroon"; "politically stable as Cameroon"; "Religious and God-fearing as Cameroon"; etc. In short, the desire to change nationalities was only entertained as long as it was believed that the country where refuge was being sought was in many ways similar to Cameroon. Cameroonians apparently would change their nationality so long as the "pain" of desertion was soothed by the belief that the new country was just like the old one.

The evidence indicates that geographical location does not produce significant variations in this one aspect of citizens' behavioral attachment to the nation. (A cross-tabulation yielded a Chi-square of 36.715 with 14 degrees of freedom which was not significant at the .01 level of significance). As such the null hypothesis was not borne out. Cameroonians, regardless of locality, generally have a high level of national pride.

Sense of Community Identity

Attention now will be directed to discovering how widespread the diffusion of this identity value is among respondents. On the strength of the factor analysis results,[22] sense of community identity will be examined along three dimensions: (1) degree of neighborliness; (2) degree of friendliness; and (3) attitudes toward cross-ethnic marriage.

i. Degree of neighborliness--Did respondents have many friends in the neighborhood in which they resided? Were visits ever exchanged between persons living in the same neighborhood and with what degree of frequency? The responses to these questions provided the material for measuring the "neighborliness" dimension of community identity. It was found to be very high in the total sample. Close to 90 per cent of the sampled population had many friends in the neighborhood where they lived. Of this proportion, only 11 per cent later said they never exchanged social visits. Thus, the overwhelming majority of respondents visited each other's homes with varying degrees of frequency.

When geographic location was controlled, it was found that degree of neighborliness was comparatively higher among plantation camp and town respondents than for village respondents.

ii. <u>Degree of friendliness</u>--This dimension of the identity subsystem involves the ease or difficulty respondents experienced in establishing friendship networks with non-ethnics. Secondly, it aims to discover the composition of respondents' friendship networks; whether recruitment and participation are solely determined on the basis of cultural similarity or other non-particularistic criteria. The data show that over two-thirds of the sampled population experienced no problems establishing friendly ties with non-ethnic people. About the same proportion of respondents also indicated that their close friends were drawn from persons who belonged to different ethnic groups.

Although the majority of respondents could be classified as friendly, this attribute varies to some extent with geographic location. As expected, more persons from ethnically heterogeneous communities (camps and towns) than from ethnically homogeneous rural villages, have no apparent difficulty establishing friendship <u>contacts</u> across ethnic boundaries. The same is true for composition of friendship network; more people from the village subsample than from the camp and town subsamples appear to have developed strong friendship bonds which exclude persons from other ethnic groups. Sixty-four per cent of the village respondents admit to having their close friends from

Table 5.9
R Factor Analysis: Rotated Factora Matrix Showing Factor Loadings on Dimensions of Inter-Group Contact

Items	Factor Ib	Factor IIc	Factor IIId	Factor IVe
Speak any indigenous language	.00388	.00140	.04970	.51630
Recognize anybody from neighborhood	.13491	.00233	.13749	.00570
Have friends in neighborhood	.59627	.09845	.14228	.06493
Ever visit with them	.61604	.00564	.01072	.01552
How often are these visits	.56104	.04203	.18019	.06498
Have difficulty making friends with non-ethnics	.14220	.04798	.55885	.14121
Close friends come from which ethnic group	.28036	.00583	.51746	.07996
Language spoken with fellow ethnic	.03664	.02798	.29605	.45278
Reaction to cross-ethnic marriage	.01405	.12040	.18246	.09063
Any preference for ethnic group	.04304	.71066	.01899	.11195
Any particular reason	.06732	.66599	.03921	.12332

aFactor I accounts for 43 per cent of the total variance, Factors II and III for 46 per cent and Factor IV 10.3 per cent.
bChildren in Family Decision-making Factor.
cImages of Parental Authority Factor.
dTypology of Family Decision-making Factor.
eTypology of Ethnic Group Decision-making Factor.

among co-ethnics while only 31 per cent of the camp respondents and 34 per cent for the town subsample share this trait--a spread of almost 30 percentage points separates town from countryside. The division parallels that which emerged in the analysis of data on neighborliness.

It is easy to see why camp and town residents appear to be more neighborly and to participate in a more varied and heterogeneous friendship network than village folk. One of the definitive characteristics of camps and towns is their heterogeneous population as opposed to ethnically homogeneous rural villages. Plantation camps and towns within Cameroon serve as magnets attracting all kinds of peoples from all over the country. These people flock into these areas for a variety of reasons-- greater educational and employment opportunities, adventure, escape from the constraints of traditional life, etc. From a purely statistical standpoint, a person living in a multiethnic urban context has a greater probability of coming into frequent contact with individuals from other ethnic groups than an isolated villager, and is therefore, most likely to participate in a wider variety of overlapping activities. Such opportunities do not exist in rural villages, and even when they do, they exist on a much lower scale. The data confirm the hypothesis that persons from ethnically homogeneous rural villages will have more difficulty establishing friendship ties with non-ethnics than those persons from camps and towns. (A cross-tabulation of location by ability to make friends with non-ethnics produced a raw chi-square of 13.389 with 8 degrees of freedom at .0991 significant level. This sustains the theoretical hypothesis that location affects cross-ethnic social relationships.)

The data also confirm the hypothesis that the actual composition of respondents' friendship group would be significantly affected by community differences, such that comparatively more camp and town respondents than village ones will have a singularly heterogeneous friendship network. So it was found, for instance, that in the village subsample 64 per cent of the respondents draw their close friends from co-ethnics. About the same proportion had difficulty making friends with persons from other ethnic groups. As expected, majorities in camp (65 per cent) and town (63 per cent) had most of their close friends from different ethnic groups.

On the whole this writer's observations draw strong support from previous studies of camp attitudes which find a high sense of community identity among workers that transcends local ethnic particularisms.[23] The most recent study by DeLancey among camp residents found on the basis of quantitative analyses that the more heterogeneous the labor camp and labor force the more diversified the sociometric patterns; i.e., a pattern of friendship networks that cuts across ethnic differences. He cites as reasons for this high level of community consciousness among plantation camp workers: (1) the fact that there are no totally exclusive neighborhoods, professions, or work places which would reinforce ethnic differences; (2) a marked preference by workers themselves for ethnically mixed living and work arrangements; (3) both (1) and (2) are supported by a deliberate policy of the employer to ignore ethnic background in job, housing, and other assignments; and (4) the fact that institutions provided by the employer--schools, clubs, sports teams, community hall activities--are generally multiethnic as are other facilities not provided by the employer but serving the entire camp, like the churches. Thus, the structural and institutional organization of camp society, reinforced by a willing disposition on the workers' part to ignore ethnic differences has led to the cementing of interethnic bonds and high level of community identity among camp workers.

iii. <u>Propensity for cross-ethnic marriage</u>--In ethnically plural societies, a good test for feelings of community identity is the extent to which members will tolerate cultural differences.

One practical way to examine this is to turn to marriage patterns in order to find out whether they are strictly endogamous or exogamous. The intensity of inter-ethnic antagonism can be expressed very sharply in the willingness or reluctance of members to participate in exogamous marital relations. Where there is a willingness, a sense of shared community identity can be inferred; but where there is a general preference for endogamy, one can conclude that feelings of community identification are absent or weak at best.

The data reveal that a substantial majority of respondents are neutral on the question of marriage across ethnic lines. On one extreme, only 12 per cent of the respondents clearly stated a preference for a non-ethnic marriage partner; while on the other, 33 per cent--a fairly high proportion--of the respondents were inclined toward endogamy. In between these were a plurality of respondents, 41 per cent of whom expressed no particular preference as to which ethnic group a marriage partner should come from.

When respondents' place of residence was taken into consideration, the data confirmed the broad patterns that have already been sketched. Within each of the three communities, the majority of respondents have no fixed preference for any ethnic group as the pool from which potential in-laws can be drawn. Fifty per cent of the camp respondents said any ethnic group was good enough, while 35 per cent of the village and town fell in the neutral zone (i.e., did not care one way or the other). Across localities, more town and village respondents (37 per cent and 34 per cent respectively) than camp respondents (27 per cent) favor endogamy. Interestingly enough, of the three localities, comparatively more of the village respondents (20 per cent) than camp (12 per cent) and town (9 per cent) respondents come out clearly in favor of cross-ethnic marriages.

The data fail to confirm the null hypothesis (raw chi-square of 16.453 with 6 degrees of freedom at .0115 significance level) of no significant relationship between place of residence and attitudes toward inter-ethnic marriages.

The data show that the sense of community identity is widespread among the anglophone Cameroon population, though it varies in intensity and geographic location. Cameroonians, it would appear, are generally friendly and outgoing. Although the majority participate in broad-based friendship networks that cut across ethnic group boundaries, there is still some hesitation to expand these networks to accept cross-ethnic marriages.

This finding sustains the conjecture that inter-group behavior is conditioned in a well-defined field of communication which is circumscribed by what one may call "permissible sectors of interaction" among ethnic groups. Such interactions are charactrized by an approach-avoidance pattern. Although members in the broad political community do establish contact based on common functional interests and associational ties, such contracts only result in interactions that operate along narrowly defined limits (e.g., friendship networks). This is so, I believe, because of powerful internal ethnocentric forces within the respective ethnic populations that constitute the political community which prevent friendship contacts from spilling over into another realm. The absence of cross-ethnic marriages does not <u>prima facie</u> indicate intense inter-group antagonism. If anything it probably reflects people's fear that such relations may seriously compromise ethnic individuality. Since a strong advocacy for exogamy is tantamount to a call for cultural suicide, a low incidence of exogamy could be interpreted as a positive sign of ethnic pride and not ethnocentrism as such.

Finally, the data also reveal that broadly speaking, people from ethnically heterogenous communities (camps and towns) have a higher level of community identity than their counterparts in the ethnically homogeneous rural villages. This distinction holds only with regard to two dimensions--degree of neighborliness and friendship. That is to say, camp and town residents tend to have a high degree of neighborliness and experience no difficulty making friends from among nonethnics. The opposite holds for rural village folk, who, interestingly enough, come out more in favor of exogamy than those persons resident in the two multiethnic communities.

The Symbol System

Many people identify with the nation through various symbols. We asked our respondents what meaning they attached to such national symbols as the anthem and flag. Since this was an open-ended item, the responses were broken down into four broad categories: (1) political meaning; (2) historical interpretations; (3) aesthetic reactions; and (4) no reactions at all. Beginning with the last category and moving up the list (see Table 5.10), more village respondents than those from town and camp attached no meaning to the Cameroon flag and anthem. A microscopic minority of respondents from both the camp and town subsamples gave to the flag and anthem an aesthetic interpretation; they enjoyed listening to the music of the anthem and/or liked the colors of the national flag. Majorities in both village and town (59 per cent and 39 per cent respondents respectively) explained that the flag and anthem reminded them of colonial rule. The responses grouped under the category of "political" were both positive and negative. The negative view of the flag and anthem saw these as harsh reminders of the denial of fundamental human rights in Cameroon. Only a very, very small proportion of respondents in the village (1.3 per cent) and town (.6 per cent) while nobody from the camp subsample mentioned this attribute. However, for the majority of respondents regardless of community, the flag and anthem evoked

Table 5.10
Symbol Subsystem: Meaning Attached to National Flag and Anthem, by Location

Meaning	Community (percentages)		
	Rural Village	Camp	Town
Reunification and National Unity	1.3	8.4	4.3
Freedom from Colonial Rule	10.7	30.3	29.8
Enlightened Presidential Leadership	1.3	11.0	6.2
Denial of Civil Rights	1.3	0.0	.6
Aesthetic Reasons	0.0	.6	.6
Reminder of Colonial Domination	58.7	23.9	38.5
It has no meaning	17.3	.6	6.2
Other	6.7	12.2	8.1
N.A.	2.7	12.9	11.8
Total	100.0%	100.0%	100.0%
N	76	155	160

$$x^2 = 30.18762 \quad p = < .0001$$

positive feelings. They symbolized for many national unity, freedom from colonial domination, and the enlightened leadership of President Ahidjo. In all these three attributes, the proportion of respondents who mentioned them was higher for the camp subsample than for the other two.

Our finding is that the acceptance of the flag and anthem as symbols of the Cameroon nation is widespread. Close to 80 per cent of respondents in the sampled universe are positively oriented toward these national symbols. Attachment to these valued artifacts of the nation was equally strong among residents of the three localities. This in our view appears to be very strong support for the symbol system of political culture in Cameroon--indeed it approaches unanimity. The high positive support found here tends to reject the hypothesis of no significant difference between localities over this particular political culture value.

Summary

Tests of independence have shown that on certain political culture dimensions locational differences are associated with contrasts in national political orientations. This was very much in evidence in the examination of the identity system which among other things was reflected in measuring how informed and critical Cameroonians are of their political system. Although all three localities reported very low scores on the political knowledge dimension, camp and town residents nonetheless were found to be generally better informed, more interested and more critical spectators of their political system than village respondents. Secondly, all three localities manifested a high sense of system pride. Respondents' sense of their "Cameroonianness" was not found to be latent or marginal but overt and long internalized. Many attributed their pride for the Cameroon nation to the President, Ahmadou Ahidjo, as the symbol of national identity and unity. However, this close and intimate identification with the Cameroon President contrasts sharply with the low degree of familiarity the population has of his cabinet ministers. On the whole citizens' behavioral attachment to the Cameroon nation was not strongly affected by locational contrasts. The data show that a sense of community identity varies with geographic location. Residents from the three localities had a tendency to participate in broadly based friendship networks that cut across ethnic group boundaries though many were reluctant to expand these networks to include cross ethnic marriages. Using extra-ethnic patterns of interactions as indicators of feeling of identification among members of a political community, the data strongly support the position that camp and town groups have a proportionately higher level of community identification than rural village people.

This is a very significant finding for it suggests that urbanization is not altogether a bad thing, as many critics have argued over the years. It has been customary to view urbanization as a phenomenon that has had a profound dislocative impact on traditional African values and institutions. Sifting through some of the literature, one is left with the impression that although these writers are in agreement that urbanization is clearly one very important dimension of that complex of irreversible transformations African societies are undergoing, they are not prepared to look beyond those problems that are, by definition, built into the urbanization process (i.e., urban unemployment, congestion, crimes, inadequate sanitation, anomic violence, etc.), in order to see some of its beneficial aspects. The data, in revealing the other side of urbanization, underscores its inherent functional role in nation-building. What the evidence suggests is that urbanism can actually help in minimizing or defusing inter-ethnic conflict (a major problem in polyethnic socieites.)[24]

Whether it is the controlled urbanization of plantation camps or the laissez-faire type characteristic of towns, the process has resulted in the bringing together of people from diverse cultural backgrounds under a common umbrella. People so pushed together by force of circumstance tend to relate to each other more on the basis of functional needs and shared interests and less on ascriptive considerations. It is through such cross-cultural interactions that people begin to develop a sense of respect for each other and become more sensitive to cultural differences. Within such situations of culture contact stereotypes are steadily replaced by knowledge. In this regard, urbanization serves the important function of broadening the scope and framework for inter-ethnic contact and interaction. It provides the basic material from which a genuine sense of national community identity can grow. From this standpoint, it is desirable and functional in the nation-building process.

That rural residents expressed such low feelings of community identity seems to suggest that people cannot remain captive in their homogeneous ethnic capsules, isolated from the other members of the national society, and still be expected to develop strong bonds of community attachments. Thus, the more isolated people are, the lower their chances for interacting with other people not from their immediate vicinity and ultimately the lower their sense of national community identity.

But the weak sense of community identity exhibited by rural people also alerts us to the fact that if change in the underlying political cultural configuration of the Cameroon nation is to take place then rural attitudes must be radically transformed. This would mean extending to the countryside those facilities that have proved helpful in raising the level of community identification among urban residents.

While many planners may deplore the large scale migration of people from rural communities (since this inevitably leads to an overload of demands on the limited facilities in the urban centers) caution must be exercised in advocating a reversal of this trend. Coercive measures aimed at arresting the flow of rural migration to cities may ease urban congestion but will not solve the underlying problem; namely, what is it that attracts people to labor camps and large towns? After all, it is in these communities that government has historically concentrated all its best efforts. When you say town or city, you immediately conjure up images of medical and public health facilities, schools, pipe-borne water, electricity, paved roads, etc., and of course greater opportunities for entry into the working force. Caught in the "revolution of rising expectations," everybody, rural and urban alike, wants a share of the national benefits. This gives rise to a tendency to evaluate the government in very instrumental terms; what does it, or can it do, for me? It is, therefore, to be expected that town residents should manifest a more favorable disposition toward the nation than their deprived rural compatriots.

Footnotes

1. Almond and Verba, The Civic Culture, op. cit., p. 13.
2. Donald J. Devine, The Political Culture of the United States: The Influence of Member Values on Regime Maintenance. Boston: Little, Brown and Company, 1972.
3. Ibid., p. 16.
4. Third Five Year Economic and Social Development Plan, 1971-1976. Yaounde: Ministry of Planning and Territorial Development, 1971, p. 39.
5. See "Communication by H. E. El Hadj Ahmadou Ahidjo, Yaounde, 11 August 1971" in Third Five Year Plan, pp. v-xvi.
6. Third Five Year Plan, p. 80 ff.
7. Wilfred A. Ndongko, "The Political Economy of Regional Economic Development in Cameroon," in Ndiva Kofele-Kale, ed., An African Experiment in Nation-Building, op. cit., pp. 227-250.
8. Donald T. Campbell & J. C. Stanley, Experimental and Quasi-Experimental Designs for Research. Chicago: Rand McNally and Company, 1966.
9. The phenomenon described here may not necessarily be alienation but what Nelson Kasfir calls "departicipation"--the end product of a process by which popular input is minimized. I am indebted to Professor Victor T. Le Vine for bringing this point to my attention. The reader should however consult Kasfir's The Shrinking Political Arena: Participation and Ethnicity in African Politics with a Case Study of Uganda. Berkeley, California: University of California Press, 1976.
10. The low information level, as Professor Le Vine, in a personal memo, suggests, could also be attributed to several other possible reasons, many of which touch on the weaknesses inherent in survey research methodology. The instrument, for instance, may have been suffering from the problem of validity in the sense that: (a) the questions asked were not the right ones; (b) respondents preferred not to answer, or when they did respond, to respond truthfully; and/or (c) respondents just did not give a damn. I am willing

to dismiss the question of low validity on the grounds that the errors generated could at the very best be considered random with built-in allowances for self-cancellation. At the worst, if respondents failed to reply truthfully on this item, then it is equally possible that they did the same on the other items. However, this remains an empirical question to be resolved through replication of this study.

A more persuasive rival explanation for the low information level may have to do with the possibility that respondents had other ideas about what (or who) was politically relevant. That is, my choice of politically relevant actors in Cameroon was not consistent with the public's. Had I asked them to identify, for example, the local prêfet or sous-prêfet, the local traditional chief, or former high officials (like Jua, Foncha, Kemcha, etc.) they would have done much better. Although this may well have been the case, I a still unpersuaded for two reasons. First, many of these former officials are still playing an active role in the CNU both at the local and national levels. Second, the close ties between government and party usually means that in all party functions, rallies, etc., the government is represented by its prêfets or sous-prêfets. Thus, Cameroonians who conscientiously participate in these rallies should not only be able to recognize important government officials but also party commissars. That they were unable to identify the latter indicates not so much differences in perception on who are the relevant political actors rather the indifference of the Cameroonians masses toward the C.N.U.

11. What follows ignores a certain amount of official party lines. It is my view, not always that of the C.N.U. leadership, of the reality.

12. Neville Rubin, Cameroun: An African Federation. London: Pall Mall Publications, 1970, p. 153.

13. Aristide Zolberg, Creating Political Order. Chicago: University of Chicago Press, 1966; and Henry Bienen, Tanzania: Party Transformation

and Economic Development. Princeton, N.J.: Princeton University Press, 1970.

14. Seventy-five per cent of the members of the 1973-78 Cameroon National Assembly were former deputies in either the now defunct state legislative assemblies or the Federal House in Yaounde. Fifteen of the deputies (out of a total of 24) representing the two English-speaking provinces owe their parliamentary seats to their long period of association with the KNDP, CPNC, and CUC--the three political parties from former West Cameroon that joined Ahidjo's ruling Union Camerounaise in East Cameroon to form the Cameroon National Union in 1966. Three English-speaking members of President Ahidjo's cabinet (as of May, 1975) also owe their positions to their former ties with the dissolved political parties from West Cameroon. It would be difficult to escape the conclusion that the CNU is a patron/elite party which has, to some extent, united and continues to reward that faction of the country's leadership that was favorably disposed toward the idea of unification.

15. It is so easy to conclude that because nothing ever seems to happen in a country everything must be in order. In acknowledging that Cameroonians have maintained one government in office for two decades is not to suggest that all is fine, the people are happy and satisfied and therefore see no need nor have any desire for change. This blanket of deceptive calmness that appears to shroud the authoritarian countries of the Third World was only recently lifted in Iran; and in the process, exploding once again the political myth that machine guns, torture chambers and secret police remain the best antidotes for combatting the revolution of rising expectations being waged by the masses. Only time will tell whether or not the price Cameroonians have paid for the country's remarkable degree of stability and leadership continuity far outweighs the benefits.

16. The purpose of the question was to pose respondents a difficult choice in order to test their attachment to the Cameroon nation. The

widespread interest in America's space explorations evidenced by the large number of Cameroonians who went to exhibitions of Apollo 13 at various U.S. consular centers demonstrates that the American documentary offered an attractive alternative to the movie on the 10th anniversary of Cameroon's independence.

17. Rubin, op. cit., p.

18. Others like the ex-seminarian-turned-politician, Dr. Bernard Fonlon of the University of Yaounde, lost his ministerial appointment but was allowed to keep the official residence. As an apologist for the current regime, Fonlon has no equal among Cameroonian intellectuals.

19. See, for instance, Parliament in Cameroon: Past and Present (1946-1971) a highly propagandistic and pedestrian piece put out by the government. It is more an encomium on Ahidjo than an objective history of party politics in Cameroon.

20. See my "Crisis in African Leadership: O.A.U.'s Secretary-General and the Lonrho Agreements," Pan-Africanist (Northwestern University Program of African Studies), No. 5 (September 1974), pp. 12-25 for a discussion of the events which led to Ekangaki's resignation from the O.A.U.

21. "Ahidjo Holds Tight the Rein," Special Correspondent, Africa, No. 77 (January 1978), pp. 52-55. See also, U.S. State Department, Country reports on Human Rights Practices for 1979. Washington, D.C.: Government Printing Office, 1980, pp. 28-33.

22. Eleven items were included in the survey instrument for measuring sense of national community. These were later submitted to a factor analysis from which three clusters of factors with loadings of .50 and above were extracted. On the basis of the factor analysis, three levels of community were discerned: (1) degree of neighborliness--the willingness on members' part to maintain good neighborly relations with persons who live in the same neighborhood irrespective of their ethnic or regional origin; (2) propensity for inter-ethnic marriage; and (3) degree of friendliness--represents members' willingness to establish

friendship networks across ethnic lines. See Table 3.8.

23. See Edwin Ardener, "Social and Demographic Problems of the Southern Cameroons Plantation Area," in Aidan Southall, ed., Social Change in Modern Africa. London: Oxford University Press, 1961; and Mark W. DeLancy, "Changes in Social Attitudes and Political Knowledge Among Migrants to Plantations in West Cameroon," unpublished Ph.D. dissertation, Indiana University, 1973.

24. There is some evidence to contradict this position. Some scholars take the view that ethnic ties and identities do get reinforced in towns (rather than disappearing). Hanna and Hanna are of the opinion that "most residents (in towns) are to some extent 'encapsulated' within their own network which serves as a barrier between them and the wider urban social system. Striking cultural differences among many groups further hamper the development of an interethnic sense of community." Hanna and Hanna, op. cit., p. 106. For the same argument, see also Jean Rouch, "Second Generation Migrants in Ghana and Ivory Coast," in A. Southall, (ed.), Social Change in Modern Africa, London: Oxford University Press, 1961, pp. 300-304; Paul Mercier, "Remarques sue la signification du 'tribalisme' actuel en Afrique noire," Cahiers Internationaux de Sociologie, 31 (1961), pp. 61-80; and Hilda Kuper (ed.), Urbanization and Migration in West Africa. Berkeley, California: University of California Press, 1965, pp. 1-22.

6
Environment and Commitment to National Beliefs and Rules

The preceding chapter explored the cohesiveness within the Cameroon nation as expressed in members' sense of common identity as well as commitment to those salient political artifacts and myths that symbolize the Cameroon nation. This chapter will be an examination of the impact of environmental change on mass attachment to regime beliefs and rules. These last two are conceived to be more directly related to the values of a specific regime (e.g., the Foncha government, the Ahidjo regime, and so on) than the identity and symbol systems which are properly concerned with the concept of a Cameroon nation as an idea which transcends particular regimes or administrations. Because this notion of the nation as an idea is not bound by time it is often employed as a measure of popular feelings toward the political system in the broadest sense of the term. The belief and rule systems are anchored in time and place, and in this specific instance serve as a measure of how Cameroonians feel toward a particular administration, Ahidjo's.

The Rule System

On the importance of the rule system in a polity, David Easton contends that:

> Unless there is a minimum convergence of attitudes in support of these fundamental rules--the constitutional principles, as we call them in Western society--there would be insufficient harmony in the actions of the members of a system to meet the problems generated by their support of a political community. The fact of trying to settle demands in common means that there must be known principles governing the way in

which resolutions of differences of
claims are to take place.1

My own investigation of the relationship between
environment and the rule system is conceived in
the Eastonian framework. But the focus here is
not on public support of specific constitutional
principles which form the basis of the Cameroon
polity. Since public discussion of the legitimacy
of Cameroon's governmental system is hardly encouraged, any attempt to measure the level of mass
support for the nation's fundamental constitutional principles had to be carried out indirectly.
So, to avoid stirring up the government, Cameroonians were instead asked to indicate their preferences from a selection of ideal prototypes of
decision-making and conflict resolution in a polity. This exercise was aimed at discovering those
preferences which appeared to command widespread
support among the governed, and to see how close
or far removed mass preferences are from what may
reasonably be expected to constitute the regime's
view with respect to the "rules of the game."

Two types of "rules of the game" were identified: (1) those rules which determine the conditions under which authoritative decisions are
to be made; and (2) the principles and institutions through which inter-personal conflicts are
resolved in a political community.

1. **Decision-Making Preferences:**

To derive a measure of Cameroonian preference of decision-making models, respondents
were asked to react to this hypothetical i-
tem:2

When a community has to make arrangement to build a road, there are
three possible ways they can arrange
things like location, and who is going to do the work. They can leave
the decision to be made by the older
or recognized leaders in the community; or instead of only a few

important families deciding, everybody in the community will be involved in the decision-making process until a decision agreeable to almost everyone is arrived; or the whole community can be summoned to a meeting, and everybody asked to vote. A decision will be arrived at based on what the majority of the people in the community agree upon. Which way of deciding do you think is usually best in such cases?

The responses were classified into three decision-making prototypes: elitist, where decisions are made by a few; consensual model in which decisions reflect the view of almost everyone in the group; and majoritarian where decisions taken are based on the will of the majority.

Of the three modes for authoritative allocation of decisions presented to respondents, the consensual approach was the least favored across localities. Support for decision-making by the majoritarian method was high in all three localities, with about one half of the village and town subsample electing this over the other two modes. The elitist position that decision-making should be left to the wisdom of elders was the third option. Camp respondents were about evenly split between this mode and the majoritarian model, while fewer village and town residents selected the elitist method, with village residents scoring it lowest. This finding is intriguing, to say the least. Why do more camp and town residents than village folk state a preference for the elitist method for decision-making? The explanation advanced here is that the relatively low village score on this dimension was undoubtedly influenced by the fact that the entire village subsample was drawn from the two segmentary ethnic groups. Conversely, the camp and town subsamples were influenced by the high contribution from the centralized groups. So the results for the village only reflect the traditional repugnance of persons from segmentary groups for oligarchical rule. Additional evidence to support this explanation can be derived from a comparison of the scores of respondents from the two different ethnic systems. The data show that only 35 per cent of the segmentary respondents, in contrast to 46 per cent for the centralized group, support the elitist mode of decision-making. Only 24 per cent of the segmentary respondents residing in the countryside indicated a preference for this mode. This is the same proportion of respondents in the village subsample (disregarding ethnic differences) that selected the elitist method for solving group decisions.

One can also account for the strong preference among camp respondents for the elitist model as a factor of sampling bias, since over 50 per cent of respondents for this subsample belong to centralized groups, where hierarchical methods for decision-making are common. What all this amounts to is that ethnic system differences, rather than situational variation, accounts for the type of decisional model preferred by respondents. However, when location is examined and the two ethnic systems are subjected to a within-system analysis, a pattern emerges which unmistakably reveals that variations in decisional preferences are related somewhat to respondents' objective location in space. More importantly, the camp situation *seems* to affect preferences within both systems in the direction of the elitist model of decision-making. The available evidence indicates that within each of the ethnic systems a higher proportion of those resident in camps prefer the elitist model of decision-making. Among the segmentary population about 36 per cent of the respondents prefer this approach, while for the centralized group 52 per cent (a clear majority) of the respondents are inclined toward a method of decision-making which leaves all the important decisions to be made by an oligarchy. Although relatively more segmentary respondents reject the elitist model in favor of the other two, yet the over 30 per cent who selected it is surprisingly high for people who traditionally resent this approach to government.

A crosstabulation of the ethnic systems with the decision-making variable controlling for environmental difference yielded raw chi-squares of 5.595 at the .4700 level of significance for the segmentary system; and 10.016 significance level of .1239 (both with 6 degrees of freedom). Overall, a cross tabulation of the combined ethnic populations controlling for location resulted in a raw X^2 of 11.508 with 6 degrees of freedom at the .0739 level of significance. However, in all three cases, the null hypothesis was not significant at the .01 level of significance and was rejected.

2. Conflict Resolution:

The second aspect of the rule system dealing with conflict resolution was measured by this item:

> Two men have a dispute over the title to a piece of land. They take the case over to the council of tribal elders for arbitration. One of the disputants, however, is very disappointed with the council's decision and so decides to seek redress somewhere else. Suppose this man approaches you for advice, what would you suggest he should do?

The responses to this item were grouped into two categories: modern-judicial, and customary institutions.

The data show wide support for the modern-judicial approach. Preference for this method, which includs such institutions as the law courts, the police, and the gendarmerie, is the first clear indication of a convergence between system member preferences and regime rules on an important political value. Forty-nine per cent of the respondents expressed a preference for conflict to be resolved within those institutions designated by the regime for that specific purpose. On the other hand, less than 40 per cent stuck to the customary law mode for solving inter-personal conflicts, i.e., judicial process operating within the ethnic groups based on customary laws. For example, among the hierarchical Grasslanders, this would mean the resolution of conflict through the Fon or those institutions designated by him to carry out such functions; while for the acephalous system, conflict resolution is traditionally handled within village councils composed of elders.

Although support for the modern-judicial mode of conflict resolution is found among one half of the Cameroonians interviewed, variations surface when environmental difference is taken into consideration. As Table 6.1 shows, more village and town respondents have high support for the modern-judicial system for the settlement of conflict. But this is not the case for camp respondents, who modally--48 per cent--preferred the traditional customary mode for conflict resolution. On the whole, the data indicate a high level of public confidence in the country's legal institutions, modern European as well as indigenous African.

The Belief System

The last of the political culture dimensions to command attention is the belief system. As used by Easton and Devine, the belief system refers to moral values or guides. It represents the central affective goal toward which political actions <u>ought</u> to be directed. The key word here is "ought" indicating that the belief system is rooted in normative concerns as opposed to descriptive or purely experiential issues. Placed in its proper context, the belief system expresses members' consensus as to what goals a good government <u>should</u> be pursuing. It is a position held irrespective of what the regime is <u>doing</u> or <u>can</u> do. This, of course, is not to imply that what a good government should do is necessarily at variance with what it does or can do.[3]

Table 6.1
Choice of Decision-Making Models by Location

Model	Rural Village	Plantation Camp	Town
Elitist	25.0%	44.5%	33.7%
Consensual	15.8	7.1	13.1
Majoritarian	53.9	45.2	49.4
N.A.	5.3	3.2	3.7
Total	100.0%	100.0%	100.0%
N	76	155	160

$x^2 = 11.508 \quad P = <.01$

This section will deal with three goals toward which political actions should be directed in society. The goals are: <u>social welfare</u>, <u>national unity</u>, and a <u>moral society</u>. Although these goals were arbitrarily selected, this in no way reduces their importance as positive values toward

Table 6.2
Choice of Conflict Resolution Models by Location

Model	Rural Village	Plantation Camp	Town
Modern-Judicial	63.2%	38.7%	51.9%
Customary	31.6	47.7	29.4
No Opinion	5.3	13.5	18.8
Total	100.0%	100.0%	100.0%
N	76	155	160

$$x^2 = 21.392 \quad P = <.001$$

deciding which governmental action should be mobilized. Above all, they represent some of the central goals of the Cameroon polity--goals which the ruling elite has defined and requested the co-operation of the populace in working toward.

(i) <u>Social Welfare</u>--The goal of social welfare is a government whose programs and policies are directed toward providing more aid for the poor, the sick, and the old. This definition of political action is influenced largely by Christian Bay's view of politics as existing "for the purpose of progressively removing the most stultifying obstacles to a free human development, with priority for the worst obstacles, whether they hit many or few--in other words, with priority for those individuals who are most severely oppressed."[4] All governments attempt to resolve those substantive problems involving the basic needs and conscious wants of their citizens. Going beyond this, some governments are interested in sustaining a stratified system in which the gap separating the wealthy from the poor is kept as wide as possible. Other governments which are committed to the proposition that a just society is one where social, political, and economic rewards are equitably distributed among citizens. Rather than permitting a wide gulf to divide its citizens, such governments direct all their energies toward closing the gap between the "haves" and "have-nots." This is what is understood here as a good government. Consequently, respondents were asked whether a good government should give high priority to the needs and wants of its most oppressed citizens--the aged, indigent, and infirm.

The data show that commitment to the social welfare goal seems relatively widely shared by Cameroonians. Fifty-five per cent of the respondents questioned agreed (strongly or somewhat) that every good government should set as one of its goals the social and economic advancement of its most deprived members. Only 36 per cent of the respondents disagreed with this proposition. Even when one adds to this figure the 9 per cent who were undecided, the total (of those who disagreed) still falls short of 50 per cent, which does not challenge the conclusion that the social welfare goal appeals to most Cameroonians.

Support for the social welfare goal varies, however, with environmental location of respondents. Substantial majorities of both village and town respondents (57 per cent and 64 per cent respectively) in contrast to 43 per cent of the camp respondents, emphasize a social welfare society as a desirable political goal. Could this mean that village and town residents experience more poverty than camp people? This is not necessarily the case and as I have already indicated in preceding chapters it is the town and camp residents who have received a disproportionate share of national goods and services. And on the issue of social welfare services, the C.D.C. has for years provided its workers and their dependents with a wide range of social benefits-- education at all levels, medical care, housing, generous retirement benefits, and so on--at little or no cost to the recipients. It is quite plausible that camp society has come to take these services for granted, which would explain the low priority accorded to the social welfare goal by camp residents.

(ii) National Unity--The pursuit of national unity ranks as one of the principal objectives on the agendas of political leaders in the emergent African states. And in Cameroon where the socio-historical landscape is gutted by political, regional, economic, and ethnic problems as well as divergent colonial experiences, this pursuit of national unity is undertaken with a sense of urgency. The theme of national unity occupies choice space in the speeches and political writings of Cameroon's leaders, most notably the President, Ahmadou Ahidjo. A sample of Ahidjo's speeches reveals a commitment to the politically desirable goal of national unity.

In Nation and Development, Ahidjo writes:

> Firstly, the State which from now on is extending the network of its administration and its communication over the whole territory is transcending regional peculiarities and manifesting in a lively and permanent fashion the unity of the community. Secondly, economic unification which is linking more and more closely together the different regions in a network of trade relationships which reinforce their solidarity all the more. Lastly, the Party which appears as a privileged framework in which is worked out the will of the community to continue in solidarity and to collectively pursue the realization of this historic destiny.[5]

While the book from which this quotation is excerpted was addressed to the intelligentsia, Ahidjo has not limited the audience to which he spells out the goals of his government. He has also raised the issue of national unity in speeches addressed to the mass public, like this one in 1964: "I think I have laid enough emphasis on what the motto for everyone of us should be, namely Unity for National Construction" (emphasis added).[6] And again, "We shall never tire of repeating as we have on other occasions, that economic development which will give a more substantial content to our independence cannot be achieved without this National Unity."[7]

If these quotations illustrate anything, it is that for the Cameroon political regime, the theme of National Unity is considered a political imperative, a goal which should be achieved with all haste. To what extent is this view shared by the public? To what extent could one confidently say that a formal (or informal) consensus exists between elite and mass as to the attainment of this goal? Respondents were asked to indicate whether they shared the belief that a good government should try to promote national unity and instill in its members a sense of pride, love, and service to the national community.

The expectations that mass and elite shared this political value was borne out by the data. Cameroonians questioned agree that the elimination of social and political cleavages so as to facilitate for national unity is a desirable political goal. In this respect, they share the commitment of their national leadership to this dimension of the belief system. A substantial majority of the sampled respondents (62 per cent) agreed (completely or somewhat), in sharp contrast to only 27 per cent who disagreed (again in varying degrees) and 12 per cent that were undecided, that the goal of national unity is the number one priority for all good governments. This high system consensus on the unity dimension is evenly spread in all three environmental locations.

Yet, when comparisons are made between localities, more camp and town respondents (66 per cent each) than village respondents (46 per cent) support the national unity value. From a statistical point of view, the chi-square (44.182 with 8 degrees of freedom at .0000 significance level) was not significant at the .01 level, thus compelling us to accept the hypothesis that a significant difference exists between localities with respect to the belief system dimension dealing with national unity as a desirable political goal.

(iii) <u>A Moral Society</u>--This investigation was conducted at a time when the Cameroon government had declared an all-out campaign against vice and corruption in the country. This campaign resulted in a spate of decrees defining permissible limits of sexual behavior and stipulating punishments that would be meted out to those deviating from the approved norm. These were contained in Law No. 65-LF-24 of November 12, 1965, and Law No. 67-LF-1 of June 12, 1967, as amended by Ordinance No. 72/16 of August 28, 1972, which addressed 18 specific areas of public and private morality including immoral earnings (section 294), prostitution (section 343), adultery (section 361), and so on.

In the absence of a Gallup or Harris-type polling agency, no systematic attempt was made to capture the reaction of the populace to these new laws. The results of this study constitute the first systematic effort to collect and analyze the opinions of Cameroonians on this important public issue. As in the case with the rule system, the issue of public support for the regime's position on moral values was not put directly, but the central issue was nonetheless adequetely conveyed. I wanted to find out how the mass of Cameroonians reacted to the government's intrusion into their private lives. Did they share in the view that one of the goals of a good government involves the passing of laws which ostensibly protect the morals of its citizens, such as the ban on cohabitation?

The results of the data show an overwhelming rejection by the sampled populace of this regime goal. Of those individuals questioned only 35 per cent agreed with the policy (completely or somewhat), while 13 per cent were undecided as to the government's role in legislating the morals and sexual behavior of its members. The majority--52 per cent--disagreed in varying degrees with such governmental intrusion into that domain of social existence. Although respondents were not asked to comment directly on the current laws, the results may reasonably be interpreted as an expression of public disapproval of the whole policy.[8] The results also reflect the collective wish of the sampled universe that government confine its programs and activities to other areas, such as promoting national unity and correcting social and economic inequalities.

Examining the environmental factor, we see that large majorities of village and town respondents (61 per cent and 66 per cent respectively) did not view the pursuit of a moral society as a desirable political goal, in sharp contrast to the camp respondents (35 per cent of whom shared this view). Thus the proportion of village and town respondents who shared in this regime goal was very small compared to the large percentage (48 per cent) of camp respondents who favored it. The hypothesis that geographic location significantly affects people's orientations to government's role in enforcing moral values is borne out by the data.

A final comment: the laws on public and private morality were passed with all good intentions. They sought to arrest the alarming decline in public morality particularly in Cameroon's urban centers with their high pregnancy rate among the youthful female population (many of whom resorted to illegal abortions often with fatal consequences); the high incidence of Cameroonian women being subjected to sexual exploitation by male pimps; and frequent sexual abuse of Cameroonian women by European male tourists. These were the problems that led Cameroonian law-makers to pass legislation to regulate public morality. Unfortunately, in trying to enforce some of these laws, especially those dealing with sexual offences and immoral earnings, all sorts of problems surfaced.

To begin with, an over-zealous <u>gendarmerie</u> frequently took the law into its own hands as it engaged in a series of highly dramatized, carelessly executed, and indiscriminate arrests of innocent citizens. For instance, many adult women found they could not walk the streets late at night without being mistaken for prostitutes and shabbily treated by these undisciplined gendarmes. Just as the streets were being emptied of most law-abiding citizens, the <u>gendarmes</u> were also moving in on the bars and other such public places. Their frequent and unannounced sweeps through the bars quickly emptied these of their precious "service girls." In all, the enforcement of the promiscuity laws greatly disrupted the tempo of social life in the country, provoking a public backlash. It would seem that in trying to make the streets of Cameroon's urban centers safe for the morally-upright citizens, the law enforcement agents only succeeded in making them <u>unsafe</u> for everybody, law-abiding or law-breaking.

The second problem with the prosmicuity laws was a difficulty in determining when a monetary exchange between two consenting adults of opposite sexes falls under the definition of prostitution and hence a punishable crime under section 294 of the New Penal Code which reads:[9]

>   SECTION 294 (new) - IMMORAL EARNINGS
>
>   (1) Whoever procures, aids or facilitates another person's prostitution, or shares in the proceeds of another's prostitution, whether habitual or otherwise, or who is subsidised by any person engaging in prostitution shall be punished with imprisonment for from six months to five years and with a fine of from 20,000 to 1,000,000 francs.
>
>   (2) Whoever lives with a person engaging in prostitution shall be presumed to be subsidised by her, unless he

shows that his own resources are sufficient to enable him to support himself.

(3) The punishment shall be doubled where:
   a) the offence is accompanied by coercion or by fraud, or where the offender is armed; or where he is the owner, manager or otherwise in charge of an establishment where prostitution is habitually practised;
   b) where the offence has been committed to the detriment of any person under the age of twenty-one;
   c) where the offender is the father or mother, guardian or person with customary responsibility....

Given that these encounters usually occured behind closed doors, it proved quite problematic to agree on who determines that money has changed hands and the circumstances under which this has happened. Many Cameroonian males who provide their women friends with "chop money" come market day were justifiably enraged by this Diktat. Did it mean that a woman who receives "chop money" from her massa is, in the eyes of the law, a prostitute? And should the law enforcement agent regard "chop money" as payment for sexual favors a girl-friend bestows on her male-friend in the course of a normal, healthy relationship? These were some of the many knotty questions Cameroonians grappled with as the official campaign against promiscuity was being waged. The low priority accorded the morality goal may well reflect public dissatisfaction with the method of enforcing the law rather than fundamental disagreement with its objectives.

Summary

In summary, the terminal goals I chose to test toward which political action should be directed seem highly accepted by the Cameroon people. There is a high positive identification with all the goals, with only one exception--the goal of government enforcement of a moral society, which was rejected by a preponderance of the respondents sampled. The expectation of sharp differences in the level of commitment to these political goals between rural and urban residents proved incorrect. In general no value conflicts between town and countryside emerged. Cameroonians, regardless of geographic location, appear to share the same political beliefs. It is also important to observe that this high belief system consensus revealed no cleavages between the mass public and the regime on desirable political goals, except, once again, with regard to camp residents' view on the issue of a moral society.

Table 6.3
Opinion of the Social Welfare Goal by Location

Respondents Who	Village	Camp	Town
Completely Agree	36.8%	24.5%	26.9%
Agree	19.7	18.7	37.5
Undecided	15.8	9.7	5.6
Disagree	9.2	34.2	20.6
Completely Disagree	18.4	12.9	9.4
Total	100.0%	100.0%	100.0%
N	76	155	160

$x^2 = 38.75279 \quad P = <.001$

Table 6.4
Opinion of the National Unity Goal by Location

Respondents Who	Village	Camp	Town
Completely Agree	18.4%	30.3%	48.1%
Agree	27.6	35.5	17.5
Undecided	13.2	16.8	5.6
Disagree	26.3	10.3	18.8
Completely Disagree	14.5	7.1	10.0
Total	100.0%	100.0%	100.0%
N	76	155	160

$$x^2 = 44.18263 \quad P = <.001$$

Table 6.5
Opinion of the Moral Society Goal by Location

Respondents Who	Village	Camp	Town
Completely Agree	9.2%	30.3%	7.5%
Agree	15.8	18.1	18.1
Undecided	14.5	16.8	8.7
Disagree	32.9	18.7	26.9
Completely Disagree	27.6	16.1	38.7
Total	100.0%	100.0%	100.0%
N	76	155	160

$$x^2 = 50.98826 \quad P = <.001$$

Footnotes

1. David Easton, "An Approach to the Analysis of Political Systems," World Politics Vol. 9 (1956-1957), p. 392. See also Donald J. Devine, The Political Culture of the United States, op. cit., pp. 136-137.
2. Item was taken from Kluckhohn and Strodtbeck, Variations in Value Orientations. Evanston: Row, Peterson and Company, 1962.
3. Cf Donald J. Devine, op. cit. and Gabriel Almond and Sidney Verba, The Civic Culture. Boston: Little, Brown and Company, 1965.
4. Christian Bay, "A Critical Evaluation of Behavioral Literature," in James Gould and Vincent V. Thursby, eds., Contemporary Political Thought: Issues in Scope, Value, and Direction. New York: Holt, Rinehart & Winston, Inc., 1969.
5. Ahmadou Ahidjo, Nation and Development. Paris: Editions Presence Africaine, 1969.
6. Ahidjo, Contribution to National Construction. Paris: Editions Presence Africaine, 1964, p. 126.
7. Ahidjo, Nation and Development, op. cit., pp. 20-23.
8. In its fight against prostitution, the world's oldest, if not most respectable, profession hardly did the government realise that it was taking on a cross-section of the adult male population in the country. Cameroonian males spend the greater portion of their recreational hours in bars. Bars in Cameroon have become the focal point of social interaction frequented by patricians as well as plebians. The factors that have contributed to making these places of entertainment so popular are many and varied, not the least of which is the presence of "service girls." These young ladies who have migrated from the hinterland areas to the coastal urban centers are usually in their late teens and early twenties with little if any formal education. They are in the cities in search of employment but their relative lack

of marketable skills limits their employment options as a consequence the majority end up working as bar girls in the zillion bars that ubiquitously dot the Cameroon urban landscape. It is these young ladies who have provided the attraction to bars that many Cameroonians find so difficult to resist. During the hours that bars are open they dotily wait on their dipsomanic male patrons and after working hours eagerly minister to their sexual needs in return for <u>chop</u> and rent money. The male patron and the service girl are symbiotically attached to each other and as such the elimination of one spells doom for the other. As it became gradually clear, following the reckless assaults on bars by gendarmes, that these social forums would soon be without their indispensable "service girls" public opposition to the promiscuity laws was predictably swift and widespread. The reverberations were felt right in the cockpit of national decision-making. In the first cabinet reshuffle following the inauguration of these laws, Achidi Achu, Minister of Justice and under whom these unpopular laws were zealously enforced, lost his cabinet position. It is generally believed that his fall from grace is not unconnected to the laws on promiscuity. Although these finely wrought pieces of legislation still grace the Cameroon penal code their enforcement is very perfunctory.

9. As part of a series of unobtrusive attempts to gauge the problems, if any, in enforcing these statutes, the author spent many hours in the law courts. I was interested in finding out the fate of cases brought under the promiscuity laws. In April of 1973, the author was present at the Tiko Magistrate's Court when two adults charged with violations under section 294 (revised) were brought to trial. The prosecuting counsel alleged that the woman had engaged in sex with the man in return for money and that the man in complying was in fact aiding and abetting in the commission of a crime. The court refused to give judgment for the state and dismissed the case on the grounds that the arresting officer was in

no position to determine if in fact the alleged violations had occurred.

7
Conculsion

This study set out to investigate empirically the if's and why's of political culture in one relatively stable and poly-ethnic African state--Cameroon. I was intrigued by the system-functionalist paradigm which holds that in every society order and system-maintenance rely heavily on a political culture fondation and reasonably aware of the many problems that beset nation-builders in the emergent African states, but I was also dissatisfied with the conventional excuses tendered by scholars to explain political choas and system disunity in these emergent polities.

Three models were identified in Chapter 1, each of which advances reasons to explain the absence of an overarching political culture in the majority of African states. The first model rationalizes this lack of commonly shared political values as a reflection of the gigantic trauma inflicted on the social fabric by colonial domination. Because colonial rule implied a break in the political evolution of these nations, the net effect has been a legacy of political institutions and values which lack historical continuity. In the absence of structures and values whose roots are deeply buried in a people's collective social, political and intellectual history attempts to create a sense of common political identity out of these become problematic. A second approach sees the experiment in national identification doomed to failure because it is faced with the pervasive ethnic fragmentation and social cleavages that mark these nation-states. The belief is that poly-ethnicity makes for a social situation in which people's primary loyalties are directed not to the overarching nation-state but to various ethnic groupings. Not until these primordial loyalties have been destroyed or domesticated can one hope for the emergence of a common sense of national identification.

Inconsistencies in patterns of socialization constitutes the third approach employed by scholars to explain why national identity appears so faint and tenuous in the new states. Not too far removed from the ethnic fragmentation model, this approach also takes as its point of departure the factor of ethnic differences. However, rather than lay the blame on ethnic loyalties per se, the socialization discontinuity model tries to examine the processes of socialization within the different types of ethnic systems in the plural society. From these it concludes that contrasts in ethnic systems are associated with variations in socialization patterns such that some systems prepare their offspring for participation in the broader framework of the nation-state while others socialize their members for participation in the local community. Faced with such contradictions and inconsistencies in socialization patterns, nation-builders have experienced serious difficulties trying to extract from these a set of values which can have uniform relevance for the entire population.

All three models have been found wanting. The first is merely descriptive and not sufficiently analytical. Its focus has been limited to extended discussions of the disruptive impact of colonial rule on these societies while treating at a very peripheral level underlying factors not necessarily connected to colonial domination but important nonetheless in explaining the slow development of national political cultures in the former colonies. Complex social phenomena cannot be adequately explained through a uni-causal approach. On a substantive level it leads one to see the African as essentially a one-dimensional man who can never be both a tribesman and a patriot. From an epistemological perspective, the choice of tribalism as the dependent variable is unfortunate given its emotive and ideological connotations; connotations which effectively reduce its value as a concept for comparative social science research. Although the third model is superior to the previous two, it suffers from some methodological deficiencies which restrict the range of generalizability of the conclusions it generates.

In this study, I have accordingly sought not only to test systematically the validity of these models but more importantly to design the investigation in such a way that it was not limited by the weaknesses of these previous studies on political culture. In so far as colonialism (and exposure to western values) has been advanced as disruptive of traditional values on the one hand and inhibitive to the growth of a common political culture on the other, one objective of this study was to hold this variable constant in such a way that it had identical value for the populations sampled. This was done by selecting the sample from among persons who were presently living (and had lived for over ten years) on the Cameroon coast. This part of the country is the only area which has enjoyed a long and continuous history of contact with the Western world and where the effects of economic and social development have been felt for a long time. To this extent, the sample was drawn from a homogeneous population. Since it has been asserted that patterns of socialization differ from one ethnic society to another producing a welter of contradictory values that tend to polarize rather than unite their carriers, my major concern was to select a representative sample of ethnic societies in Cameroon. To avoid the methodological weakness of the socialization discontinuity model, ethnic societies were varied according to political organizations. Thus I had essentially two different types of traditional political systems--hierarchical chiefdoms and segmentary societies. I then compared the attitudes of their respective populations to certain political values to see how qualitatively different they really are; i.e., whether political structures are associated with certain types of political values and socialization processes. Furthermore, unlike the previous studies under the third model which were limited in their comparative range, this one tried to compare and analyze ethnic group value orientations and national political attitudes across three types of environmental locations--rural villages, plantation camps, and towns. By varying the traditional systems and environmental situations I sought to maximize the generalizability of the results. In sum, the overall goal of this investigation was to collect evidence demonstrating that the three models fall far short of explaining variations in national orientations because none make any effort to consider some plausible rival hypotheses.

I began the analysis with two assumptions: (1) that loyalty to ethnic group values does not necessarily inhibit positive orientations toward the nation-state; and (2) that variations in identification with the national political system can be explained as a function of the impact of environmental influences on people, which condition their individual and collective perceptions of the political regime. Thus, environmental location was the variable selected to explain contrasts in level of political identification with the Cameroon nation; while sense of attachment to ethnic group values was retained as the major plausible rival explanatory variable. It was then argued that if one varied one or both explanatory variables and corresponding variations were observed in the level of political orientations, one could then infer the existence of a relationship between the two. If on the other hand the independent variables failed to produce concomitant variations on the dependent variable, the conclusion would be that there is no association between the two sets of variables.

My program was then to demonstrate that only differences in the locality in which people were resident properly accounted for their differential dispositions toward the national political system. To execute this plan, I had first to eliminate attachment to ethnic group values--the rival hypothesis--as a serious explanatory variable. I therefore proposed that these attachments to fundamental values that give shape to ethnic societies are usually passed on to each successive generation early in life; once internalized, these values remain with ethnic group members throughout life, regardless of where they are geographically located. That is, I did not expect to find urban groups significantly different from rural groups with respect to their collective orientations toward ethnic group values. Let us briefly review the findings.

Contrasts Between Two Structurally Different Traditional Societies

Differences in the political structures of ethnic groups are associated with patterns of decision-making at the societal level. Segmentary societies have a more representative form of decision-making. For these societies decisions are arrived at within a framework which places emphasis on the principle of majority rule. In contrast, centralized hierarchical societies adopt an elitist approach to decision-making. Here decisions that affect the entire group are usually made by authority figures like the <u>fon</u> (king) or paramount chief or his authorized lieutenants. When environmental differences are considered, the distinction between segmentary and hierarchical societies on the basis of authority and decision-making patterns at the group level becomes blurry. Segmentary people who reside in villages and towns prefer the principle of majority control in decision-making while their counterparts in camps are more inclined toward the elitist model. It is in the camp locality that the distinction between centralized and segmentary systems melts inasmuch as the majority of residents from both societies chose to define decision-making within an elitist framework. The propensity for camp residents regardless of traditional systems to select the elitist model for decision-making can be explained in terms of the authority structure within plantation camps.

Plantation camps, I have argued, are organized into a hierarchical command system. The institutionalized relationship between plantation management and labor force is one of superiordinacy, and subordinacy, control and submission. This elitist pattern of authority relationships has become so deeply ingrained into camp society that it has finally overpowered the resistance of even those people who are traditionally consensual and representative in their approach to decision-making. The shift by segmentary camp residents is highly significant because it goes against their traditional decisional patterns; for the centralized residents, however, the elitist model operating in camps is consistent with the traditional approach.

The effects of environmental change are also evident in the switch by the majority of centralized town residents from their traditional elitist position to one of endorsing the principle of majority rule in decision-making. Since the majoritarian model is a characteristic of segmentary systems and since the town sample was drawn from coastal towns whose indigenous populations are organized into segmentary systems, the obvious inference is that centralized peoples resident in towns have gradually been assimilated into the host culture. Differences between the two traditional systems were observed in their orientations toward change. People from segmentary societies were least resistant to change and generally favored a modernist approach to innovative values. In contrast, people from centralized systems defined change within a neo-traditionalist framework. It follows that people's receptivity to innovation is associated with the structural features of the traditional societies from which they originate. The data fail, however, to confirm the conventional view that people from traditionally hierarchical societies are usually least resistant to change. What the data show is in fact the opposite of this position.

Similarities Between Two Structurally Different Traditional Societies

The data turned up a wide range of similarities between segmentary and centralized societies. Things such as people's images of parental authority, patterns of decision-making within the family, and the degree of intra-group contact and solidarity were found to hold equally for the two systems. Parental authority for members of both systems brought out recollections of an authoritarian and domineering father in contrast to a permissive mother. The structure of decision-making within the family was basically the same for both systems. It was unrepresentative since participation was not extended to the children in the household but limited only to parents and other elders. The structure was yet more lopsided since it was biased in favor of the father, who made all the important decisions, sometimes with the help of his spouse. Within both systems a high level of group pride and solidarity was observed. This was expressed in the pride people took in speaking their indigenous languages whenever in the company of group members. It was also interesting to note that segmentary systems, in spite of their fissiparous tendencies, still manifested a sense of solidarity and cohesion as intense as that observed for centralized people. The impact of environmental differences did not significantly change the tenor of these findings. Regardless of geographical location, a high degree of support for most of these values was observed.

To sum up, the data show that there are certain traditional values and group attitudes that are not associated with particular forms of social organizations and structures. There is a high degree of similarity, if not uniformity, between the two structurally different traditional political organizations with respect to a wide range of values. Finally, the data also suggest that these values do not lose their relevance even in situations of culture contact. The major conclusion here is that support for ethnic group values is strong for the universe sampled.

Although the study was not specifically concerned with ordering the population groups (within systems and across communities) in respect to the strength of their attachments to ethnic system values, it is still possible to say that such attachment to ethnic groups is a property shared by the universe studied and as such can be considered a systemic characteristic. If it is a "universal" feature, I argue, it cannot be employed to explain differences with regard to some other variable--in this case, national political orientations. Since the data showed that support for ethnic group values is a systemic characteristic (here system is used to refer to members of the Cameroon political system taken as a homogeneous unity), intrasystem differences on other important variables have to be explained by factors that are not held held in common by system members.

Consequently, the analysis was moved to the level of environmental groups. The findings of comparisons between environmental groups with respect to their orientations toward the national political system will now be reviewed.

Environment and Political Culture System

Tests of independence showed that on certain political culture dimensions environmental differences are associated with contrasts in national political orientations. First the identity system. I was interested in, among other things, measuring how informed and critical Cameroonians are of their political system. Although all three environmental groups reported very low scores on the political knowledge dimension, nonetheless camp and town residents were found to be generally better informed, more interested spectators of their political system. Secondly, all three environmental groups manifested some sense of system pride. Respondents' sense of their Cameroonianness was not found to be latent or marginal but overt and long internalized. (The counter-indication however is that many respondents would be willing to change nationality.) Many attributed their pride in the Cameroon nation to the president, Ahmadou Ahidjo, as the symbol of national identity and unity. However, this intimate identification with the Cameroon president contrasts sharply with the low regard the population has for his cabinet ministers. On the whole citizens' behavioral attachment to the Cameroon nation was not affected by environmental contrasts.

I did find that sense of community identity varies with geographic location. Residents from the three environmental communities (this was less true of villages) had a tendency to participate in broadly based friendship networks that cut across ethnic group boundaries, though many were reluctant to expand these networks to accept cross-ethnic marriages. Using extra-ethnic patterns of interactions as indicators of feeling of identification among members of a political comunity, the data strongly support the position that camp and town groups have a higher level of political community identification than rural village people.

This is a very significant finding, for it suggests that urbanization may contribute to nation-building. It has been usual to view urbanization as a phenomenon that has had a profound dislocative impact on traditional African values and institutions.[1] While most students of African urbanication are in agreement that urbanization is clearly one very important dimension of that complex of irreversible transformations African societies are undergoing, yet few are prepared to look beyond those problems that are by definition built into the urbanization process (i.e., urban unemployment, congestion, crimes, inadequate sanitation, anomic violence, etc.), in order to see some of its beneficial aspects. The data exposed urbanization's inherent functional role in nation-building. We are urged to view urbanism as something that can actually help in minimizing or defusing inter-ethnic conflict (a major problem in the majority of plural societies.)[2]

Whether it is the controlled organization of plantation camps or the laissez-faire type characteristic of towns, the process has resulted in the bringing together of people from diverse cultural backgrounds. People so pushed together by force of circumstance tend to relate to each other more on the basis of functional needs and shared interests and less on ascriptive considerations. It is through such cross-cultural interactions that people begin to develop a genuine sense of respect for each other as they become more sensitive and understanding of cultural differences. Within such situations of culture contact stereotypes are steadily replaced by knowledge. Urbanization thus serves the important function of broadening the framework for inter-ethnic contact and interaction. It provides the foundations on which a genuine sense of national community identity can be erected. From this standpoint it is desirable and functional in the nation-building process.

No significant environmental differences are associated with orientations to the symbol system of political culture. Attachments to the flag and anthem as symbols of the Cameroon nation are equally strong among residents of the three localities. This feeling is vividly captured in this statement by a twenty-two year old youth: "When I see the flag and hear the anthem, I immediately think of my very peaceful and independent country and say aloud 'LONG LIVE CAMEROON!'" It could not have been better expressed.

In our examination of the rule system, two procedures were considered: decision-making and conflict resolution. Environmental differences do somewhat affect decision-making preferences. The consensus across all three communities was for the majoritarian form of decesion-making, although camp dwellers leaned toward an elitist model. The preference by the masses for a participatory form of decision-making runs contrary to the elitist approach that is the hallmark of the national power structure. First, there is the problem of mass participation in the political process. With only one single political party, clearly the principle of mass participation in the decision-making process is a theory yet to be translated into objective practice. Secondly, one is confronted with the reality of a very exclusive national policy-making structure headed by a president (who is at the same time leader of the party) and the Political Bureau; with the latter just as unrepresentative as the other organs of the political party. Because the constitution concentrates so much power in the hands of the president, he rules virtually as an imperial leader.[3] Thus, the two dominant policy-making institutions, the national party and the Presidency, cannot truly be considered answerable to the sovereign will of the electorate, and to that extent they are elitist. The public, however, states a preference for an open and participatory decision-making process, as opposed to the present form which is elitist in orientation and excludes effective mass participation and input.

With respect to preferred rules for resolving conflict in the nation, there was a high system consensus for the <u>modern-legalist</u> model but when environmental differences were taken into account concomitant shifts were observed in group preferences. Village and town residents showed a preference for the modern-legalist approach to conflict resolution. In contrast, camp residents expressed a marked preference for "traditional" methods of conflict resolution. Village and town residents' support for the modern-legalist model for resolving conflict indicates a meeting of the minds between mass preferences and regime rules with respect to this political value. Village and town residents, the data show, are more likely to appeal to the regime's values and institutions to resolve interpersonal and intra-societal conflict. On the other hand, the selection of traditional methods by camp residents could be interpreted as reflecting this community's lack of confidence in regime models for conflict management and resolution.

Environmental differences do not significantly affect mass attitudes with respect to those political goals toward which governmental action should be directed. Support was widespread for the social welfare and national unity goals, though low on the "moral society" value (camp dwellers are again the exception). The belief that a good government should give top priority to the problem of social and economic inequality while on the other hand laying down a solid foundation for national unity is shared by an overwhelming majority of the Cameroon people. The very strong support for these goals is significant in that it reveals a shared commitment of the mass public and national leadership to goals both feel are desirable and necessary for national progress. However, such was not the case with the morality goal. Although the national leadership considers itself duty bound to lay down some stringent moral laws regulating sexual behavior, this view was not shared by the mass public, which suggests a fundamental difference of opinion between national elite values and mass public desires over the issue of government's role in legislating moral behavior. Clearly the people's position is that areas of interpersonal relations are out of bounds for government.

On two of these goals--moral society and social welfare--town and rural residents are closer to each other than they are to their counterparts in camps; that is to say, rejection of the one and commitment to the other is proportionately higher for town and village populations than camp residents. On the other hand, on the national unity goal, village residents find themselves isolated from the rest of the universe as a realignment takes place between camp and town.

Several conclusions can be derived from these observations. First, the data show that people were able to retain their attachments to certain ethnic group values and institutions and still maintain a fairly high level of identification with the nation-state, a finding which has distinct implications for national integration. It is generally agreed that the term "integration" covers a vast range of human relationships and attitudes. Although the concept lends itself to several definitions, the common element is the search for those factors which contribute toward system unity. Interest here is in that level of national integration which Myron Weiner has defined as: "The process of bringing together culturally and socially discrete groups into a single territorial unit and the establishment of a national identity."[4]

In an ethnically pluralitic society, national integration involves the interplay between ethnic group attachments and national loyalties. Two schools of thought dominate the social science approach to the question of national integration in Africa. The first view sees the emergence of a common nationality/identity as contingent on the systematic destruction of ethnic loyalties and attachments. In order to become a functional and an integral part of the nation, the convert must disavow his ethnic group attachments, since these tend to detract from the new national loyalty.

In opposition to this first view of national integration is a second model which recognizes the permanance of ethnic groups in African societies and seeks, therefore, to include them in the calculus of national integration. Rather than define a common nationality in terms of a homogeneous society, emphasis is placed on creating a heterogeneous nation with unity in diversity as the ultimate goal.

I find the second model theoretically sound. For empirically the first model--which sees the

African as a one-dimensional man incapable of relating concurrently to the ethnic group and nation-state--has not been borne out in this study. Africans do not define loyalty as a zero-sum phenomenon in which the new national loyalty necessarily detracts from the old ethnic group loyalty. From this study it is clear that those social engineers and academicians who persist in identifying tribalism as the single most disruptive factor in the integrative revolution have erred. For it seems to me that it is not attachments to various ethnic groups per se that necessarily lead to social dislocation; rather it is in the process of politicizing these attachments that conflicts in demands and interests find expression. The solution is not to rid tribalism of its putative dysfunctional aspects, but to depoliticize ethnic groups. Other agencies and institutions need to be created to articulate political demands in which criteria for participation and recruitment are not ascriptively defined.

To be sure, my conclusions are not definitive, largely because of limitations imposed by the research instrument. For instance, the instrument did not include items to tap the difference in quality of loyalties directed to both the ethnic group and nation-state. Ethnic group and nation were conceptualized and presented to our respondents not as two mutually exclusive groups competing for the individual's allegiance, but complementary to each other. The ethnic group has been viewed as the primary socializing agency in the individual's maturation process (and we have found evidence to support this) and the experiences forged here are later generalized into the broader framework of national society. It was taken for granted that people derive differential satisfaction by associating with these various groupings. For me then, it was a question of overlapping memberships and multiple loyalties. Professor Guetzkow has commented on the importance of overlapping membership and loyalties, though in a context slightly different from this:

> The object of one loyalty may be dependent upon the survival of the object of another loyalty, so that loyalty to the latter involves support to the former. Or the object of one loyalty may be seen as equivalent to the object of another loyalty . . . [or] individuals develop habit-patterns, so that training in loyalty to one object is generalized and may be transfered in his reaction to other objects of loyalty. He learns appropriate ways of supporting objects, and these habits of expressing loyalty can then be attached to new objects.[5]

This is consistent with my position that ethnic group loyalty and national identification, though analytically distinct, do not, in real life, operate according to the rules of a zero-sum game.

Secondly, the data suggest that variations in political orientations are associated with contrasts in environmental localities. The results have shown that people from rural villages react differently to the national political system than urban residents. For instance, residents from ethnically heterogeneous centers have a relatively higher level of information and are more interested in and critical of their government than village folk. These differences in perceptions of the nation (its leaders, institutions, laws, etc.) reflect contrasts in levels of development between town and countryside. The notion of "development" was simply defined as the material rewards in the form of amenities obtained by an environmental community due to its advantageous location vis-a-vis the political regime; amenities such as schools, factories, pipe-borne water, paved roads, and the like. We argued that urban communities, almost by definition, were more endowed with these artifacts than other areas. Furthermore, we argued that the distinction between town and countryside was one conditioned by historical and sociological forces too self-evident to warrant any extended discussion. It is a distinction which reflects the reality of socio-economic stratification. The two environmental communities can be viewed as two distinct social classes and economic groupings: on the one hand, a poor, illiterate, rural folk, and on the other, a literate urban folk living, in relative affluence.

What this amounts to is that residence in any given environmental location implies certain advantages and disadvantages. Those communities which enjoy a disproportionate share of national goods and services would be more likely to hold favorable perceptions of the political system. National orientations, for me, then, are not a set of reflex actions, inborn or biological, but rather are response-dispositions arising from the fact of living within a given spatio-temporal setting. These orientations are, as some have already contended, states of mind which provide the reservoir of support from which the national political system draws its legitimacy. One way to look at national orientation is to regard it as a disposition in people in response to specific inducements from the national political system. It then becomes the sum of the perceptions held as to the performance capability of national institutions. Throughout this study, I have assumed that town residents generally interpret governmental performance in very favorable terms only because towns are endowed with certain material benefits that villages do not have.

Town and countryside also manifest fundamental differences on another significant dimension: ethnic complexion and opportunities for interethnic contact and interaction. Ethnic diversity and cross-ethnic contact, I argue, have some influence in terms of conditioning people from plural societies to accept each other as members of the same political community. It was suggested that residents from multiethnic centers (plantation camps and towns) would have greater access to opportunities for interethnic contact than those from ethnically homogeneous rural villages. Town and camp dwellers would, therefore, be in a better position to develop strong community ties through participation in friendship networks that span ethnic backgrounds. This position also found support from the data.

Future research on political culture should be directed at drawing up a hierarchy of loyalties in order that intensity of identification with the nation can be measured. We may want to look at national orientations using Guetzkow's model of multiple loyalties. Three types of national loyalties are distinguished in this model: instrumental, autonomous, and complaint. Instrumental orientation is what Guetzkow refers to as "loyalties as means." These are loyalties directed toward the nation because it is perceived to be supportive of the goals aspired to by the holder. To the extent that the nation is believed to be satisfying the individual's needs, instrumental orientations would be directed toward it. Such orientations are usually inspired by the desire for goal-attainment and sustained through rewards or perceived rewards accruing to the holder. Since an instrumental orientation is based on a quid pro quo, it loses its strength once the pay-off ceases. Instrumental orientations could also mean vicarious satisfaction gained by identifying with the nation and sharing in its achievements, characteristics, status, and possessions.

The second category of orientations is what Guetzkow calls "loyalties as end values." These are orientations which exist independently of the goods and services that the nation provides for its members. They are generated by considerations the member holds as to the intrinsic value of the nation, i.e., the nation is considered as an end in itself. It is this type of orientation which supports the attitude: "My country right or wrong." Finally, there are orientations formed through fear and punishment. Because acts of disloyalty are frowned upon and severely punished, members are compelled to exhibit outward signs of conformity. When not fear-induced, such orientations may also mean member supportive behavior toward the nation because it is believed to be the "embodiment of legitimate authority" (Guetzkow's phrase). Such an orientation is by definition passive since all the individual does is accept and observe the laws of the nation without questioning their validity "merely because it is traditional and right to accept such commands as premises for action."[6] Members therefore pay their taxes, attend party rallies, buy party cards, and so on, because that is the way things are done and, besides, everybody else does them.

Using such a model which has already differentiated varieties of national loyalties makes the job relatively easier. The data that will be gathered from such an approach might well enable one to talk in more meaningful terms not only about the <u>direction</u> but the <u>quality</u> of national orientation.

Footnotes

1. Hanna and Hanna, <u>Urban Dynamics in Black Africa</u>, op. cit., especially chapter 5.
2. There is some evidence to contradict our position. Some scholars take the view that in towns, ethnic ties and identities get reinforced (rather than disappear) because as Hanna and Hanna write, "Most residents are to some extent 'encapsulated' within their own network which serves as a barrier between them and the wider urban social system. Striking cultural differences among many groups further hamper the development of an interethnic sense of community." In Hanna and Hanna, op. cit., p. 106. For the same theme, see also Jean Rouch, "Second Generation Migrants in Ghana and Ivory Coast," in Aidan Southall, ed., <u>Social Change</u>, op. cit., pp. 300-304; Paul Mercier, "Remarques sur la signification du tribalisme actuel en Afrique noire," <u>Cahiers Internationaux de Sociologie</u>, 31 (1961), pp. 61-80; and Hilda Kuper, ed., <u>Urbanization and Migration in West Africa</u>, Berkeley, California: University of California Press, 1965, pp. 1-22.
3. See Mbu Etonga, "An Imperial Presidency: A Study of Presidential Power in Cameroon," in Ndiva Kofele-Kale, ed., <u>An African Experiment in Nation-Building: The Bilingual Cameroon Republic Since Reunification</u>, Boulder, Colorado: Westview Press, 1980, pp. 133-157.
4. Myron Weiner, "Political Integration and Political Development," in Finkle and Gable, eds., <u>Political Development and Social Change</u>, op. cit., p. 551.
5. Harold Guetzkow, <u>Multiple Loyalties: Theoretical Approach to a Problem in International Organization</u>, Princeton, N.J.: Center for Research on World Political Institutions, 1955, pp. 18-30.
6. <u>Ibid</u>.

Bibliography

CAMEROON: ETHNOGRPPHY

Articles

Chilver, E. M. and Kaberry, P.M. "The Kingdom of Kom in West Cameroon," in Forde, D. and Kaberry, P.M., eds. West African Kingdoms in the Nineteenth Century. London: O.U.P., 1967.
_____. "Traditional Government in Bafut, West Cameroon," The Nigerian Field, XXVIII (January 1963).
Doumbe-Molonge, M. "Origins et Migrations des Duala," Abbia, 20 (June 1968).
Mafiamba, P-C., "Notes on the Polyglot Populations of Nkambe," Abbia, 21 (January-April 1969).
Ruel, M. J. "Migrations in Two Southern Cameroons Tribes: The Banyang of Mamfe Division," in Ardener et al., Plantation and Village in the Cameroons.

Books

Ardener, Edwin W. Coastal Bantu of the Cameroons. London: International African Institute, 1956.
Chilver, E. M. and Kaberry, P.M. Traditional Bamenda: Precolonial History and Ethnography of the Bamenda Grassfields. Buea: Ministry of Primary Education & Social Welfare, 1964.
Kale, P. M. A Brief History of Bakweri. Lagos: Tika-Tore Press, 1939.
McCulloch, Merran, Littlewood, Margaret and Dugast, Idelette, Peoples of the Central Cameroons. London: International African Institute, 1954.
Ritzenthaler, Robert and Ritzenthaler, Pat. Cameroon Village: An Ethnography of the Bafut. Milwaukee: Public Museum Publications in Ethnography 8, 1962.

Unpublished Documents

Allen, J. G. E. Intelligence Reports on the Clans and Village Groups of Victoria Division, 1938 Buea: West Cameroon Archives.
Anderson, A. C. A Preliminary Assessment Report of the Banyang Tribal Area, 1929. Buea: West Cameroon Archives.
Anonymous. Native Customs for the Victoria Division 1921. Buea: West Cameroon Archives.
Bridges, W. M. and D. A. F. Shute. Intelligence Reports on Bakweri, Victoria Division, 1935-1938, 2 vols. Buea: West Cameroon Archives.
Gorges, E. H. F. Banyang Tribal Area Assessment Report, 1930. Buea: West Cameroon Archives.
Hawkensworth, E. G. Assessment Report 1926. Buea: West Cameroon Archives.

CAMEROON: POLITICS, HISTORY AND SOCIETY

Articles

Ardener, Edwin W. "Social and Demographic Problems of the Southern Cameroons Plantations Area" in Aidan Southhall, ed., Social Change in Africa, ed., London: Oxford University Press, 1961.
_____. "The Nature of the Reunification of Cameroon" in Arthur Hazlewood, ed., African Integration and Disintegration: Case Studies in Economic and Political Union. London: Oxford University Press, 1967.
_____. "The Political History of Cameroon," The World Today Vol. 18, No. 8 (August 1962).
Bayart, J. F. "One-Party Government and Political Development in Cameroon" in Ndiva Kofele-Kale, ed., An African Experiment in Nation-Building: The Bilingual Cameroon Republic Since Reunification. Boulder, Colorado: West-Westview Press, 1980.
Brutsch, Jean-Rene. "A Glance at Missions in Cameroon," International Review of Missions, 39, 155 (1950).

Chem-Langhee, Bongfen and Njema, Martin Z. "The Pan-Kamerun Movement, 1949-1961" in Ndiva Kofele-Kale ed., An African Experiment in Nation-Building: the Bilingual Cameroon Republic Since Reunification.

Etonga, Mbu. "An Imperical Presidency: A Study of Presidential Powers in Cameroon," in Ndiva Kofele-Kale, ed., An African Experiment in Nation-Building: the Bilingual Cameroon Republic Since Reunification.

Le Vine, Victor T. "A Contribution to the Political History of Cameroon," ABBIA, No. 24 (January-April, 1970).

Ndongko, Wilfred A. "The Political Economy of Regional Economic Development in Cameroon," in Ndiva Kofele-Kale, ed., An African Experiment in Nation-Building: the Bilingual Cameroon Republic Since Reunification.

Ruel, M. J. "Migration in Two Southern Cameroons Tribes: the Banyang of Mamfe Division," in Shirley Ardener, E. W. Ardener, and W. A. Warmington, Plantation and Village in the Cameroons. Oxford: Oxford University Press, 1969.

Special Correspondent. "Ahidjo Holds Tight the Rein," Africa No. 77 (January, 1978) pp. 52-55.

Books

Ahidjo, Ahmadou. Contribution to National Construction. Paris: Editions Presence Africaine, 1969.

_____. Nation and Development. Paris: Editions Presence Africaine, 1964.

Ardener, Edwin W. and Ardener, Shirley and Warmington, W. A. Plantation and Village in the Cameroons: Some Economic and Social Studies. Oxford: Oxford University Press, N.I.S., 1960.

Banfield, Edward C. The Moral Basis of a Backward Society. Glencoe, Illinois: the Free Press, 1958 and 1962 editions.

Bederman, Sanford. *The Cameroon Development Corporation: Partner in National Growth.* Bota, West Cameroon: C.D.C. Publication, 1958.

Benjamin, Jacques. *Les Camerounais Occidentaux.* Montreal: Les Presses de l'Universite de Montreal, 1972.

Beti, Mongo. *Main basse sur le Cameroun: autopsie d'une decolonisation.* Paris: Francois Maspero, 1972.

Bouchand, J. *La Cote du Cameroun dans l' historie et Cartographie des a l' annexation allemande.* Yaounde: I.F.A.N., Centre Camerounaise, 1952.

Clignet, Remi. *The Africanization of the Labor Market.* Berkeley and Los Angeles: University of California Press, 1976.

Gardinier, David. *Cameroon: United Nations Challenge to French Policy.* London: Oxford University Press, 1963.

_____. *Political Behavior in the Community of Douala, Cameroon: Reactions of the Duale People to Loss of Hegemony, 1944-1955.* Athens, Ohio: Center for International Studies, University of Ohio, 1966.

Gonidec, P. F. *La Republique federale du Cameroun.* Paris: Berger-Levrault, 1969.

Johnson, Willard R. *The Cameroon Federation: Political Integration in a Fragmentary Society.* Princeton University Press, 1970.

Joseph, Richard A. *Radical Nationalism in Cameroun.* Oxford: Oxford University Press, 1977.

Kale, P. M. *A Political Evolution of the Cameroons.* Buea: Government Printer, 1967.

Kofele-Kale, Ndiva, ed., *An African Experiment in Nation-Building: the Bilingual Cameroon Republic Since Reunification.*

Kuczinski, P. R. *The Cameroons and Togoland: A Demographic Study.* London: Oxford University Press, 1939.

Le Vine, Victor T. *The Cameroon Federal Republic.* Ithaca, New York: Cornell University Press, 1971.

_____. *The Cameroons from Mandate to Independence.* Berkeley and Los Angeles: University of California Press, 1964.

Meek, C. K., *Land Tenure and Land Administration in Nigeria and the Cameroons*. London: Her Majesty's Stationery Office, 1957.

Ngwa, J. A. *An Outline Geography of the Federal Republic of Cameroon*. London: Longman's Green and Company, 1967.

Njeuma, M. Z. *The Origins of Pan-Cameroonism*. Buea: Government Printer, 1964.

Rubin, Neville. *Cameroon: An African Federation*. London: Pall Mall Publications, 1970.

Rudin, Harry, *Germans in the Cameroons 1884-1914*. New Haven: Yale University Press, 1938.

Ruel, M. J. *Leopards and Leaders: Constitutional Politics Among a Cross River People*. London: Tavistock Publications 1969.

Vernon-Jackson, H. O. H. *Language, Schools, and Government in Cameroon*. New York: Teachers College Press, 1967.

Victoria Centenary Committee ed., *Victoria, Southern Cameroons: 1858-1958*. Victoria: Basel Mission Book Depot, 1958.

Welch, Claude, *Dream of Unity: Pan Africanism and Political Unification in West Africa*. Ithaca, New York: Cornell University Press, 1966.

Wells, F. A. and Warmington, W. A., *Studies in Industrialization: Nigeria and the Cameroons*. London: Oxford University Press, 1962.

Official Publications

Cameroon Development Corporation, *Annual Reports*, 1950-73.

League of Nations, *Report by His Majesty's Government to the League of Nations on the Administration of the Cameroons* 1924, 1932, and 1938.

Ministry of Economic Affairs and Planning, *Main Results of the April 1976 General Population and Housing Census*. Yaounde: Central Bureau of the Census, 1978.

Philipson, Sir Sydney, *Report on the Financial, Economic and Administrative Consequences to Southern Cameroons of Separation from the*

Federation of Nigeria. Buea: Prime Minister's Office 1959.

United Nations, Report by His Majesty's Government to the United Nations on the Administration of the Cameroons, 1949 and 1950.

Unpublished Documents

Clignet, Remi and Foster, Philip. "Blue and White Collar Workers: An Analysis of the Camerounian Modern Labor Force," Northwestern University, 1973.

Delancy, Mark W. "Changes in Social Attitudes and Political Knowledge Among Migrants to Plantations in West Cameroon," unpublished Ph.D. Dissertation, Indiana University, 1973.

Secretary's Office, "Presbyterian Church in Cameroon: Church Census 1972."

POLITICAL CULTURE AND SOCIALIZATION

Articles

Almond, Gabriel. "Comparative Political Systems," Journal of Politics, 18 (3) August, 1956.

Brown, A. "Introduction" in Brown A. and Gray, J., eds. Political Culture and Political Change in Communist States. New York: Holmes and Meir, 1977.

Buchanan, William. "Political Identification," International Encyclopedia of the Social Sciences, pp. 632-644.

Easton, Dennis. "An Approach to the Analysis of Political Systems," World Politics, Vol. 9 (1956-1957).

_____ and Hess, R. D. "The Child's Political World," Public Opinion Quarterly, XXIV (1960).

_____ and Hess, R. D. "Youth and the Political System" in Lipset, S. M. and Lowenthal, Leo eds., Culture and Social Character. New York: The Free Press of Glencoe, 1961.

Frey, Frederick W. "Socialization to National Identification Among Turkish Peasants," Journal of Politics, 4 (November, 1968).

Gorer, G. "National Character: Theory and Practice" in Mead, M. and Metraux, R., eds., The Study of Culture at a Distance. Chicago: University of Chicago Press, 1953.

Greenstein, Fred I. "The Benevolent Leader: Children's Images of Political Authority," American Political Science Review, LIV (1960).

Grundy, Kenneth W., "The 'Class Struggle' in Africa: An Examination of Conflicting Theories," The Journal of Modern African Studies, 2, 3 (1964).

Hayward, Fred W. "A Reassessment of Conventional Wisdom About the Informed Public: National Political Information in Ghana." American Political Science Review, Vol. 70 (1976).

_____. "Rural Attitudes and Expectations About National Government: Experiences in Selected Ghanaian Communities," Rural Africana, 18 (Fall 1972).

Jennings, Kent M. and Langton, Kenneth P. "Mother Versus Father: The Formation of Political Orientations Among Young Americans," Journal of Politics 31 (May 1969).

_____. "Political Socialization and the High School Civics Curriculum," The American Political Science Review, 67 (September 1968).

Kim, Young C. "The Concept of Political Culture in Comparative Politics," Journal of Politics, 26, 2 (May 1964).

LaPalombara, Joseph. "Italy: Fragmentation Isolation and Alienation," in Lucian W. Pye and Sydney Verba (eds.) Political Culture and Political Development. Princeton: Princeton University Press, 1965.

Leites, Nathan. "Psychological Hypotheses about Political Acts," World Politics, 1 (1948).

Levine, Robert. "Political Socialization and Culture Change," in Clifford Geertz, ed., Old Societies and New States, New York: The Free Press 1963.

_____. "The Internalization of Political Values in Stateless Societies," Human Organization XIX, 2 (Summer 1960).

_____. "The Role of the Stimulus Generalization Hypotheses," Behavioral Science, V (1960).

McClelland, David C. "The Achievement Motive in Economic Growth," in Finkle and Gable, eds., Political Development and Social Change.

Mead, Margaret, "National Character," in International Symposium on Anthropology, New York. Anthropology Today: An Encyclopedic Inventory (ed.) A. L. Kroeber, Chicago: University of Chicago Press, 1952.

_____. "The Study of National Character," in Daniel Lerner and Harold D. Lasswell, eds., The Policy Sciences, Stanford: Stanford University Press, 1951.

Miller, Robert A., "Elite Formation in Africa: Class, Culture, and Coherence," Journal of Modern African Studies, 12, 4 (1974).

O'Connell, James. "Sènghor, Nkrumah, and Azikiwe: Unity and Diversity in the West African State," The Nigerian Journal of Economic and Social Studies, Vol. 5, No. 1 (March, 1963).

Paden, John, "Urban Pluralism, Integration, and Adaptation of Communal Identity in Kano," in Ronald Cohen and John Middleton, eds., From Tribe to Nation in Africa. Scranton, Pennsylvania: Chandler Publishing Company, 1970.

Patterson, Samuel C., "The Political Cultures of the American States," Journal of Politics, 1, 30, 1968.

Pye, Lucian, W. "Personality and Changing Values," in his Aspects of Political Development. Boston: Little, Brown and Company, 1966.

Rustow, Dankwart A., "Turkey: The Modernity of Tradition," in Lucian Pye, and Sydney Verba, eds., Political Culture and Political Development, op. cit.

Schaar, John H. "Loyalty," International Encyclopedia of the Social Sciences, pp. 484-488.

Verba, Sydney. "Germany: The Remaking of Political Culture," in Lucian W. Pye and Sidney Verba, eds., <u>Political Culture and Political Development</u>. Princeton: Princeton University Press, 1965.

Weiner, Myron. "Political Integration and Political Development," in <u>Political Development and Social Change</u>. eds., Finkle and Gable, pp. 551-562.

Yambo, Mauri. "Political Culture in Contemporary Kenya," Unpublished thesis. The University of Dar es Salaam, Tanzania, March, 1972.

<u>Books</u>

Almond, Gabriel and Powell, Bingham G. <u>Comparative Politics: A Developmental Approach</u>. Boston: Little, Brown and Company, 1966.

_____ and Verba, Sidney, <u>The Civic Culture</u>. Boston: Little Brown and Company, 1965.

Beer, S. A. and Ulam, B. A., (eds.) <u>Patterns of Government</u>. 2nd ed. New York: Random House, 1968, chapter 3: Political Culture.

Benedict, Ruth. <u>Patterns of Culture</u>. Boston: Little, Brown and Company, 1958.

_____. <u>The Chrysanthemum and the Sword: Patterns of Japanese Culture</u>. Boston: Little Brown and Company, 1946.

Bienen, Henry. <u>Tanzania: Party Transformation and Economic Development</u>. Princeton, N.J.: Princeton University Press, 1970.

Dawson, Richard E. and Prewitt, Kenneth. <u>Political Socialization</u>. Boston: Little Brown and Company.

Devine, Donald J. <u>The Political Culture of the United States: The Influence of Member Values on Regime Maintenance</u>. Boston: Little, Brown and Company 1972.

Enloe, Cynthia. <u>Ethnic Conflict and Political Development</u>. Boston: Little, Brown, and Company, 1973.

Fagen, Richard. <u>The Transformation of Political Culture in Cuba</u>. Stanford: Stanford University Press, 1969.

Finer, S. F. The Man on Horseback. New York: Praeger, 1962.

Finkle, J. and Gable, R. W., eds., Political Development and Social Change. New York: John Wiley and Sons, Inc., 1966.

Gorer, G. Exploring English Character. New York: Norton, 1955.

──────. The American People: A Study in National Character. New York: Norton, 1948.

Guetzkow, Harold. Multiple Loyalties: Theoretical Approach to a Problem in International Organization. Princeton, N.J.: Center for Research on World Political Institutions, 1955.

Hess, R. D. and Torney, Judith V. The Development of Political Attitudes in Fragmentary Society, Princeton: Princeton University Press, 1970.

I. Shida, T. The Political Culture of Japan: Conformity and Competition, Tokyo: Tokyo University Press, 1970.

Kavanagh, Dennis, Political Culture. London: Macmillan Press, 1972.

Langton, Kenneth P., Political Socialization, New York: Oxford University Press, 1969.

Laumann, Edward O., Bonds of Pluralism. New York: Wiley, 1973.

Lenski, Gerhard, The Religious Factor. Garden City, New York: Doubleday, 1961.

Litt, Edgar. The Political Culture of Massachusetts. Cambridge, Massachusetts: The M.I.T. Press, 1965.

Mair, Lucy, The New Nations. Chicago: University of Chicago Press, 1963.

Mayer, Lawrence, Comparative Political Inquiry. Homewood, Illinois: Dorsey Press, 1972.

Post, K. W. J. and Vickers, Michael, Structure and Conflict in Nigeria 1960-65. London: Heinemann Educational Books Ltd., 1973.

Pye, Lucian W. Aspects of Political Development. Boston: Little, Brown and Company, 1966.

──────. Politics, Personality, and Nation-Building: Burma's Search for Identity. New Haven: Yale University Press, 1962.

_____. The Spirit of Chinese Politics: A Psychological Study of the Authority Crisis in Political Development. Cambridge, Massachusetts: M.I.T. Press, 1968.
Pye, Lucien W. and Verba, Sidney, eds. Political Culture and Political Development. Princeton: Princeton University Press, 1965.
Rose, Richard. Politics in England. London: Faber and Faber Ltd., 1964.
Rudolf, L. and Rudolf, S. H., The Modernity of Tradition: Political Development in India. Chicago: University of Chicago Press, 1967.
Verba, Sidney and Nie, Norman H., Participation in America. New York: Harper and Row, 1972.
Wilson, R. W., Learning to be Chinese: The Political Socialization of Children in Taiwan. Cambridge, Massachusetts: M.I.T. Press, 1970.
Young, Crawford. The Politics of Cultural Pluralism. Madison: University of Wisconsin Press, 1976.

TRIBE, ETHNIC GROUP, TRIBALISM AND ETHNICITY

Articles

Anber, Paul. "Modernization and Political Disintegration: Nigeria and the Ibos," Journal of Modern African Studies, 5, 2 (September, 1967).
Antunes, George and Gaitz, Charles M., "Ethnicity and Participation: A Study of Mexican Americans, and Whites" American Journal of Sociology, 80 (1975).
Apter, David. "The Role of Traditionalism in the Political Modernization of Ghana and Uganda," World Politics 13 (October, 1960).
Argyle, W. J. "European Nationalism and African Tribalism," in P. H. Gulliver ed., Tradition and Transition in East Africa. London: Routledge and Kegan Paul, 1969, pp. 41-58.
Beals, R. C., "Urbanism, Urbanization and Acculturation," American Anthropologist, III, 1 (January-March, 1951).

Brown, Paula. "Patterns of Authority in West Africa," <u>Africa</u>, XXI, 4 (October, 1951).

Clignet, Remi, "Environmental Change, Types of Descent, and Child Rearing Practices," in Horace Miner, ed., <u>The City in Modern Africa</u>. New York: Praeger, 1967.

Geertz, Clifford, "The Integrative Revolution, Primordial Sentiments and Civic Politics in the New States," in Clifford Geerts, ed., <u>Old Societies and New States</u>. New York: The Free Press, 1963.

Gluckman, Max. "Tribalism in Modern British Central Africa" in Irving L. Markovitz ed., <u>African Politics and Society</u>, New York: The Free Press, 1970.

Greeley, Andrew M., "Political Participation Among Ethnic Groups in the United States: A Preliminary Reconaissance," <u>American Journal of Sociology</u>, 80 (1974).

Gulliver, P. H. "Introduction" in Gulliver ed., <u>Tradition and Transition in East Africa</u>. London: Routledge and Kegan Paul, 1969.

Hannerz, Ulf. "Ethnicity and Opportunity in Urban America" in Abner Cohen, ed., <u>Urban Ethnicity</u>, London: Tavistock Publications, 1974.

La Fontaine, J. S. "Tribalism Among the Gisu: An Anthropological Approach," in P. H. Gulliver, <u>Tradition and Transition in East Africa</u>.

Mafeje, Archie. "The Ideology of Tribalism," <u>Journal of Modern African Studies</u>, Vol. 9, No. 2 (August, 1971).

Mercier, Paul. "Remarques sur la signification du 'tribalisme' actuel en Afrique noire" <u>Cahiers Internationaux de Sociologie</u>, 31, (1961).

_____. "On the Meaning of 'Tribalism" in Black Africa" in Pierre Van Den Berghe, ed. <u>Africa: Social Problems of Change and Conflict</u>. San Francisco: Chandler, 1965.

Mitchell, J. C., "Urbanization, Detribalization and Stabilization in Southern Africa: A Problem of Definition and Measurement" in

UNESCO, *Social Implications of Industrialization and Urbanization in Africa South of the Sahara*. Paris: UNESCO, 1956.

Murdock, George, "Review of the Folk Culture of Yucatan," *American Anthropologist* 45 (January-March 1943).

Nadel, S. F. "Witchcraft in Four African Societies: An Essay on Comparison," *American Anthropologist*, Vol. 54 No. 1 (January-March 1952).

Nelson, Dale E. "Ethnicity and Socioeconomic Status as Sources of Participation: The Case for Ethnic Political Culture," *American Political Science Review*, Vol. 73, No. 4 (December 1979).

Parenti, Michael, "Ethnic Politics and Persistance of Ethnic Identification," *American Political Science Review* LXI, 3 (September, 1967).

Rothchild, Donald. "Ethnic Inequalities in Kenya," *Journal of Modern African Studies*, Vol. 7, No. 4, 1969, pp. 689-711.

Smock, Audrey Chapman. "The N.C.N.C. and Ethnic Unions in Biafra," *Journal of Modern African Studies*, Vol. 7, No. 1 (1969).

Twaddle, Michael, "Tribalism in Eastern Uganda," in P. H. Gulliver *Tradition and Transition in East Africa*.

Wallerstein, Immanuel, "Ethnicity and National Integration," in Harry Eckstein and Davbid Apter, eds., *Comparative Politics*, New York: The Free Press, 1963, pp. 665-668.

Wolpe, Howard, "Port Harcourt: Ibo Politics in Microcosm," *Journal of Modern African Studies*, Vol. 7, No. 3 (1969), pp. 469-493.

Books

Banton, Michael, ed. *Political Systems and the Distribution of Power*. London: Tavistock Publications, 1965.

Brown, Radcliffe and Forde, D., eds. *African Systems of Kinship and Marriage*. Oxford: Oxford University Press, 1959.

Buell, Raymond L. *The Native Problem in Africa.* 2 Vols. New York: Archon Books, 1928.

Busia, Kofi A. *Report on a Social Survey of Sekondi-Takoradi.* London: Crown Agents, 1960.

Cohen, Abner. *Custom and Politics in Urban Africa: A Study of Hausa Migrants in Yoruba Towns.* Berkeley and Los Angeles: University of California Press, 1969.

Cohen, Ronald and Middleton, John, eds. *Comparative Political Systems: Studies in Politics of Pre-industrial Societies.* N.Y.: Doubleday, Natural History Press, 1967.

_____. *From Tribe to Nation in Africa: Studies in Incorporation Process.* Scranton, Pennsylvania: Chandler Publishing Company, 1970.

Drake, St. Clair and Cayton, Horace R. *Black Metropolis: A Study of Negro Life in a Northern City.* New York: Harper and Row, 1962.

Epstein, A. L. *Politics in an Urban African Community.* Manchester: Manchester University Press, 1958.

Forde, Daryll and P. M. Kaberry, eds. *West African Kingdoms in the Nineteenth Century.* London: Oxford University Press, 1967.

Fortes, Meyer and Evans-Pritchard, E. E., eds. *African Political Systems.* London: Oxford University Press, 1940.

Kasfir, Nelson. *The Shrinking Political Arena: Participation and Ethnicity in African Politics of Uganda.* Berkeley, California: University of California Press, 1976.

Lewis, Oscar. *Life in A Mexican Village: Tepoxtlan Revisited.* Urbana: University of Illinois Press, 1951.

Lopreato, Joseph. *Italian Americans.* New York: Oxford University Press, 1970.

Ndem, Eyo B. E. *Ibos in Contemporary Nigerian Politics.* Onitsha: Etudo Ltd., 1961.

Nelli, Humbert S. *Italians in Chicago, 1880-1930: A Study in Ethnic Mobility.* New York: Oxford University, 1970.

Suttles, Gerald D. *The Social Order of the Slum: Ethnicity and Territory in the Inner City.* Chicago: University of Chicago Press, 1968.

Wilson, Godfrey. An Essay on the Economics of Detribalization in Northern Rhodesia, Rhodes-Livingstone Institute (Livingstone, 1941-42), Papers 5 and 6.

GENERAL

Articles

Adepoju, Aderenti, "Migration and Socio-Economic Links Between Urban Migrants and Their Home Communities in Nigeria," Africa Vol. 44 1974).

Baker, Tanya and Bird, Mary. "Urbanisation and the Position of Women," The Sociological Review, VII, 1 (July, 1959).

Bay, Christian. "A Critical Evaluation of Behavioral Literature," in James Gould and Vincent V. Thursby, eds., Contemporary Political Thought: Issues in Scope, Value and Direction. New York: Holt, Rinehart and Winston Inc., 1969.

Beattie, John. "Checks on the Abuse of Political Power in Some African States: A Preliminary Framework for Analysis," in Cohen, Ronald and Middleton, John, eds., Comparative Political Systems: Studies in the Politics of Pre-Industrial Societies.

Crane, Robert I. "Urbanism in India," American Journal of Sociology 60 (1955), pp. 463-370.

Ginsburg, Norton. "The Great City in South East Asia," American Journal of Sociology, 60 (1955).

Gugler, Josef. "Life in a Dual System: Eastern Nigerians in Town, 1961," Cahiers d' Etudes Africaines, Vol. II (1971).

Hoselitz, Bert F. "Urbanization and Economic Growth in Asia," Economic Development and Cultural Change, Vol. 6 (1957).

Huntington, Samuel P. and Dominquez, J. I. "Political Development" in Greenstein, Fred I. and Polsby, N. W., eds., Macropolitical Theory, Handbook of Political Science, Vol. III

Menlo Park, California: Sage Publications, 1970.
Ki-Zerbo, Joseph. "African Personality," in Apter and Coleman, eds., Pan-Africanism Reconsidered. Berkeley, California: University of California Press, 1962.
Kilson, Martin L. Jr., "Nationalism and Social Classes in British West Africa," Journal of Politics, XX, 2 (May, 1958).
Kofele-Kale, Ndiva. "Crisis in African Leadership: O.A.U.'s Secretary General and the Lonrho Agreements" Pan Africanist (Northwestern University, Program of African Studies), No. 5 (September 1974).
_____. "Our Colonial Mentality: Europe Legalegacy to Africa," The Pan-Africanist, No. 3 (December, 1971).
Kopytoff, Igor. "Socialism and Traditional African Societies" in William H. Friedland and Carl G. Roseberg, Jr., eds., African Socialism. Stanford: Stanford University Press, 1964.
Leeds, Anthony, "Location Power in Relation of Supralocal Power Institutions," in Aidan Southall ed., Urban Anthropology: Cross-Cultural Studies in Urbanization. New York: Oxford University Press, 1973.
Leith-Ross, S. "The Rise of a New Elite Amongst the Women of Nigeria" International Social Science. Bulletin, VII, 3 (1956).
Merton, Robert. "A Paradigm for the Study of the Sociology of Knowledge" in Paul F. Lazarsfeld and Morris Rosenberg, eds., The Language of Social Research. New York: The Free Press, 1955.
Miner, Horace. "The Folk-Urban Continuum" American Sociological Review, 17 October, 1952.
Nyerere, Julius. "Ujamaa: The Basis of African Socialism," in Friedland and Roseberg, eds., African Socialism. Stanford: Stanford University Press, 1964.
Redfield, Robert. "The Folk Society" American Journal of Sociology, 52 (January, 1942).
Rouch, Jean. "Second Generation Migrants in Ghana and Ivory Coast," in Aidan Southall, ed.,

Social Change in Modern Africa, London: Oxford University Press, 1961.
Scheuch, Erwin K. "The Cross-Cultural Use of Sample Surveys: Problems of Comparability," in Stein Rokkan, ed. Comparative Research Across Cultures and Nations, Paris: Mouton, 1968.
Sklar, Richard. "Political Science and National Integration--a Radical Approach," Journal of Modern African Studies Vol. 5, No. 1 (May, 1967).
Stavenhagen, Rodolfo. "Classes, Colonialism and Acculturation," in J. A. Kahl, ed., Comparative Perspective on Stratification: Mexico, Great Britain, Japan. Boston: Little, Brown and Company, 1968.
Tignor, Robert L. "Colonial Chiefs in Chiefless Societies," Journal of Modern African Studies, 9, 3 (1971).
Weiner, Myron, "Political Integration and Political Integration and Political Development," in Finkle, Jason, and Gable, eds., Political Development and Social Change. New York: John Wiley and Sons, Inc., 1966.
Wirth, Louis. "Urbanism as a Way of Life," American Journal of Sociology 44 (January, 1938).
Wriggins, Howard W. "Impediments to Unity in New Nations" in Finkle, Jason and Gable, eds., Political Development and Social Change.

Books

Allsop, Kenneth. The Bootleggers. London: Hutchinson, 1961.
Apter, David E. and Coleman, James S., eds. Pan-Africanism Reconsidered. Berkeley, California: University of California Press, 1962.
Bell, Daniel. The End of Ideology: On the Exhaustion of Political Ideas in the Fifties. New York: Collier Books, 1961.
Cabral, Amilcar. Revolution in Guinea. New York: Monthly Review Press, 1970.
Caldwell, John C. African Rural Urban Migration: The Movement to Ghana's Towns. New York: Columbia University Press, 1969.

Campbell, Donald T. and Stanley, J. C. Experimental and Quasi-Experimental Designs for Research. Chicago: Rand McNally and Company, 1966.
Cohen, M. A Preface to Logic, New York: Meridian, 1956.
Coleman, James S. Nigeria: Background to Nationalism. Berkeley and Los Angeles: University of California Press, 1963.
Cressey, Donald R. Theft of the Nation: The Structure and Operations of Organized Crime in America. New York. Harper and Row, 1969.
Durkheim, Emile. The Division of Labour in Society, Trans. George Simpson. New York: Mac-MacMillan Company, 1933.
Fanon, Frantz. The Wretched of the Earth. New York: Grove Press, 1967.
Foster, George M. Traditional Cultures and the Impact of Technological Change. New York: Harper and Row, 1962.
Friedland, William H. and Roseberg, Carl G., eds. African Socialism. Stanford: Stanford University Press, 1964.
Glazer, Nathan and Moynihan, Patrick. Beyond the Melting Pot. Cambridge, Massachusetts: MIT Press, 1963.
Gordon, Milton M. Assimilation in American Life. New York: Oxford University Press, 1964.
Gugler, Josef and Flanagan, William G. Urbanization and Social Change in West Africa. London: Cambridge University Press, 1978.
Handlin, Oscar. The Uprooted: The Epic Story of the Great Migration that made the American People. Boston: Little, Brown and Company, 1952.
Hanna, William John and Hanna, Judith Lynne. Urban Dynamics in Black Africa: An Interdisciplinary Approach. Chicago: Aldine-Atherton, 1971.
Hayakawa, S. I. Symbol, Status, and Personality. New York: Harcourt Brace and World, 1953.
Herskovits, Melville. Man and His Works. New York: Alfred A. Knopf, 1948.
Hodgkin, Thomas. Nationalism in Colonial Africa. London: Muller, 1956.

Huntington, Samuel P. *Political Order in Changing Societies*. New Haven: Yale University Press, 1968.

Jones, Maldwyn Allen. *American Immigration*, Chicago: University of Chicago Press, 1960.

Kerlinger, Fred. *Foundations of Behavioral Research*. New York: Holt, Rinehart and Winston, Inc., 1964.

Klare, Caroline F. *Greenwich Village 1920-1930: A Comment on American Civilization in the Post-War Years*, New York: Harper and Row, 1965.

Kluckhohn, F. and Strodtbeck, F. *Variations in Value Orientations* Evanston: Row, Peterson and Company, 1961.

Kuper, Hilda, ed. *Urbanization and Migration in West Africa*. Berkeley, California: University of California Press, 1965.

Maine, Henry. *Ancient Law*. London: J. Murray, 1961.

Mayer, Lawrence, *Comparative Political Inquiry* Homewood, Illinois: Dorsey Press, 1972.

Merton, Robert K. *The Sociology of Science*. Chicago: University of Chicago Press, 1973.

Milbrath, Lester W. and Goel, L. M. *Political Participation*. Chicago: Rand McNally, 1972.

Moore, W. *Social Change*, Englewood Cliffs, N.J.: Prentice-Hall, 1974.

Nkrumah, Kwame. *Class Struggle in Africa*. New York: International Publishers, 1970.

_____. *Consciencism*. New York: Monthly Review Press, 1970.

Nesbit, Frank Ford. *Language, Meaning and Reality*. New York: Exposition Press, 1955.

Parsons, Talcott, *Essays in Sociological Theory*. Glencoe: The Free Press, 1954, 2nd edition.

Pelling, Henry. *American Labor*. Chicago University of Chicago Press, 1960.

Pfefferman, Guy. *Industrial Labor in the Republic of Senegal*. New York: Praeger, 1968.

Przeworski, Adam and Teune, Henry. *The Logic of Comparative Social Inquiry*. New York: John Wiley Interscience, 1970.

Redfield, Robert. *Tepoxtlan: A Mexican Village*. Chicago: University of Chicago Press, 1930.

Rokkan, Stein, ed. *Comparative Research Across Cultures and Nations*. Paris: Mouton, 1968.

Roiyard, Hellman E. *A Sociological Study of An Urban Native Slum Yard*. Capetown: Oxford University Press, 1948, Rhodes-Livingstone Institute Paper, No. 13.

Seibel, Hans Dieter, Industriearbeit and Kulturwandel in Nigeria: *Kulturelle Implikationen des Wandels von Einer Traditionellen Stammesgesellsch Ordo Politicns*. Koln/Opladen: Westdeutscher Verlag, 1968.

Senghor, Leopold Sedar. *On African Socialism*. New York: Praeger, 1964.

_____. *Report on the Principles and Programme of the Party* (English Translation). Paris: Presence Africaine, 1959.

Shivja, Issa. *Class Struggle in Tanzania*. New York: Monthly Review Press, 1976.

Sigmund, Paul E., ed. *The Ideologies of the Developing Nations*. New York: Praeger Publishers, 1967.

Simms, Ruth, *Urbanization in West Africa: A Review of the Current Literature*. Evanston, Illinois: Northwestern University Press, 1965.

Southhall, Aidan, ed. *Social Change in Modern Africa*. London: Oxford University Press, 1961.

_____. *Urban Anthropology Cross-Cultural Studies in Urbanization*. New York: Oxford University Press, 1973.

Spengler, Oswald. *The Decline of the West*, 2 vols. New York: Knopf, 1945.

Summer, William Graham. *Folkways*. Boston: Ginn and Company, 1907.

Tonnies, Ferdinand. "Gemeinschaft and Gessellschaft" (1st edition, 1887) Translated and edited Loomis, Charles P., *Fundamental Concepts of Sociology*. New York: American Book Company, 1940.

White, Leslie A. *The Science of Culture*. New York: Farrah, Straus and Cudahy, 1946.

Whyte, William Foote. *Street Corner Society: The Social Structure of an Italian Slum*. Chicago: University of Chicago Press, 1943.

Zolberg, Aristide. *Creating Political Order*. Chi-
    Chicago: University of Chicago Press, 1966.
Zorbaugh, Harvey. *The Gold Coast and the Slum*.
    Chicago: University of Chicago Press, 1939.

Name Index

Achu, Achidi, 303n
Adepoju, Aderanti, 229, 240n
Ahidjo, El Hadj Ahmadou, 24-25, 71n-72n, 259, 261-265, 274, 276, 280n-283n, 285, 302n, 313
Allen, J.G.E., 141n, 143n, 207n
Allsop, Kenneth, 67n
Almond, Gabriel, 8, 10-11, 44, 61n-62n, 87, 138n, 244, 280n, 302n
Alphonse V., King, 143n
Anber, Paul, 36, 68n
Anderson, A.C., 143n
Apter, David E., 13, 47-49, 63n, 73n-74n, 140n, 181-182, 203, 208n
Ardener, Edwin W., 5n, 69n-70n, 85-86, 88, 113, 136n-139n, 141n, 152, 178, 206n-207n, 284n
Ardener, Shirley, 69n, 143n
Argyle, W.J., 66n
Aristotle, 8
Azikiwe, Nnamdi, 66n

Baker, Tanya, 240n
Banfield, Edward C., 51-52, 74n, 87, 139n
Bay, Christian, 292, 302n
Bayart, J.-F., 22, 26, 64n
Beals, R.C., 209, 239n
Beattie, John, 144n
Bederman, Sanford, 139n, 240n

Beer, S.A., 10, 61n
Bell, Daniel, 67n
Benedict, Ruth, 8, 61n
Benjamin, Jacques, 72n
Bienen, Henry, 281n
Bille, Chief of Isuwu, 141n
Bird, Mary, 240n
Bouchaud, Joseph, 142n
Brown, A., 62n
Brown, Paula, 129-130, 132, 144n
Busia, Kofi, 229, 241n

Cabral, Amilcar, 15, 63n
Caldwell, John C., 229, 241n
Campbell, Donald T., 280n
Cayton, Horace R., 67n
Chem-Langhee, Bongfen, 70n
Chilver, E.M., 133, 140n-141n
Clignet, Remi, 63n, 206n, 239n
Cohen, Abner, 58, 67n-68n
Cohen, M., 75n
Cohen, Ronald, 140n, 144n, 211, 239n
Coleman, James S., 5n, 13, 63n, 72n, 74n
Crane, Robert I., 137n

-347-

Cressey, Donald R., 67n

Daoudu, Sadou, 263
Dawson, Richard E., 61n
DeLancey, Mark W., 284n
Devine, Donald J., 8, 280n, 291, 302n
Dominguez, J. I., 62n, 73n
Drake, St. Clair, 67n
Dugast, Idelette, 140n
Durkheim, Emile, 51, 73n
Dyer, Cherry, 206n

Easton, David, 8, 12, 52, 62n, 73n, 285-286, 291, 302n
Eckstein, Harry, 140n
Edel, May, 33, 66n-67n
Ekangaki, Nzo, 24-25, 264-265, 283n
Endeley, E.M.L., 2, 31, 179-180, 192, 263
Enloe, Cynthia H., 64n
Epstein, A.L., 140n, 220
Etonga, Mbu, 323n
Evans-Pritchard, E.E., 129, 139n, 214

Fanon, Frantz, 65n
Finkle, Jason, 69n, 323n
Flanagan, William G., 283n
Fonlon, Dr. Bernard, 283n
Foncha, John Ngu, 2, 39, 179, 264, 281n, 285
Forde, D., 190n
Fortes, Meyer, 129, 139n, 214
Foster, George M., 136n, 138n, 206n

Frey, Frederick W., 52, 74n, 87
Friedland, William H., 65n

Gable, Richard N., 323n
Gaitz, Charles M., 69n
Geertz, Clifford, 21, 64n, 72n-73n
Ginsburg, Norton, 137n
Glazer, Nathan, 67n
Gluckman, Max, 209-211, 239n
Goel, M.L., 66n
Gomes, Fernao, 142n
Gordon, Milton M., 66n
Gorer, G., 8, 61n
Gorges, E.H.F., 143n-144n
Gowon, General, 42
Gravenreuth, Freiherr von, 110
Gray, J., 62n
Greeley, Andrew M., 69n
Greenstein, Fred I., 62n
Grundy, Kenneth 28, 65n
Guetzkow, Harold, 321-322, 323
Gugler, Josef, 229, 240n-241n
Gulliver, P.H., 66n

Hazlewood, Arthur, 70n, 139n
Handlin, Oscar, 68n
Hanna and Hanna, 284n, 323n

Hawkesworth, E.G., 141n, 143n
Hayakawa, S.I., 240n
Hayward, Fred W., 74n
Hellman, E., 239n
Hess, R.D., 12, 62n, 73n
Hodgkin, Thomas, 182, 208n
Hoselitz, Bert F., 80, 136n
Huntington, Samuel P., 62n

Ishida, T., 62n

Jennings, Kent M., 73n
Johnson, Willard R., 5n, 66n, 70n, 72n, 93, 139n, 154, 207n, 259
Jones, Maldwyn Allen, 68n
Joseph, Richard A., 69n
Jua, Augustine, 263, 281n

Kaberry, P.M., 102, 133, 140n-141n
Kahl, J.A., 64n
Kale, P.M., 2, 5n, 136n, 142n, 192, 207n
Kangsen, Rev. J. C., 193
Kasfir, Nelson, 280n
Kavanagh, Dennis, 44, 72n
Kemcha, P.M., 281n
Kilson, Martin L., 65n
Kim, Young C., 61n
Ki-Zerbo, Joseph, 74n
Klare, Caroline F., 67n
Kluckhohn, Florence, 180, 207n-208n, 302n

Knopf, Alfred A., 74n
Kofele-Kale, Ndiva, 64n, 70n, 207n, 280n, 323n
Kopytoff, Igor, 65n
Krabbes, 80
Kuper, Hilda, 284n, 323n

LaFontaine, J.S., 30-31, 34, 66n
Langton, Kenneth P., 73n
LaPalombara, Joseph, 51-52, 74n
Lasswell, Harold D., 61n
Laumann, Edward O., 69n
Lazarsfeld, Paul F., 63n
Leeds, Anthony, 75n
Leith-Ross, S., 240n
Lenski, Gerhard, 69n
Lerner, Daniel, 61n
Levine, Robert, 47-49, 72n-73n
Le Vine, Victor T., 5n, 72n, 136n, 154, 203, 207n
Lewis, Arthur W., 21, 64n
Lewis, Oscar, 74n
Lipset, S.M., 73n
Littlewood, Margaret, 140n
Loomis, Charles P., 73n
Lopreato, Joseph, 67n
Lowenthal, Leo, 73n

McCulloch, Merran, 140n-141n

McNally, Rand, 66n
Mafeje, Archie, 19-20, 30, 34, 64n, 66n, 72n
Maine, Henry, 33, 51, 73n
Mair, Lucy, 63n
Mansfield, 117
Markovitz, Irving I., 239n
Mayer, Lawrence, 9-10, 61n
Mvodo, Ayissi, 265
Mead, Margaret, 8, 61n
Meek, C.K., 138n-139n, 142n
Mercier, Paul, 34, 67n, 284n, 323n
Merton, Robert, 18, 32, 63n, 67n
Metraux, R., 61n
Middleton, John, 140n, 144n, 211, 239n
Milbrath, Lester W., 66n
Miller, Robert A., 29, 64n-65n
Miner, Horace, 74n, 137n, 239n
Mitchell, J.C., 239n
Montesquieu, 8
Moore, W., 239n
Motomby-Woleta, Peter, 31
Moynihan, Daniel Patrick, 67n
Muna, Solomon Tandeng, 25, 263
Murdock, George, 74n

Nadel, S.F., 136n
Ndem, Eyo B.E., 39, 70n
Ndongko, Wilfred A., 280n
Nelli, Humbert S., 67n
Nelson, Dale C., 69n

Ngu, Anomah, 264
Ngwa, J.A., 136n
Nie, Norman H., 66n
Njeuma, M.Z., 69n-70n
Nkrumah, Kwame, 65n-66n
Ntumazah, Ndeh, 2
Nyerere, Julius, 65n

O'Connell, Father, 66n

Paden, John, 140n
Parenti, Michael, 69n
Parsons, Talcott, 78, 136n
Patterson, W., 73n
Pelling, Henry, 68n
Pfefferman, Guy, 240n
Philipson, Sir Sydney, 70n
Plato, 8
Polsby, N.W., 62n
Post, W.J., 69n-70n
Powell, Bingham G., 62n
Prewitt, Kenneth, 61n, 73n
Przeworski, Adam, 139
Puckler-Limburg, 117
Puttkammer, Jesco von, 80
Pye, Lucian W., 11, 61n-62n, 72n, 74n

Radcliffe-Brown, 141n
Redfield, Robert, 73n, 84, 137n
Ripert, A.M., 143n
Ritzenthaler, Robert and Pat, 105, 140n-141n

Rivkin, Arnold, 63n
Rokkan, Stein, 138n
Rosberg, Carl G., Jr., 65n
Rose, Richard, 43, 72n
Rosenberg, Morris, 63n
Rothchild, Donald, 68n
Rouch, Jean, 284n, 323n
Rubin, Neville, 206n, 259, 281n,-283n
Rudin, Harry, 136n, 139n, 142n, 144n, 155
Rudolf, L., 62n
Rudolf, S.H., 62n
Ruel, M.J., 85, 119-120, 125-126, 137n, 143n-144n
Rustow, Dankwart A., 74n

Saker, Reverend Alfred, 82-83, 110, 148-149, 153
Scheuch, Erwin K., 138
Seibel, Hans Dieter, 229n-240n
Senghor, Leopold Sedar, 33-34, 65n-67n, 69n
Shivji, Issa, 20, 29, 38, 64n-65n
Sigmund, Paul E., 65n
Simms, Ruth, 216
Sklar, Richard, 38, 46, 72n
Smock, Audrey Chapman, 68n
Southhall, Aidan, 75n, 142n, 239n, 284n, 323n
Spengler, Oswald, 180, 207n
Stanley, J.C., 280n
Stavenhagen, Rodolfo, 20, 29, 64n

Strodtbeck, Fred, 207n-208n
Sumner, William Graham, 32, 67n

Tabi, Egbe, 302n
Teune, Henry, 139n
Thursby, V., 302n
Tignor, Robert L., 16-18, 63n
Tonnies, Ferdinand, 51, 73n
Torney, Judith V., 73n
Twaddle, Michael, 66n

Ulam, B.A., 10, 61n

Van den Berge, Pierre, 67n
Verba, Sidney, 8, 11, 44, 61n-62n, 66n 72n, 74n, 87, 138n 244, 302n
Vickers, Michael, 69n-70n

Wallerstein, Immanuel, 140n
Ward, Robert, 43
Warmington, W.A., 69n, 139, 143n
Weiner, Myron, 317, 323n
Welch, Claude, 70n
Wells, 139n
White, Leslie A., 240n
Whyte, William Foote, 68n
Wilson, Godfrey, 209, 239n
Wilson, R.W., 62n
Wirth, Louis, 74n
Wolpe, Howard, 68n

Wriggins, Howard W., 38, 69n

Yaya, Moussa, 263

Zintgraff, Count Eugene von, 103, 117
Zolberg, Aristide, 281n
Zorbaugh, Harvey, 68n

Subject Index

Administration
- British/United Kingdom, 93, 138n, 144
- German, 79, 89, 117-118, 148, 206n

African Politics, 16, 22, 28
African Socialism, 28, 65n
African Societies, 18, 28-30, 35, 44, 129, 153, 214, 228, 313, 317
Age Sets/Groups, 106, 114-115, 122-123, 144n
Ashanti Confederation, 49
Associations, 107, 115, 124-127, 129-133, 144n, 181
Attitudes, 10-11, 14, 16, 51-52, 57, 73n, 200
Authority Patterns, 49, 144n, 160, 167, 214
- Domestic Authority, 214-215, 269
- Egalitarian Authority, 221
- Parental Authority, 215, 218, 221
Authority roles, 129, 220
Authority Systems, 129, 131, 133-134

Bafaw, 31
Bafut, 103-107, 119, 127-128, 133-134, 140n

Bakweri Land Committee, 137n, 178, 207n
Bakossi, 31
Balondo, 31
Bantoid-Speaking, 94-95
Bantu-Speaking, 94
Banyang, 85, 87, 96, 98-101, 115-117, 119-120, 122-124, 127, 132, 134, 139n, 143n-144n, 145-147, 153-154, 156-170, 172-177, 183-186, 188-193, 196, 198-201, 203-204, 214-215, 218-219, 221, 223, 230
Belief Systems, 3, 291, 295-296, 300
Beliefs, 8-10, 86, 300
Biafran State, 42
Black Power, 34
British Commonwealth Development Corporation (COMDEV), 93
Buganda Kingdom, 49

Cameroon Development Corporation (CDC), 38, 82-83, 92-93, 96, 139n, 147, 195, 293
Cameroon
- Anglophone/English-Speaking, 1-4, 7, 24, 69n, 77, 80-82, 93-94, 98, 102, 146, 148-154, 178-180,

194, 197, 199, 206n, 250, 260, 263, 273, 282n
- East, 1, 4, 25, 282n
- Francophone/French-Speaking, 3-4, 42, 69n-70n, 193, 206n, 250, 260, 263
- Northern, 1
- Southern, 1-2, 4-5n, 31, 39-40, 70n, 92-93, 137n, 142n-143n, 179, 193, 196, 207n, 284n
- West, 1, 4, 42, 70n-71n, 80, 82, 143n, 148, 260, 282n, 284n

Catholic Newspapers, 44
Centralized Chiefdoms, 96, 99, 105, 126-127, 214
Chamba, 100, 140n
Christianity, 105, 177
Class Struggle, 15, 28, 63n-64n, 69n
Colonial Administration, 49, 81, 262
Colonial Africa
- Post-Colonial, 16-18, 28, 265
- Pre-Colonial, 16, 28, 68
Colonial rule, 274-275, 305
Colonialism, 13, 15, 17-18, 20, 64n, 71n, 110, 193, 307
Commercial Bourgeoisie, 39
Community Identification/Identity, 56-57, 60, 62n, 267, 273, 277-278

Conflict Resolution, 105, 112, 120, 286, 290, 292, 315
Constitutional Change, 256-257
Coup d' etat, 20
Creole, 83-84
Cross-ethnic Marriage, 173-175, 267-268, 270, 274, 283n
Culture
- Cross-Cultural Contact, 85
- Cultural-Exchange, 80
- Cultural Values, 11, 33
- Political Culture, 3, 7-21, 43-44, 46, 48, 51, 53, 55, 59, 61n, 69n, 72n-74n, 77, 87, 96, 139n, 243, 260, 275-276, 312, 321

Decentralization, 250
Decision-making, 159-160, 162-169, 201-202, 205, 213-219, 221-222, 235-236, 240n, 269, 286-289, 291, 303, 309-311, 314-315
Decision-making Models
- Elitist, 287-288, 291, 310, 314-315
- Consensual, 287, 291
- Majoritarian, 287, 291

-354-

Democracy, 9, 12, 260
Demographic Characteristics, 145
Detribalization, 209-211, 239n
Duala, 68n, 77, 79, 109-110, 114

Economic Development, 250-253, 261-262, 280n, 295
Efik, 40-41, 94
Ekoi, 41
Elite, 3, 12, 22, 25, 28, 64n, 136, 259, 282n, 292, 295
Elitist Model, 287-288, 291, 310, 314-315
Environment, 3, 7, 209, 212, 236, 243
Environmental Change, 3, 7, 212, 215-216, 221-222, 239n, 285, 310
Ethnic Balance, 23-24
Ethnic Group
 - Centralized, 204, 214, 216-217, 225-227, 230, 231-237, 288-289, 311
 - Hierarchical, 181, 201-203, 205, 307, 309-310
 - Segmentary, 94, 126-129, 168, 201-205, 213-216, 223-227, 233, 235-237, 288-289, 307, 309-311
 - Stateless Society, 47, 72n
Ethnic group values, 3, 157, 187-188, 209, 211, 213, 231, 237, 308-309, 312, 317
Ethnic Systems, 288, 289

Ethnicity, 3, 7, 19, 23, 25, 28-29, 33-34, 38, 40, 50, 66n-67n, 69n, 140n, 209, 212, 280n
Ethnicization, 187, 191
Ethnocentrism, 32

Federation, 1-2, 5n, 25, 70n, 98, 193, 264
Fon (King), 103-108, 127, 133-134, 141n, 192, 290, 309
Fulani, 68n, 102

Grassfields, 98-102, 139n-140n, 145-147, 149, 153-154, 156-159, 162-169, 170, 172-180, 183-193, 196, 198-201, 204, 207n, 214, 216, 218-219, 221, 224, 228, 230, 290
Gusii, 47, 49

Hausa-Fulani, 36, 42
Heterogeneity, 97
Historical Discontinuity, 13-14, 16-17
Homogeneity, 99

Ibophobia, 39
Ibo "Problem," 36
Ibo, 36, 38-42, 68n, 70n
Identification, 172, 177, 184, 202-203, 244, 276, 305, 308, 313

Identity System, 243, 276
Imperialism, 15, 32
Independence, 2, 5n, 72n, 89, 93, 260-261
Indirect rule, 18, 81, 105
Institutions, 14-18, 45, 56-57
Integration, 5n, 16, 70n, 72n, 139n-140n, 193
Intra-group Cohesiveness, 225, 228
Inter-group Contact, 157
Intra-group Contact, 170, 201, 202
Isuwu, 77, 108-109

Kinship, 106, 114, 129-133, 141n, 181, 209, 229
Korup, 94
Kpe, 31, 68n, 77, 79, 81-83, 85, 86, 87, 96, 98-101, 108-112, 114, 118, 120, 127-129, 132-133, 137n-139n, 141n-142n, 145-147, 153-154, 156-167, 170-171, 173-180, 183-186, 188-201, 203-204, 206n, 214-215, 218-219, 221, 223, 230
Kpe-Mboko, 77, 83, 141n-142n

Labor Unions, 44-45
Laissez-Faire, 24, 58, 214, 277, 314
Language, 222-228, 269
Leaders, 13, 22-23, 25-26, 28, 31-32, 39, 45, 55, 128-129, 132-134, 143n, 254-260, 263, 265, 294, 319
League of Nations, 1, 90, 138n
Loyalties, 21-22, 27, 29, 32, 36, 43-45, 48, 172, 203, 220, 305, 317-319, 321-322

Mandate/Trusteeship, 1, 4, 5n, 72n, 91
Modern judicial System, 290, 292
Modernization, 13, 36, 38, 55, 73n
Molongo, 31
Moral Society, 291, 296-297, 300-301, 316

Nation-States, 18, 34, 37, 48, 305-306, 317
National Assembly, 98, 251, 264, 282n
Nation-building, 277, 313-314
National Consciousness, 7, 26, 28, 56
National Identity, 19, 55-56, 243-244, 276, 305
National Unity, 291, 294-297, 301, 316
Nationalism, 5n, 39-40, 65n, 72n
Native Authority Court System, 105
Nigerian Civil War, 42
Nuer, 47, 49

Organization of African Unity (OAU), 25, 71n, 264, 283n
Orientations, 180-185, 201, 203-204, 207n, 231-233, 234, 236, 238, 243, 258, 308, 310, 314-315, 320-322

Pan-Africanism, 70n, 74n
Pan-Kamerun Movement, 70n
Participation, 43, 65n-66n, 69n, 126, 164, 167, 175, 202, 220, 222, 249, 269, 280n, 306, 311, 318
Plantation Agriculture, 89, 110
Plantation Camps, 87, 88, 90, 100, 111, 139n, 157, 172, 199, 211, 217-218, 220-222, 227-228, 230, 232, 233, 245-246, 252-255, 260-262, 266, 270, 272-277, 287, 291-294, 300, 310, 316, 320
Plebiscite, 2, 39, 193
Political Awareness, 204, 244-246, 260
Political Consciousness, 179, 191
Political Development, 5n, 16, 61n, 64n, 69n-70n, 72n, 74n
Political Evolution, 5n
Political Knowledge, 252, 256, 276, 284n, 312
Political Orientations, 3, 7, 10, 14, 47, 50, 52, 54, 59, 73n, 87-88, 94, 96-97, 100, 167, 185, 237, 276, 280n, 312, 319
Political Parties, 38, 44, 72n, 254
- Cameroon National Union (CNU), 96, 256, 258-260, 263, 281n-282n
- Cameroon People's National Convention (CPNC), 31, 193, 259, 282n
- Cameroon United Congress (CUC), 259, 282n
- Cameroon Youth League, 179
- Kamerun National Congress (KNC), 2, 192-193
- Kamerun National Democratic Party (KNDP), 2, 98, 192-193, 259, 282n
- Kamerun People's Party (KPP), 2, 192
- One Kamerun Party (OK), 2
- Union Camerounaise (UC), 259-260, 263, 282n
Political Power, 23, 35, 37-38, 180
Political System, 8-9, 12, 35, 38, 43, 47-48, 51, 55, 59, 61n-62n, 73n, 103-104, 111, 118-119, 129, 132-133, 139n, 144n, 184, 199,

238, 243-244, 256, 276, 285, 307-308, 312, 319-320
Political Values, 3, 8, 10, 13-15, 17, 19, 47-48, 50, 72n, 190, 199, 204, 290, 307, 315
Politicization, 34, 37, 69n, 190, 198
Poly-ethnic Societies, 12, 38, 57
Primordial Attachments, 28, 32, 44
Prostitution, 296, 298-299, 302n
Public Custodian, 90, 91

Religious Affiliations
- Animists, 154
- Basler Evangelische Missionsgesellschaft, 148-149, 153-155, 206n
- London Baptist Mission, 82, 110, 142n, 148-152, 155-156
- Native Baptist Church, 149-152
- North American Baptist, 149-154, 156
- Presbyterians, 148-152, 154-156, 193
- Roman Catholic Church, 148-156
Reunification, 2, 39, 64n, 70n-71n, 93, 98, 193, 263-264, 275
Rural-Urban Continuity, 229
Rural Villages, 57-58, 74n, 79, 84, 86-87, 139n, 159, 199, 209-214, 218, 227-228, 230, 232-233, 245, 245, 252-255,

261-262, 266, 268, 270, 272-278, 287, 291-293, 295, 297, 300-301, 308, 315-316, 320
Rule Systems, 285-286, 289, 296, 314

Social Welfare, 291-294, 300, 316
Socialization, 11, 14, 19, 33, 46-48, 50, 56-57, 61n-62n, 72n-73n, 185, 187, 200, 204, 306-307
Socio-economic Development, 26, 52-53, 55-56, 81, 266, 307
Socio-ethnographic, 3, 77
Socio-political Organization, 97, 126-127
- Organizations, 97, 126-127, 205
- Relations, 20, 29
- Values, 145, 160
Succession and Inheritance, 106, 113, 123-124, 127-128
Symbol Systems, 243, 274-275, 285, 314,
Systems-Functionalist, 8, 52

Theoretical Explanation, 18-19
Theoretical Framework, 50, 59
Third World, 11, 20, 52, 282n

Tikar, 100, 102, 116, 140n
Traditional Institutions, 3, 77, 85
Traditional Systems, 12, 58, 127, 139n, 181, 213-214, 226, 231, 234-235
Traditional Values, 3, 32, 85, 182, 209, 313
Traditions of Origin, 109-110, 115
Tribalism, 7, 14, 19-20, 22-23, 25, 28-34, 37-38, 43, 45-46, 64n-67n, 239n, 247, 318
Tribe, 209-210, 248

United Nations, 2, 31, 92, 137n, 178, 193
Urban Centers/Towns, 57-58, 74n, 79, 80, 85-88, 111, 159, 172, 199, 209-214, 215, 217-218, 220-221, 223, 227-229, 230, 232-233, 245-246, 251-255, 260-262, 266, 268, 270, 272-276, 278, 284n, 287, 291-293, 295, 300, 301-302n, 308-309, 315-316,
Urbanization, 58, 75n, 79, 136n, 239n-241n, 276, 277, 313-314

West Afrikanische Pflanzunsgesellschaft, Victory (WAPV), 89
Widekum, 100, 102-103, 140n

Yoruba, 36